Teeming re\

"Instead of reinventing the wheel while setting up an organization, why not look at cooperatives that have been around for millions of years? Tamsin Woolley-Barker uses modern knowledge of animal societies to show us what works, how it works, and why animals from ants to our fellow primates perhaps know something that we don't."

—Frans de Waal, PhD, author of *Chimpanzee Politics* and *Are We Smart Enough to Know How Smart Animals Are?*

"This is a terrific book. As with colonies of ants, packs of wolves, schools of fish, and gatherings of any other social organisms, a swarm of humans—whether a rally, an army, or a corporation—does not behave like the sum of its individual parts. *Teeming* offers a scintillating, provocative, mind-bending marriage of sociobiology, biomimicry, and organization theory, chock-full of facts and theories that help explain these often-mystifying superorganisms composed of people like you and me."

—Denis Hayes, Founder of Earth Day, author of *Cowspiracy*

"In this groundbreaking and highly entertaining book, Dr. Tamsin details the unified theory of how all organizations will operate in the 21st Century. Beyond theory, the most effective firms already use TEEMING principles to scale—underlying what nature has understood for eons. Read before your competitors!"

—Verne Harnish, CEO Scaling Up, author of *Scaling Up (Rockefeller Habits 2.0)*

"With millions of species and time-tested strategies to draw from, bio-mimicry offers endless creative potential. Ensuring we get nature's lessons right requires being true to the science, translating nature's design principles with integrity, and making that wisdom accessible to those who put it in practice. Woolley-Barker gracefully does all three—honoring the science, teasing out the deep patterns, and spinning a compelling vision of a better future. This is a rich resource, and one worth taking the time to enjoy. The principles are easy to apply, and it's not far-fetched to say your organization will thrive like the ants and fungus if you do. *Teeming* is your go-to resource for making that happen."

—Dayna Baumeister, PhD. Principal Biomimicry 3.8;
co-director Biomimicry Center at Arizona State University

"Teeming is clearly a labor of love, with a lifetime of research, experience, and thought poured into it. These are not facile sound bites, and they deserve a good read. You will certainly get your money's worth. Start reading, and go about your business—Dr. Woolley-Barker's superorganisms will jump out at you everywhere you go—at work, at home, and even on the evening news. Working together can work a whole lot better if we learn from nature. Not just that, but there is a real person inside these pages—one we'd like to know. Tamsin weaves a rich conversation full of entertaining adventure—a journey of the mind and spirit, and one you won't forget."

—Jay Harman, CEO PAX Scientific and author of
The Shark's Paintbrush

"Evolutionary biologist Woolley-Barker draws on the ancient R&D of living systems to show how nature can help us challenge Silicon Valley's vertical hierarchies and billion-dollar unicorns with self-organized systems that are functional, flat, agile, adaptive and resilient. *Teeming* is a timely, insightful, inspiring and enjoyable exploration of one of the deepest challenges facing not only the sustainable movement but all modern organizations—how to ensure the adaptive benefits of emergent coordination without the deadening impacts of command and control."

—Gil Friend, Chief Sustainability Officer, City of Palo Alto;
Founder, Natural Logic, Inc.

"Teeming is a full and excellent account of the Whys and the Hows of organizational biomimicry for enterprises and teams. It is packed full of biological examples and fascinating anecdotes, all beautifully written in a personal, engaging, and thoughtful style. Well done!"
—Ken Thompson, author of *Bioteams* and *The Networked Enterprise*

"Tamsin Woolley-Barker does a superb job explaining what we can learn from other super social species, ranging from naked mole rats, ants and bees, to elephants and humpback whales, to become happier, more creative, and more successful members of companies, organizations, and society."

—Peter Gloor, Author *Swarm Creativity*, Research Scientist,
MIT Center for Collective Intelligence

"Have you ever found yourself stuck in an endless, pointless business meeting, wondering how we could operate in a better way? Well, wonder no more! *Teeming* is chock-full of relevant wisdom from our most reliable and ancient source, Nature herself. Tamsin Woolley-Barker's training as an evolutionary biologist and biomimicry professional are evident on every page, as she illuminates lessons from the natural world that can dramatically improve our businesses, our teams, and our lives."

—Katherine Collins, Founder, Honeybee Capital and
author of *The Nature of Investing*

"An easy-to-digest book with profound implications for the future of our social systems, *Teeming* overflows with poetic and scientific insight. It is also an entertaining read. This timely book explores how competition and cooperation play out in all social systems. With gracious ease Dr. Woolley-Barker blends her passion and expertise for sociobiology, facilitation, ecology and systems thinking to provide the theoretical insight and practical application we sorely need in redesigning our organizational systems to flourish far into the future. Diverse, self-organizing, collaborative, and purposeful superorganisms provide powerful insight into how the firms of the future can adapt and thrive in these transformative times, while creating the conditions conducive for life to flourish. A must-read for those with an eye on what our future could hold."

—Giles Hutchins, author of *Future Fit* and *The Nature of Business*

"I consider this book a must-read for anyone with a manager title in my organization. Tamsin Woolley-Barker masterfully teaches us how nature gets the job done—without drama and overhead. Crisp, intentional, audacious."

—Reza Sadeghi, PhD, Chief Strategic Officer,
BIOVIA/Dassault Systems

"As a systems communicator, I'm always looking for ways to unlock nature's tenuous genius. At last, the solution has arrived. Woolley-Barker is the fresh and futurist voice our Age of Biology has been waiting for."

—Zem Joaquin, Founder, Near Future Summit & ecofabulous,
Huffington Post Editor at Large

"*Teeming* should be required reading for everyone working in (or managing) a team. Creative and design teams will find invaluable insight into applying the lessons of Nature to their own company, culture and process. I wish I had this book 20 years ago!"

—Eric Corey Freed, Architect, Author, and Facilitator,
Institute for Living Futures

"Truly a fascinating and inspiring read! Using the principles of Biomimicry, Sociobiology, and Evolution, Dr. Woolley-Barker shows how to transform your own company by emulating nature's most efficient natural models and systems—all forged over billions of years of trial and error. Only the winningest systems have survived—why reinvent the wheel when you can take advantage of 3.8 billion years of optimization driven by natural selection? *Teeming* goes even further. By demonstrating that humans are an evolutionary novelty—'ant-like apes' with deeply biological adaptations for ensuring equity, fairness, and cooperation—*Teeming* makes the case that termite mounds and slime molds have something uniquely relevant to teach us about doing business. This 'Stone Soup' cookbook will entertain you and blow your mind, while tangibly showing how to tailor your own superorganism for sustainable success."

—Paul T. Telfer, PhD, Managing Director, Congo Conservation Company and Sabine Plattner African Charities

"Teeming is of great value to anyone interested in self-organization in nature and how we can apply our understanding of it to human organizations. We know how the cells in our bodies work together, but we know so little about what drives us as individuals within our larger groups. Woolley-Barker describes powerful principles we can borrow from nature's societies to help our own organizations evolve to cope with rapid change. For me, as an expert in system theory and sociobiology, this book is now a permanent resident on my desk."

—Olga Bogatyreva, PhD, DSc, Director of BioTRIZ Ltd, and author of *Inventor's Manual* and *Biomimetic Management*

"What a fun read! Culturally transformative nature porn for the closet biologist in all of us!"

—Taryn Mead, PhD, Symbiosis Group

"What might be possible if we could lead our organizations to become thriving interconnected networks of collaboration, ingenuity, and self-organized wealth accumulation? If we could transform our society and economies into structures that embody and contribute to the evolutionary power of life itself? In this critical time, Tamsin Woolley-Barker peers into nature's enduring intelligence to show us how we might do it. This book is a great read, and a must for any leader curious about the simple rules that can lead us to a better future, together."

—Toby Herzlich, Founder, Biomimicry for Social Innovation and Senior Trainer, Rockwood Leadership Institute

"*Teeming* is a revolutionary book that literally turns the world as we know it upside-down to provide us with a new way to look at and solve the immense challenges facing our world today. Tamsin Woolley-Barker is a brilliant and approachable writer with an immense knowledge about how our fellow travelers on this planet have survived and prospered much longer than we humans. We strongly recommend that you read this book if you want to create more sustainable companies, organizations or communities."

—Barbara and John McDonald, co-owners of MycoMesh, a bio-inspired organization for social innovation

TEEMING

How
Nature's
Oldest Teams
Adapt
and Thrive

Tamsin Woolley-Barker, PhD

(drtamsin@teeminnovationgroup.com)

Cover design by Christy Collins
Interior design by Lieve Maas
Interior art by Cultura Creativa
Author photo by Marcy Browe

Second edition: 2021

Printed and bound in the United States of America
ISBN: 979-8-9851760-0-1

Published by BioInspired Ink Press

To the kindest, most loving and thoughtful offspring a biologist could ever wish for—Desmond Wildan, Ingo Zephir, and Roan James—and to the best ancestors a girl could ever have—my parents, Jim and Margaret Barker. You made it all possible.

Anyone who believes exponential growth can go on forever in a finite world is either a madman or an economist.
—KENNETH E. BOULDING

Look at you, you madman!
Screaming you are thirsty and dying in a desert,
when all around you there is nothing but water!
—KABIR

TABLE OF CONTENTS

Prologue

[The ants] have been dominant elements of most of the land habitats
for at least 50 million years . . . It gives great pleasure to think that
they stung or sprayed formic acid on many a dinosaur that
carelessly trampled their nests.
—E. O. WILSON

Did you ever see that old black-and-white Disney nature documentary, where hundreds of lemmings jumped from the Norwegian cliffs to their death for the good of their species? It made a deep impression on the four-year-old me. Their instinct for self-sacrifice was so moving.

Humans should do that! I thought.

But we don't. Why not? I'm embarrassed to say I devoted way too much time over the next three decades trying to figure out how lemming suicide could evolve, though I gave up trying to trigger it in humans pretty quickly. This somber scene inspired an entire life and a dissertation trying to understand how behavior and evolution worked. It was only a few years ago (at my son's science fair, strangely enough) that I discovered the film crew had tossed those lemmings off by hand for a little extra drama. The whole thing was a hoax—evolution just doesn't work that way. Nobody does anything for the good of their species.

This is not a tree-hugging book, though I've hugged my fair share of trees—even dated a guy that lived in one for a while. It's not about giving everything away or turning companies into communes (though some might actually like keeping their workers from ever leaving). I'm not advocating a return to some mythical innocence of our idyllic nature. I am an evolutionary biologist and I study social systems. I know firsthand that predators and parasites are real, and that every group of collaborators needs to protect their collective wealth from them. Competition does indeed drive life's radical innovations, "honing wondrous form to function." Life really is survival of the fittest.

I first learned this math of evolution in the tidepools where I spent a lot of my time as a child. Thumping waves and piercing UV blasted the rocky shores twice a day, and a good piece of real estate was (and still is) hard to find. Collaboration doesn't jump out at you here—everyone is seeking opportunity at someone else's expense. It's winner-take-all on the reef. A nudibranch eats a stinging anemone, borrowing its paralyzing chemistry to make predators think twice. Hermit crabs slide into the spiraling safety of shells discarded by the snails that made them—these are one-time transactions, not relationship builders. Thanks, and bye. Reputations aren't built here. It's every man—or mussel—for himself. Beloved writer John Steinbeck saw these pools as a tranquil, lovely, murderous metaphor for human endeavor[1]—creatures scratching desperately for a patch of rock to call their own, then holding on for dear life once they found it. A barnacle retreats deep into his home, sealing shut to protect its soft, tender body from the harsh realities of life. If one anemone creeps too close to another, the cranky carnivores shoot tiny harpoons of paralyzing toxin at one another until the rival moves on. It's eat or be eaten on the reef.

Our lives feel like this frequently, but on Wall Street it's that way all the time. Business is premised on the tidepool-capturing market share, securing proprietary assets, monopolizing commodities. It's a dog-eat-dog world and the unsentimental competitor cleans Mr. Nice

Guy's clock every time. Well, not exactly, because the game of life isn't played in a vacuum in business or on the reef. The next level of growth demands alliance. Competition and cooperation go hand-in-hand, ebbing and flowing like the tides to drive the magic of evolution.

As an undergraduate I studied biology in California's coastal redwood forests—fog dripping from spindly, needle-like leaves, each drop condensed and harvested in eerie silence. Mushrooms popped up, eager for a sip of moisture beneath the tallest creatures on the planet scrapping it out for sunlight high above them in the gloom. The trees carpeted the forest floor with their acidic needles, poisoning any who dared shadow their seedlings.

But there was more to the story than just a feverish arms race for sun. These plants needed other things too—water, fertilizer, mates—and these could be spread far and wide. If they couldn't get what they needed rooted in place, they had to partner with someone who could.

The trees cook up sugar—lots of it—and trade it with quicker creatures in exchange for their more mobile services. Deep in the soil, the redwoods roots intermingle with a pulsing network of fungi—exchanging a steady stream of water and fertilizer for sugar fuel. Other plants do business here too. Perfumed and nectar-rich flowers tempt busy honeybees, who smear their sexual pollen from one flower to another in the nearby meadows, while candy-colored sugarberry shrubs tempt squirrels and jays to plant them or splatter along the streams in moist packets of fertilizer. All life is intertwined in a tight dance of hungry bodies, and the next level of growth demands alliance.

Like most backyard biologists, I spent a lot of my childhood scrabbling around in the dirt watching ants. I'd scratch out their invisible trails with a stick, tricking them into following the wrong ones. They spoke in a chemical code—*Food's over here! Who moved our cheese?* Each seemed to be a brainless machine cruising in dopey circles, but together they always figured it out. You could stop a few, but more were always on the way. They never ate on the spot either, but took it home to share. I'd pour a pool of Log Cabin syrup and time them with my swim team stopwatch. They were good at their work—industrious and easygoing, running in endless cheerful loops. It never took long.

One day, my mom took me to visit a friend of hers ten minutes east, to where the planned-housing frontier met the wild chaparral. I hot-footed it along the ill-conceived black slate patio looking for a patch of shade, when a furious red mass began teeming up my leg from a crack in the pavers. Like the peaceful little black ants, there was no stopping these hot-pepper red ones either. I shrieked and stomped in agony, rubbing my legs as my mom whisked me to safety and a hose. *Wow!* I was struck with respect for these angry red soldiers, and happy to leave them behind.

I never saw those red ants again. San Diego's native Southern fire ants are gone from those chaparral hills now, wiped out by the mellow little black ants. How could that be? It turns out the black ants are the descendants of Argentine banana boat stowaways from decades before. All claimed the same clan—super-sisters with the same chemical fingerprint. Today, their vast super-colony spans across California, displacing the natives as it goes. The black ants just have more friends than the red ones.

Collaboration was the key to their success, as Professor Robert Trivers drove home for me one lucky day in 1989 when the fates conspired to bring me to his lecture hall.

I was taking a class on neurobiology, and planning a career in it. I wanted to know what kind of animal human beings were, and the answer seemed to lie with our swollen brains. I was eager to find out. Unfortunately, neurobiology required studying a litany of horrifying experiments, each more disturbing than the last. How could the researchers stand it? Spinning mice in centrifuges until their bones grew wrong, keeping kittens in boxes until their eyes stopped working—how could the scientists go home at night and make dinner for the kids like nothing had happened? Was *this* the nature of the human animal? Repulsed, I stopped attending lectures and sped through the textbook. Figuring I ought to go to class before the final, I showed for the very last class—but the regular professor wasn't there! We had a guest lecturer.

I had no idea who Robert Trivers was, but I've never been the same since.

Trivers told us about something called sociobiology[2]—the study of social evolution. He spoke of vampire bats taking turns to cough up blood for a hungry friend who would return the favor another night, and how closely related he'd have to be to someone to make jumping in a river to save them genetically worthwhile. He said he might do it anyway—probably—and explained why that might be. He showed us the simple math of good deeds, in ant colonies and baboon troops, and showed us mathematically how a man might invest less in his offspring if he couldn't be sure he was the father, or why a male lion could be expected to kill all the cubs when he took over a pride, and why siblings will fight for their parents' attention to the point where an eaglet could push his brother from the nest to his death. I was electrified—bolt upright in my seat. This explained everything.

The rest of the hippies in the audience didn't seem to care much for this. What about free will, empathy, and fairness? What about equality? They didn't like this biological determinism. But Trivers didn't give two figs about any of that. Nature was just math. There was no should be, only what it is. I thought it was pretty dynamite stuff. I was tired of sanctimonious hippies anyway.

I've been a sociobiologist ever since.[3] I study the evolution of social systems, and how social systems drive evolution in turn. Sociobiology has a cold kind of logic to it: it's society with the skin peeled off, an unflinching vision of our social lives. It's certainly not for the moralistic or reactive. It's a little like passing a grisly car accident on the freeway—you don't want to see it, but it is the raw naked truth. Part of you is compelled to look. You might be deeply repulsed by what you see, because it's not in our nature to do math when we're making social decisions. No matter—the math is baked into us. Evolution has done it for us. Sociobiology goes beyond what we think ought to be, to try and understand what actually is and why. It's a fresh way to look at the familiar social choices we make every day, and gain insight into things we think we know. It provokes disturbances in our thinking that open space for new possibilities.

There's an unexpected wrinkle to this story, by the way. It turns out society doesn't evolve quite the way biologists used to think it did. Free will, empathy, and fairness are actually important, and baked into our biology as well, as you'll see. These are what bind us together as human beings, allowing us to create far more than we could on our own. These are the keys to what could be.

Since that day in Trivers' class, I've applied sociobiology to orca whales in the Bering Sea (and to the fishermen I lived with on that boat way too long), baboon mating behavior in Ethiopia (and to newlyweds at our old photography studio, not too different really). I even applied it to my colleagues at the biotech where I worked as a bench scientist—not nearly as interesting as whales or baboons, but a good sight better than brides and fishermen.

Nowadays I apply the evolutionary lens to companies, helping them evolve. I work as a biomimicry consultant with a Fortune 500 and entrepreneurial clientele, developing biologically inspired solutions to the most difficult challenges. We search for life's deep principles and technologies, and help R&D translate them into workable applications. The innovations we discover emerge from every facet and scale of biology, everything from material science to automotive design, packaging, cosmetics, medical devices, business models, and everything in between. Anything you can frame as "how does nature do it?" is fair game for us.

As a scientist, I see everything through the lens of sociobiology and evolution. I look for patterns, and try to find what lasts. Sharks are virtually unchanged since they appeared on Earth 400 million years ago—their way of life works even as the world changes. Ant societies have been toiling together for 100 million years, and the fungi still network through the soil as they did a billion years ago. These ways of life continue to work, through dramatic upheaval and radical change.

After studying social evolution all this time, there's one thing I've come to understand about our organizations, and our whole way of life really: we can't keep structuring things the way we do. We can't expect hierarchical pyramids to grow without collapsing, or adapt to change effectively.

You don't need a sociobiologist to tell you this—any kid playing with blocks can show you: if you build it tall, the base must be wide. Even then you can only go so high. There are limits to vertical growth. The dinosaurs grew very large indeed, but they required huge bones to support all that weight. Only the smallest, lightest, and most mobile have survived to the present day—birds!

Our global organizations are like those old dinosaurs—ponderous behemoths, sitting ducks for cosmic collision. As hierarchies grow, the cost of management rises steeply along with the risk of error. It's a mathematical fact: if each manager earns three times the amount of a base-level employee, and there is one manager for every ten people, management will eat a quarter of your payroll. That starts to be a very large sum as organizations grow. Furthermore, decisions get bigger as you move up the chain of command, while the number of people making them shrinks. The most powerful managers are those furthest from the front lines—overwhelmed with decisions. Management is the lumbering skeleton that struggles to keep us from collapsing under the weight of our own complexity. The beast slows and begins to sway. When change comes—and it will—they falter and fail. There are limits to hierarchical growth. Vertical only scales so far.

Extracting growth and profit from a vertical structure is limited, and responding to change much more difficult. That's a problem, since a hard rain's a gonna fall, make no mistake. And it's no coincidence either—as top-heavy structures grow more complex, the slightest wind might trigger collapse. The way we design our organizations, and society at large for that matter, instability is inevitable. Between exponentially growing technologies and social revolution, climate change and peak-everything, we are inhabiting an increasingly unpredictable world of our own design. Multinational corporations span many divisions and market segments; our teams cross cultures, languages, time zones, and political regimes. Supply chains and customer needs shift suddenly, and resources grow scarce, making prices volatile. Change is sudden, unexpected, and calamitous. These beasts will fall.

To be clear, there is nothing inherently wrong with hierarchies. They have important biological functions, and nature uses them all the time. A hierarchical system of cells stops cancer from proliferating, while the Department of Corrections keeps the inmates from running the prison. Hierarchies boost important signals in our brains—amplifying good signals and suppressing noise to build coherent patterns. Hierarchies are useful. But they aren't the right structures for adapting to change.

As people who inhabit lively social networks, hierarchies drive us nuts. We have ideas and something to say, and hierarchies filter us out. We are noise in the system—hierarchies are designed to remove it. As organizations struggle under the burgeoning weight of managing complexity, individuals begin to disengage. One in three workers don't care about the work they do, and a quarter of us hate our jobs. Most of us live for the weekend. We just aren't that motivated to make a billion-dollar bonus for a handful of executives and shareholders we've never met, or repetitively hawk toxic pieces of plastic crap that will be in the trash in six months before floating around the planet forever. Pushing faceless numbers around, going to endless meetings—it's a soul-crushing bore. Our daily mottos could be "Grow but don't collapse today!" "Delay the inevitable!" or "Do more with less!"—none compelling reasons to get up in the morning, no matter how high up the chain you are. Most of us lack the decision-making authority or the time to do anything of significance.

Our work is a paycheck, just a way to feed the family and keep the kids in school. We do the same pointless things, the same stupid ways, though we know we could do them better if we had free rein and cared. Turnover, disengagement, and a fair degree of hopelessness result. It's not good for business—you have to keep replacing people who hit the revolving door, and a lot of the talent you keep gets left on the table as folks stop bringing their whole self to work. Their noise is going to be filtered out anyway.

Here we stand—on the edge of a dwindling planet, staring down the barrel of a ten-billion-human population explosion, at the brink of the Sixth Extinction. The summers get hotter, the winters weirder, and no one seems to be doing anything about it. The truth is, few of us can. We lack the time and energy after running in our hamster wheels all day. The relentless pressure for growth has us gripped in a vise, caught between a rock and a hard place at every level. Most of us are asleep at the wheel, and why not? The car is going there anyway, and we need more freaking sleep. Another election? Throw those bones to the wolves.

There is hope for us, however. The giant dinosaurs are long gone, but tiny, nimble birds and mammals have inherited the earth in their place. Ancient and furtive fur- and feather-balls have diversified into everything from elephant shrews to platypus, blue whales to bats, penguins, eagles, kiwis, and ostriches. One of these species is us, and just look! We are everywhere, transforming everything we touch. After four billion years, nature's diversity is dazzling.

There are other creatures as well, some even better at surviving change. Hard-working teams of termites and ants built wealth along-side the dinosaurs, and they still do today.[4] A single termite or ant may not survive for long, but together they are wildly successful to our lasting dismay. These are the superorganisms—colonies that act quite literally as one animal.

Fourteen of the hundred most invasive species in the world are superorganisms,[5] including fire ants and yellowjackets, and we're locked in perennial battle with the termites. There are at least 14,000 species of ant, if not twice as many, and each and every one lives in a superorganism society. All those ants in a sack would weigh about the same as all of humankind. Globally, the termites weigh 27 times more than us or ants—there's a cow's worth of them for every one of us. Social insects represent a quarter of the Amazon Basin's animal biomass and 80% of the total weight of insects in the world. That's some serious creepy-crawly factor.

But there are societies even more successful and ubiquitous than these. Beneath the soil you walk on lies a half-billion-year-old nutrient superhighway, a dense network of fungal fuzz on the hunt for matter to digest and minerals and water to absorb. If a meal is out there, they will find it. When they do, those nutrients will flow throughout the system, shuttled to wherever they are needed most— because the fungi are fused into one. Each individual does better this way than they could on their own.

I imagine you're thinking, *Oh, now I know where she's going with this. This sounds like thinly-veiled socialism! I'm pretty sure THAT'S not good for business!* But hear me out. Like I said, this isn't a tree-hugging book. I want to get you thinking about leading, managing, and responding to change the same way life's proven successes capitalize on opportunity, ride out disturbance, stay resilient, and grow future wealth and potential. How do they spark innovation, nurture collaboration, and lead their teams? How do they seed the present for lasting and growing returns on their investment? Most importantly, how can we structure our own global superorganisms for the same kind of returns?

This book offers a new and deeply biological way to do business. In fact, it is a new way to organize our entire global society as we do the hard work of adapting to a finite earth. This isn't a recipe for despair, scraping by, or doing less harm while delaying the inevitable death spiral, nor am I suggesting we become an army of automaton clone ants, or assimilate into the Borg. The ant way of life conjures up images of the *Iliad's* myrmidon warriors—self-sacrificing ants transformed into people in order to repopulate a plague-decimated island.[6] This book isn't like that—just the opposite in fact. "Teeming" is a recipe for unbounded optimism, abundance, individuality, and creativity, as we find new ways to live and grow faster than any species has done before, and just as sustainably.

The ants are not choking on smog or stuck in traffic. The fungi aren't counting carbon credits or worrying about the Pacific Garbage Patch. Termites don't have slums. All have grown and prospered for hundreds of millions of years, through all kinds of radical change, with the same metabolic needs we have. Why can't we do it too? I'm certain we can.

I know we can, because it's been done before. It's being done now. Evolution's simple math of cooperation and competition rolls on. If you want your organization to adapt nimbly, continuously, with no fossilized, rigid, slow and costly management, you need a living thing.

What you need is a superorganism. This book will show you how.

Introduction

The single greatest lesson the garden teaches is that our relationship to
the planet need not be zero-sum, and that as long as the sun
still shines and people still can plan and plant, think and do,
we can, if we bother to try, find ways to provide for
ourselves without diminishing the world.
—MICHAEL POLLAN

You need a superorganism. The good news is you already have one! Every human network is a superorganism, just like an ant nest or a beehive. We are an invasive species too, of course—colonizing the entire glow in the faintest flutter of an evolutionary eye, displacing other species along the way. Like honeybees, we did it by working together, coordinating tasks no chimpanzee could ever contemplate.

Everything we do requires collaboration, and our actions ripple collectively through our seven-billion-human family. Like ants, we expect our fellow simians (mostly strangers) to coordinate with us (reasonably politely). We drive on one side of the street, obey the stop signs, keep to our lane, wait patiently for our lattés, hold doors open for people, say please and thank you and excuse me. But if for one second you remember (as I always do) that we are 98% chimpanzee, you will see these good manners are astonishing!

Upon visiting the London Zoo's first chimpanzee exhibit in 1835, Queen Victoria judged them "painfully and disagreeably human."

With apologies to Dr. Jane Goodall's furry colleagues, the Queen was correct. Chimps are not good people. A friend of mine lost the better part of his hand to an especially nasty one, and Dr. Goodall observed male patrols systematically exact genocide upon the males of a neighboring troop.[1] There is a profound difference between us and them, but genetically, we are 98% alike. If we turned back the evolutionary clock just the tiniest sliver on every airline passenger, Starbucks customer, coworker, and passerby, a horrifying bloodbath would ensue.[2] But it doesn't. We just board the plane and assume we'll reach our destination with hands and ears intact. And we do.

My children often jump around like curious little chimps. It drives them bananas when I look at them that way. *Mom! Stop looking at us like we're chimpanzees!* But I can't help it—that's what they are. All of us are. Look at these fancy chimpanzees, standing up, wearing clothes, riding bikes. What magnificently kind, talented, well-mannered creatures. I have photoshopped chimp clients at my ex-husband's photo studio, facilitated leadership workshops for chimp scientists making the jump to chimp C-suite, and helped earnest chimpanzees extract their head from their recycling bins as a sustainability consultant. Everywhere I go, these fancy apes impress me with their thoughtfulness, creativity, and kindness. Don't be offended if I ogle you a little, it's just that you're amazing! What other ape can swim like Michael Phelps or sing like Nina Simone? Show me the ape that can replicate DNA in a tube, build a plane or a sandwich, style their hair, read a book, or give up their seat to someone struggling on the subway, and I will hand you a mirror. The 2% difference is right there.

What is it exactly? And why should companies care? As an evolutionary anthropologist and sociobiologist, I believe humanity's radical breakthrough was combining all the political and problem-solving abilities of a chimpanzee with the collaborative teamwork of ants. In many ways, we have more in common with termites and honeybees than our powerfully individualistic ape brethren. Our ancestors were the first ant-like apes.

We are certainly apes—political, shortsighted, and self-serving, but also tender and caring and imaginative. We are also responsible honeybees, swelling with civic duty; industrious ants moving earth and tending gardens; DIY paper wasps driven to create; and densely networked fungi supporting whole ecosystems of teeming life. People are superorganisms too.[3]

Every living thing is driven by a single overwhelming purpose: to nurture the next generation and ensure its success. At its core, that is the nature of value. We've all inherited a talent for creating it, because four billion years of our ancestors did it before us. The drive to make more for the future runs deep. For superorganisms, however, nurturing the next generation isn't just a personal endeavor, it's a collective one. The future belongs to all, not just the parents among us. We may not agree what the future should look like or how to get there, but we are in it together regardless. That's something only an ant-like ape could understand.

When a hungry wolverine hunts rabbit, it must find, catch, and devour it alone. Superorganisms are not like this. We do it together. It's the old stone soup fable: a hungry stranger enters a starving village, and knocks on doors to beg for a meal. No one will answer. The people hide in their homes, miserable behind closed doors. Finally, the stranger goes to the town square and collects bits of downed wood here and there to make a fire. He pulls a pot from his pack, draws water from the town well, and puts it on to boil. Then he adds a simple stone and waits, warming his hands by the fire. After a while, a few curious children come to see what he's up to.

I'm making stone soup, he says. *You're welcome to join me. But it does need a little something.*

The children start to bring him things: an old potato, a shriveled carrot, a stick of wood for the fire. Their parents start to come too, and soon a delicious aroma is wafting up from the pot. The suspicious villagers eye the growing crowd from their windows, but they too can smell the soup. More people come, adding a bit of dried sage and some salt. It gets competitive. Someone busts out a squawking chicken, and all the neighbors cheer. All who shared eat, those who trust are full. An old man pulls out a fiddle, a woman opens a dusty bottle she's been hoarding. Singing and dancing break out around the fire and conversation runs deep into the night. What else might they do together?

This is how superorganisms thrive in the landscapes of scarcity that exclude other species. You'll find ants all over the deserts of Australia, termites in the parched Kalahari, naked mole rats pushing dirt around Somalia. How do they do what they do?

Superorganisms succeed by gathering and curating tiny scraps of value that aren't worth the effort for other creatures: shattered splinters of wood, bits of chopped up leaves, specks of pollen, molecules of water and fertilizer. They partner with other creatures to transform this concentrated goodness into something of real heft and value. In this way, superorganism colonies accumulate great wealth.

These species have big footprints. Like us, ants and termites have kept their tender tropical skin and preference for warmer climates, and learned to adjust the world around them instead. They build elaborate air-conditioned structures, cultivate crops, and herd and milk domestic animals just as we do. Hundreds of thousands—even millions—of individuals work together on these complex tasks, with no management of any kind. Together, they sense and respond to their environment faster and more efficiently than any managed hierarchy or independent individual could on their own.

Superorganism societies are focused entirely on one thing: making each generation more successful than the last. To do that, they must continuously compound their wealth. They've acquired some interesting tricks for this—five simple patterns and twelve principles by my reckoning. They build with infinite things, as far as evolution is concerned: sunlight and carbon, the complexity, diversity, and interconnectedness of networks, and their organizations grow from the edges out, seeking and responding to opportunity and threat on the front lines. There are termite mounds in the Congo that have been continuously occupied for 2,400 years, and one humongous fungus in Oregon is over 8,500 years old. These superorganisms are as close to immortal as living things get, and their ancient way of life is a recipe for success.

How do superorganisms make more each generation? They spill the value they create out into the larger ecosystem, feeding the life that feeds them. They have to do it, because it's the only way to regenerate value for their future offspring. Abundance spirals outward in widening circles of opportunity.

Sounds good, right? This kind of shared purpose can bring out the best in a team. Superorganism value and the principles they use to create it can change the world. It has already in fact—many times over in the history of Earth. I believe they can do it again.

Emulating other superorganisms may sound like a radically new way to do business and restructure society. It may sound vast and daunting—but I don't believe it is. Superorganisms operate on a dozen simple principles, and because we are superorganisms too, they feel natural to us. It's easy to reimagine our companies as platforms for collective value creation, nurtured and cared for by our tiny, distributed, self-organized and creative contributions. It's the way we ant-like apes like to work, and the way we work best. Everything is connected—if you can find the right leverage points, the whole thing may flip on a dime. Revolutions and tipping points often surprise us.

I'm guessing you might be a little mystified by now. What is she on about? Creepy crawlies, subterranean fungi, angry chimps? What does any of this have to do with my business? Fair enough. I invite you to come see for yourself. Imagine you are an intrepid naturalist searching the globe for exotic specimens, or the source of the Nile—you are Charles Darwin, Mary Kingsley (the woman who navigated the Congo in full Victorian dress), Jane Goodall, Jacques Cousteau, or Matt Henson, the African-American gentleman who, with Robert Peary, was the first person to reach the North Pole.[4] You are about to discover a wild frontier of possibility, so keep an open mind and open eyes. And you'll need a map and compass, because this is uncharted territory.

Part One

Of Ants and Apes

In Part One, we'll explore the nature of superorganisms, from fungal networks to ant colonies to the ant-like ape you see each day in the mirror. How do other superorganisms solve the kinds of problems we face? How might the ant and ape within us expand our superorganisms for global success? I lay out the biological roots of these things, because to me, nothing makes sense except in light of evolution.[5] You are welcome to bring your faith, by the way. Darwin did. He felt that science and spirituality occupied different spheres of understanding, and there was no competition between them. Even Jehovah's Witness' magazine, *The Watchtower,* has long featured a terrific Biomimicry Backpage—celebrating life's exquisite miracles, accompanied by intriguing open-ended questions like: "Does life only appear to be designed?" and "If the copy requires a designer, what about the original?" I think these are lovely questions to explore on your next nature walk. There are plenty of ways to get to our destination, and you'll get no argument from me which path you choose. But a warning: bring the Cortizone cream. Things are gonna get itchy.

Part Two

Design your own Superorganism: Collective Intelligence

In Part Two, we'll learn how superorganisms work together on a daily basis to regenerate value from the bottom up. I'll offer some prescriptions, biological stories, and examples of real companies applying these ideas today, though it's unlikely they study naked mole rats to get there. There is no top-down plan beyond their DNA blueprints, and no one gives orders, yet surprisingly complex behaviors result. This collective intelligence is a critical element of superorganism success. We'll get down in the dirt and play in the mud, so dress accordingly. And pack lightly—you can leave your preconceptions at home. You won't need them where we're going.

Part Three

The Urge to Procreate: Swarm Creativity

Our ape nature gives us extraordinary talents: we see the big picture, imagine various outcomes, and figure out how to generate them. Our maker instinct is insistent. When combined with our small world superorganism networks, novel adaptations move outward quickly like ripples in a pond, recombining with local context to create the future as they go. That's swarm creativity. Meanwhile, our connective technologies allow us to network far beyond immediate circles. This digital sprawl has potential…but how do we structure it for adaptability and parasite prevention?

Part Four

The Sweet Spot between Order and Chaos: Distributed Leadership

Growing value from the bottom up is the cornerstone of superorganism success, but it's just one piece of the puzzle. All these bits of information are noisy, confusing, and often contradictory. How do superorganisms make sense of it all? Part Four shows how we bridge the gap between bottom-up production and top-down vision through distributed leadership. Understanding these principles can help us consciously design and lead our own superorganisms, to find the sweet spots they thrive in.

Part Five
The 2% Difference: Trust and Transparency

This section looks at the fourth African ape—us—and how our own superorganisms work. The differences between people and other apes are profound. Genetically speaking, we are 98% identical to our closest relatives, bonobos and chimpanzees. You can easily see the creativity and empathy and talent for political maneuvering we share with them. But that remaining 2% is quite something different. To me, it represents our superorganism strategies for maintaining equitable cooperation and preventing parasitism. Think about it: giving up part or all of your reproductive fitness is an enormous investment in the commons that our collective offspring will inhabit. You better be sure the colony will protect it. What this looks like for ant-like apes is intriguing. I can't speak to the genetic specifics of our 2% difference—despite my poetic abstractions, we aren't chimps with good manners any more than you can wipe the superorganism shine off an ant and find an ancient solitary wasp underneath. We are human all the way down. What's of interest to me here is the way we ant-like apes collectively establish and maintain moral communities that grow the social capital we need for collective intelligence to go to work. This is how big things get done quickly.

Part Six
Make More Life with Your Life: Regenerative Value

Finally, in Part Six, we'll explore how superorganisms create and regenerate enduring value. The great biologist EO Wilson estimates that all the ants on earth are about equal to us in biomass, yet they aren't drowning in their own plastic waste or choking on the air they exhale. The difference is simply that these organisms build their compounding wealth with virtually infinite things: sunlight and carbon, diffuse specks of water and nutrients, complexity, diversity, connection, and trust. Their teams grow from the edges out, in modular, self-managed units that seek and respond to opportunity and risk on the front lines, and they leverage symbiotic partnerships to unlock untapped value. This is no pyramid scheme; these are infinite things. By focusing systematically on shared purpose, building with infinite stuff, and spilling collective value into the larger ecosystem, they compound their future wealth. This is regenerative value.

Superorganisms are all around us. They've dramatically outlasted the dinosaurs, and the opportunities to consult their collaborative logic are endless, the results proven and enduring. If they can do it, why can't we? There's no reason why not. The future is uncertain, but others have done it before us, some with no brains at all! It can be done, and we have millions of implacable mentors to show us how. Reach out and introduce yourself, because life did not take over the globe by combat, but by networking![6] Watch and learn, grasshopper, as your organization and all the life it touches grows and profits from infinite stuff. We have all the ingredients we need to make great stone soup. Let's get cooking!

The Mycelial Way:
A Quick Guide to *Teeming*

How does nature grow infinite wealth on a finite planet? I've distilled five broad patterns and twelve deep principles that unite superorganisms in their quest for compounding value. We can apply them to our own endeavors for the same kind of teeming returns.

Pattern #1. Superorganisms cultivate collective intelligence:

Principle #1.   *Facilitate self-organized networks.*

Principle #2.   *Aggregate scattered scraps into something greater.*

Principle #3.   *Cultivate individual diversity and independence.*

Principle #4.   *Maintain open always-on conversations between diverse independent individuals.*

Principle #5.   *Trigger tipping-point cascades with simple if-then rules and feedback loops.*

Pattern #2. Superorganisms nurture swarm creativity:

Principle #6.   *Align action around a compelling shared purpose: creating value for a collective future.*

Principle #7.   *Launch multiple low-investment experiments.*

Principle #8.   *Tune social networks to spread innovation or suppress it.*

Pattern #3. Superorganisms rely on distributed leadership:

Principle #9.   Zip small specialized modular teams together as needed.

Principle #10:   Integrate local specifics with global vision.

Pattern #4. Superorganisms establish and maintain trust in reciprocity:

Principle #11.   Choose good partners, share work and wealth, and protect collective value from parasites.

Pattern #5. Superorganisms regenerate the systems they depend on:

Principle #12.   Build with abundant things, feed the life that feeds you, and grow future potential.

This book is not the first to take the biomimetic approach to organizations. Ken Thompson's *Bioteams* is an old favorite.[1] Thompson is a business coach, not a biologist, yet his prescriptions for creating high-performance teams are strikingly similar to my own. When different organisms converge on the same way of doing something, it generally means the idea is a good one!

Ant and honeybee colonies are characterized by some deep recurrent patterns:

- Emergence, in which surprisingly complex group behaviors arise from many simple (and not necessarily stellar) actions by diverse and independent individuals.
- Independence. Any individual may contribute and make a difference, and diverse strategies are necessary for effective collective intelligence to emerge.

- Self-management. Superorganisms flatten traditional permission structures and leverage personal accountability, transparent information flows, and shared purpose instead.
- Always-on, blanket communication. There are no orders. Individuals broadcast information to the whole group, using signals that require no reply or confirmation, but simply trigger action in the receivers.
- Redundancy. Mistakes by one individual don't matter too much because others are working on the same problem their own way. One of these parallel experiments will likely succeed. This way, multiple backup systems evolve along their own trajectories, and can ultimately be repurposed for something else. If organizations lack redundancy, it's harder to trust individuality and experimentation—failures may be catastrophic.

Add to this the 2% difference: our human superorganisms rest on latent ape-inherited dominance hierarchies, and we are driven to negotiate everything we do. We are inherently political creatures. Peer accountability, transparency, and a moralistic and collectively enforced belief in the rightness of equitable sharing are our superorganism workarounds. We hide and suppress the urge to dominate, and work to neutralize dominance tensions. Overt maneuvering isn't considered polite.

I realize not every very busy and important person like yourself has the time or inclination to read a book like this, so for you (yes, just for you!) I have put the key points here so you can get where I'm going. You won't be able to talk slime mold intelligence at a cocktail party or know what folks mean when they ask about your wuzzle, but that's okay. The important thing to know is that consciously emulating other superorganisms can help scale our endeavors for future success.

Part One
Of Ants and Apes

*It is easy to remember when we were small and lay on our stomachs
beside a tide pool and our minds and eyes went so deeply into it that
size and identity were lost, and the creeping hermit crab was our size
and the tiny octopus a monster. Then the waving algae covered us and
we hid under a rock at the bottom and leaped out at fish.
It is very possible that we, and even those who probe space
with equations, simply extend this wonder.*
—JOHN STEINBECK

Chapter One

Supersaurus Wrecks

It is not the strongest of the species that survive, nor the most intelligent, but the one most responsive to change.
—CHARLES DARWIN

Responding to the winds of change by building higher walls is like plugging a leaky dike with your fingers. It doesn't work. You can only extract so much profit and growth this way, and the next decade promises massive upheaval; the leaks are increasing. We desperately crave change—require it in fact—but we are afraid of what it will look like. Many of us cling fearfully to a past when we enjoyed more certainty. Hierarchical organizations used to provide that. They try and still tell us where to go and when, what to do and how, which provides some illusion of stability. But decision-making is increasingly distant from the front lines of everyday life. Executives and managers might have the big picture, but they lack vital local detail. Those of us actually on the front lines are just the hired help for someone else's purpose—their tame, wingless aphids ready for milking.

Our waking hours are rented out to corporate shareholders—they own our time at work. When do we get to live for ourselves, for our family's and community's future? When do we get to procreate what really matters to us? We put those things off to the end of our useful working lives, hoping we'll still have the good health and financial means to enjoy it. We dream of the novel we'll write, the bed and breakfast we'll open, where we will live when we retire. We spend our time fantasizing about escape. The dinosaurs are gone, but the writing is on the wall for today's dinosaurs too. Grow—but don't collapse today.

Meanwhile, executives reorganize the furniture in search of the perfect *Titanic* deck chair arrangement. A few omniscient leaders at the top suspend the laws of gravity and time for a moment to pull the legs out from under things and stick them back magically someplace else. Presto! Stability is comforting, predictable, controllable, and efficient…but of course, change is none of these things. Shift happens, and you'll have to reorganize when it does. Restructure all you like—you're always designing the adaptability out of the future.[1]

Our problem is that we're trying to design organizations like machines: thinking happens at the top, doing at the bottom. Managerial visions pass through many layers to reach the front lines. Narrow, routine-based jobs and functional units are fixed: input x and out comes y.

But living systems are nothing like this. Life organizes as it goes, accumulating matter and energy from the bottom up, with no preconceived plan or destination. Life senses and responds to change in the moment, whenever and wherever it occurs.

If you've ever been out on a late spring evening, just as dusk begins to fall—maybe having a beer on the deck with friends—and had a great fat flying VW bug of a beetle buzz along and smack into you, then back up to bang into someone else like a kid on a bumper car ride, before zooming off into the twilight, you probably wondered how such a stupid creature could survive. But there's an excellent reason why the junebug flies this way: he doesn't know where his target is. He must compare one patch of air to the next, moving always toward the one with more molecules of the right scent—the female junebug. He has to build his trail one patch at a time. Evolution works this same way. Molecules, cells, and creatures organize themselves moment to moment to make the most of whatever they find. Life just moves to the next best possibility—whatever works best now will make more later.

If we want organizations to adapt continuously, without expensive and distant top-down management, we need them to become living things. Not big, fat junebug bumper car living things, though. We need something special. We need superorganisms.

Chapter Two

Ask a Local

*If the age of the Earth were a calendar year and today were a
breath before midnight on New Year's Eve, we showed up a scant
fifteen minutes ago, and all of recorded history has blinked by in
the last sixty seconds. Luckily for us, our planet-mates—
the fantastic meshwork of plants, animals, and microbes—
have been patiently perfecting their wares since March, an
incredible 3.8 billion years since the first bacteria. . .
After 3.8 billion years of research and development, failures
are fossils, and what surrounds us is the secret to survival.*
—JANINE BENYUS

Junebugs remind me of Charles Darwin, one of my all-time heroes.
He was a huge beetle fan. Once, up in a tree somewhere in South
America, he caught a fascinating beetle in his hand—as naturalists
do, when suddenly another, even more incredible species crawled past
him. He snatched it up with his other hand, before coming face to
face with an extraordinary third species—the best one of all. Darwin
couldn't bear to lose any of these specimens, so he did the only logical
thing. He popped it in his mouth.

With unspeakable disgust and pain he identified his catch: a bombardier beetle, the only animal known to mix a boiling hot chemical

44

explosion inside its own body. Shooting livid acid down his throat, all three beetles escaped.[1]

Producing boiling poison inside your body is a major feat of engineering,[2] but the bombardier's delivery system is even more impressive. A pair of swiveling, deadly rocket launchers shoot high pressure clouds of hot acid gas, maiming predators and disgusting any who would put them in their mouths. In South Africa they call them eye-pissers, because they'll nail you in the eye just for looking at them.

Special cells inside the beetle produce highly reactive chemicals including hydrogen peroxide, collecting them in separate reservoirs. When threatened, a tiny muscle-controlled valve opens, emptying the chemicals into an indestructible combustion chamber. Essentially, this guy's got a homemade pressure-cooker bomb on his ass. The fluid begins to boil, and the high-pressure vapors force open a valve at the tip of his abdomen. It would kill the beetle if it happened all at once, but instead, the venomous steam blasts forth in a series of imperceptibly tiny bursts. The solution is so good it evolved twice—completely independently.

As you might imagine, this spray system is the envy of engineers. A company called [µ]Mist has figured out how to mimic it, applying bombardier brilliance to everything from fuel injection to drug delivery, fire extinguishers, and asthma inhalers. I relate this to you because today's problems are big, complex, and explosive, and rarely fit in the compartments we devise for them. Yet, if you get the right mix of stuff, the results may surprise you. *Here, put this in your mouth.*

The bombardier—all species, in fact—have perfected their survival strategies over billions of years. Every adaptation has succeeded against great odds. They work. Delivering these biological solutions to companies is a lot of fun. Our design teams discover all kinds of bio-inspired innovations, then work with corporate engineers to translate these principles into human solutions. These answers are usually more pleasant than the bombardier's technology, and often just as powerful.

More and more companies are venturing outside the organization for innovation and inspiration.—Why not go all the way outside? From the tidepools to the rainforest and every place in between, nature's proven strategies and structures inspire and instruct us. From the humblest creatures to the most humbling, nature's four-billion-year-old R&D labs offers a treasure trove of time-tested, energy-efficient, life-friendly solutions. It's not unusual for us to stumble on a truly disruptive technology—every project brings surprise and delight.

Jay Harman[3] of PAX Scientific knows this. He spent his free time at the beach, as a kid, surfing and seeking shells. The best and brightest engineers had long assumed that the shortest way for energy and matter to get from point A to point B was a straight line—but Jay observed that energy and matter spiral in vortices, the same way waves and shells do. Applying this observation to fans and turbines yielded significantly quieter and more efficient results.

This is biomimicry—careful observation of the living world, distilled into deep principles that stand the test of time, applied to our human challenges. This recipe for radical innovation breaks the narrow bounds of our experience on Earth, opening a portal to a world of superpowers. It's actually a very old world, one that is all around us and always has been. Earlier humans were quick to observe and imitate mating calls, behaviors, and signals of animals around them. In this way, they radically broadened their problem-solving toolkit. Biomimicry continues the tradition of imitating nature's genius for innovation.

Today, our thirst for new ideas brings us from the Age of Information to the Age of Biology. Ultimately, all innovation comes from this biological wellspring. BioTRIZ founders Nikolay and Olga Bogatyreva[4] were able to show that nature's solutions are truly novel 88% of the time— something we just haven't tried. Radically disruptive ideas seem to come out of nowhere, transformative, surprising, and yet somehow obvious. Bumps on the leading edge of the humpback whale's flippers minimize turbulence, and wind turbine blades that mimic them are 40% more efficient. Water beads up and rolls off the lotus leaf, cleaning dirt from their surface in the process. Lotus-San paints leverage this self-cleaning property, saving maintenance costs, energy, and ourselves from toxic cleansers. Meanwhile, a chip in your smartphone mimics the way your ears and brain work, separating and amplifying signal from noise.

Life's genome is a vast repository of the ancient past. The diversity is staggering. 90% of the eight to thirty million species we guesstimate exist have yet to be discovered. Scientists each year report 15,000 more, while new species turn up forgotten in old museum drawers. It's impossible to keep pace. Just a spoonful of soil may contain 10,000 different species of bacteria, each with a unique set of adaptations for thriving.[5] They face the same kinds of problems we do: drought, the need for fuel and transportation, keeping precious things safe, warm, and dry. Each has its own patch of ground to set seed and spread upon, and a ruthlessly honed strategy for doing so.

No matter what challenge, nature has a clever bag of tricks to deal with it. Nature's lessons are a vast ancient library of ideas that anyone can borrow—completely open-source and unclassified. But like Julius Caesar's armies at the Gates of Alexandria, we've been burning the library down as fast as we can. We'll never know what we've lost or the value that lost intelligence might have brought us. When you look at what we've done to this planet, to one another, and the other creatures that live here with us, it's easy to feel overwhelmed. But I really believe life's proven patterns offer the big answers we need. Just a few big tipping points can flip our way of life on a dime.

It's been done before, after all. Nature's processes, materials, structures, and compounds are universally efficient, sustainable, and healthy to make and operate. Life assembles itself, in water or air, at room temperature, from abundant natural materials, in beautifully efficient yet flexible ways. Other species don't pull vast quantities of yesterday's sunlight out of the ground, toss away things no other species has evolved to eat, or poison the places their own seedlings grow. If any ever did, they are not around today. But we are nature too—just naked, clever apes that went down the fossil fuel rabbit hole to suckle at the beguiling teat of yesterday's sunlight.

Some believe we were created by a higher power to steward the rest of creation or use it as we see fit—until a bite of the devil's apple got us 86-ed. Others see humanity as an overpopulating, cancerous parasite that has overstepped its bounds to sap our planet dry. Either way, we've gone off the reservation—and I mean that as a statement of defiance against those who think the future and the boxes we've been put in are foregone. Everyone—other than madmen, economists, mycorrhizal fungi, and Argentine ants—knows you can't grow indefinitely on a finite planet. But we also know that ending that growth would wreak unacceptable economic devastation. How do we make the changes we need without breaking what we've got?

Our bio-inspired design teams mimic proven designs like the whale flipper or the lotus, as well as biological *processes*, like photosynthesis or ecosystem succession. How does nature grow ecosystems around other species' waste? How does nature find and expand a new niche? Innovate and spread innovation? Organize for compounding wealth? Protect that value from parasites? How does nature lead a team?

These questions lead to where superorganisms excel. This book aims to tease teamwork, leadership, innovation, and value creation apart—in other species as well as ourselves—in order to discover and apply deep patterns and principles for scaling our own nascent superorganisms.

Complex adaptive systems like economies and political regimes actively resist change. Every component is attached to something else—when one thing shifts, everything else adjusts too. Such systems are hard to knock off course. That's good when you're trying to maintain order—like a forest recovering from a fallen tree or a termite mound trying to rebuild after an aardvark has a go at it. But just because a system has persisted a few decades doesn't mean it works over evolutionary time. Unsustainable systems are just as hard to change—though natural selection will eventually remove them. This is part of what we call the *naturalistic fallacy*: if something occurs in nature, it must be okay. If other birds and beasts engage in adultery, infanticide, cannibalism, incest, and slavery, does it make it all right for us too? The opposite failure of logic arises as well—if we don't see gay sex in every corner of the animal kingdom, it must be unnatural and therefore wrong (this is false—same-sex relations are widespread in social species. Three-quarters of bottlenose dolphin males form same-sex pair bonds, and many are mated for life. By the way, a dolphin same-sex orgy is called a wuzzle. You're welcome.). Biomimicry has to watch out for these fallacies all the time—we can only say nature's strategies have worked long enough to persist. On whether we would like to live that way, nature is mum.

The very notion of sustainability implies sustained effort. The word conjures Sisyphus, rolling his stone up the mountain, or Atlas groaning under the weight of the world. If it sounds like wartime rations, it's because that's what it is. We are fighting a war for our quality of life, staring down the barrel of a 10-billion-person shotgun pointed right at our little blue marble. Our dilemma lacks easy solution. Our economies and companies must keep growing, according to our capitalist assumptions, but our planet's resources are finite. Is this war even winnable? Many of our most dedicated soldiers (and beloved children) are strung out on the edge of despair. It's heartbreaking. But I suggest we've been thinking small. I like Bob Johansson's observation that disruptive innovation occurs when two opposing concepts come together to shatter the frame of constraint—like sunshine and showers exploding into rainbows.[6] We have to find a new way to live, that much is certain, but the most ancient superorganisms have already solved this dilemma. Multiple times in fact—and we are superorganisms too. Our antennae and mycelia are at the ready.

So, how does the rest of nature grow infinite wealth on a finite planet?

Roll up your sleeves and wash your hands, because it's time to go to work on a proven recipe for abundance. We're going to make stone soup. Let's get started!

Chapter Three

The Meek Shall Inherit the Earth

No man is an island, entire of itself;
every man is a piece of the continent, a part of the main.
—JOHN DONNE

As the C-suite shuffles the deck chairs, the iceberg looms larger. How deep does it go? The crew relies on the captain to guess as best he can, but there's really no way to know. Contrast this with the BBC's *Frozen Planet* episode in which a pod of Antarctic orcas lazily circle an ice floe, eyeing a resting seal. They turn without warning, speeding in formation towards the seal, driving a perfectly timed wave before them. The ice tips hard and pitches down, exploding back up with a wall of spray. The seal bleats and struggles to keep his perch. As the whales reach the ice, they dive below, and speed in front of their wave. As one, their tails form a shallow reef. The swell looms, crashing down to wash the seal helplessly into the sea. *Snack time.*

The image is a little macabre—sociobiology at work again. But these orcas are superorganisms too, by my reckoning. Their approach is creative, flexible, unique, and collaborative. No other pods exhibit this seal-pitching behavior; the clan invented it. What if your organization was like this? Now, the ice is not a problem, it's an opportunity. This is how nature approaches things, and we can approach our own challenges the same way.

Homo sapiens' ability to adapt and collaborate has turned us into a spectacular success. We colonized the whole globe in the faintest flutter of an evolutionary eye, and we did it by working together. Everything we do requires collaboration. From farmer to roaster, distributor to barista, how many people had a hand getting your latté to you this morning? How many of us grow, process, and sew all the clothes on our backs; harvest, raise, and butcher all the food that we eat? There are few folks that do—and those are probably trapped on some forgotten island and would like to get off. Guaranteed they aren't getting laid.

This degree of cooperation is rare in nature. Most species live and forage alone, coming together only to mate or raise young. The black widow has so little use for others that she will eat her mate once she gets what she needs. Some creatures, like mackerel and zebra, group together—relying on many eyes and ears to alert them to predators. Their hope is that the shark or lion will get their friends instead. Ultimately, it's every mackerel for himself.

Most group-dwelling species only collaborate if and when it suits them. It's hard to do otherwise. The more similar they are, the more their individual niches overlap, and the more they compete. There is safety in numbers, but density brings competition—an uncomfortable line to walk.

Nature has tried-and-true ways of reaping the benefits of cooperation while minimizing the cost of competition. One way is to be genetically identical. A grove of aspen trees breaks the wind and weathers wildfires together, but like Utah's trembling giant, a single 80,000-year-old 6-and-a-half-ton individual, they are really one big clone connected at the roots. The trees are competing for the same stuff, but it's all the same as far as evolution is concerned. This is one being.

Pyrosomes are also like this. You've probably never heard of these fantastical beasts, but these 60-foot-long fluorescent ocean tubes are big enough for a man to swim through! They glow white as they move—a bloom of pyrosomes luminescing on a dark night in the warm south seas is said to be a rare and magical sight. Each of these startling creatures is actually a colony of tiny jellyfish-like animals called zooids. The zooids are clones, each containing thousands of bioluminescent bacteria that flash in synchronized waves that let the zooids coordinate their movements. By sticking together and communicating, the pyrosome moves through the water, catching and digesting anything that falls in—even penguins!

Though these colonies are made up of clones, slight mutations do accumulate. If some zooids eat more than their share or do less work—if they cheat—the whole colony will clog with food and sink to its collective death on the seafloor. It's one for all and all for one when you are a pyrosome.

Our bodies are like this too: a collection of genetically identical cells, physically glommed into one beast that can do things a single cell never could. Our cells are united by common purpose: getting our bodies to meetings on time and finding other bodies to mate with, not necessarily in that order. In fact, we don't even think about the miracle of cellular cooperation until it stops. Our cells aren't supposed to compete with each other, but mutations do occur, and cells go rogue. We call that cancer. It's happening all the time, but a hierarchical cellular system generally weeds these bad apples out. If a cancerous cell does escape hierarchical control, the mutant's selfish success will be short-lived; the whole team may fail and perish with them in it.

Most group-living vertebrates, like mackerels and zebras, are not clones. They aren't really all that cooperative either, but sticking together has important benefits so they tolerate it, relying on a linear pecking order to resolve their tensions. The biggest guy takes what he wants—food, mates, or a spot to sit—and everyone else gets out of his way. Individuals don't waste too much time or effort fighting about it; just size each other up and submit.

Some social animals, like chimps and wolves, do genuinely cooperate on complex tasks. Chimp males form alliances to intimidate bigger and more aggressive individuals, hunt together, or patrol the edges of their territory against rival groups. The spooked look on their faces as they slink through the forest is straight out of a Vietnam war flick. A twig snaps and they huddle, grasping each other's penises for comfort like groomsmen at a wedding. So I'm told. Once they catch their prey, the females cluster around begging for scraps. The most desirable booty calls receive them. Wolves go even further in this kind of cooperation—adults hunt together, taking preferred positions and roles while sharing the meat. One dominant female controls the breeding rights, and the rest are her grown-up babies, helping out with the pups. Neanderthal society may have been like this.

But modern people and ants are something else. We aren't like cells or zooids, aspen trees or wolves. We work together on all kinds of tasks, often in large groups of unrelated strangers. We have different talents and personalities. Our dominance hierarchies are still present, but weak and diffuse, and we work hard to suppress them, banding together against those who boss us around, take more than their share, or shirk their responsibility to the team. We teach our children to be nice and play fair, and they understand these things instinctively.[1] This is unique among apes.

Entomologist William Morton Wheeler invented the term superorganism back in 1911 for ant colonies, which he thought of quite literally as organisms composed of individual ant cells.[2] To Wheeler, a superorganism was more than a metaphor. The queen is the colony's ovary, and the few males little more than flying sperm. Yes, they fly. Different castes of workers specialize in different roles, much like skin cells or neurons and firefighters or teachers. In our bodies or an ant colony, components are tightly aligned around reproducing the entity as a whole. That's what makes them an organism. But if that was all there was to being a superorganism, we wouldn't need a new word to describe it. "Decentralized organism" would do fine. But the cells of a superorganism are not clones, and this diversity yields surprising emergent powers.

Merriam-Webster says a superorganism is "an organized society that functions as an organic whole." Wikipedia defines it as "an organism consisting of many organisms." These definitions are accurate, but not especially inspired or useful. The term superorganism isn't really a biological one, which is partly what I like about it. As a scientist, it allows me to offer my own slightly wider and fuzzier definition, and cherry-pick the species I think should go in it. Not everyone will agree with me—and they can go write their own book!

Most biologists reserve the word superorganism for animals that are eusocial, a strict biological term with a very precise meaning: "eusocial groups contain overlapping generations of adults, with whole classes that do not reproduce, but help others rear the groups' collective offspring instead."[3] These are hard-and-fast criteria that few animals meet: only two vertebrates by traditional reckoning.

When I use the word "superorganism" I am describing something a little fuzzier: a group of genetically distinct individuals of the same species, in which members take on different tasks, whole classes of non-sibling adults help others raise their young, and no one can survive and thrive on their own for long. That, to me, is a superorganism.

These are literally or figuratively amoeba-like societies where individuals move about independently but fundamentally depend on one another. No one can do everything that's required, and the whole is more than the sum of the parts. Some honeypot ant workers are so full of nectar they can't move—they just hang from the ceiling storing food for the colony. Other workers take care of them while satisfying the group's more active requirements. Similarly, a termite soldier defends her colony from ant attacks with trap-jaws so big she can't feed herself. No matter. Other workers willingly do it for her. If it takes a village to survive, it's a superorganism.[4]

Superorganisms have only evolved a half-dozen times or so in the history of Earth. Most are insects, and their strangeness, elegance, and beauty are a biologist's endless delight. Among ants, a single queen pumps out the colony's eggs, while the workers are all sterile females, each with a job to do. Some work indoors, caring for the brood or maintaining the nest, while others work outside as foragers or soldiers. The few males are just flying sperm. They do no work, and their sisters heartlessly expel or kill any extras once mating season is over. *Bye boy,* you're just an extra mouth to feed. Some species form very small colonies, with as few as four ants, while others number in the tens of millions. Most are predators of one kind or another, but some gather seeds, and others are gardeners. In every case, sterile colony members work together while leaving reproduction to the queen and drones.

There are many kinds of ants, but the biggest, most complex societies—the leafcutters, weavers, and swarm-raiding species—have the most to tell us about the workplace.

The leafcutter story may even sound familiar to you, though the timeline will not. These ants laid aside their hunting, gathering way of life some 70 million years ago, and settled down to farm. They built teeming cities, each containing millions of ants. Their ancestors ate the mushrooms that grew on rotting leaves, and at some point, began harvesting fresh leaves to make compost to feed the fungus inside their nests.

Today, these ants maintain huge underground fungal farms. The colony can't survive without them; the fungi are their stomach. These tiny mushrooms live here and nowhere else, passed down from one generation of ants to the next—each colony has its own strain. A bucket brigade of workers cuts and carries half a ton of fresh leaf fragments to the nest each year, with progressively smaller ants relaying the scraps toward the nest. Smaller ants ride upon the larger ones, fending off the parasitic flies that dive-bomb them, in an attempt to lay eggs on live prey. Finally, the smallest workers masticate the leaves into a pulp, passing it to the tiniest workers of all, those who tend the compost inside the nest. Meanwhile, another caste harvests the nutrient-rich mushroom fruit, delivering it to the colony's growing larvae. Finally, deep in the royal chamber lies the queen, her monstrous bulk churning out eggs for the future as her royal retinue attends to every need, moving her eggs to the nursery like a conveyor belt.

The swarm-raiding species—South American army ants, African driver ants, and Asian marauder ants—are impressive and best given respect. More slime mold than ant in their ways, these nomads form huge raiding columns that spread like giant amoebae as much as 150 feet across. Worker castes differ vastly in size—an African soldier may be two inches long. Up close, these colonies are a teeming mass, with millions of ants running back and forth from a temporary bivouac formed of their own living bodies. The queen and her brood lie within this palanquin. The raiders pour forth from it each day, fanning into a branching front that ruthlessly overcomes any animal unlucky enough to be in its path. Even lions and elephants back away. Some tribes use the ants as surgical sutures, tempting soldiers to seize the edges of the wound with their mandibles before twisting off the body.

Weaver ants are perhaps the most complex. These fearless tree-dwellers work together, making silken tents of folded leaves. Regimented brigades of workers pull the edges of the leaves together into tubes, while others fetch the larvae, wagging them back and forth along the seams, stroking them to emit sticky threads that stitch the tents together with each sweep. It's like a handheld sewing machine—nice 3D printer concept, no?

Honeybees are another familiar superorganism. Domesticated by humans 10,000 years ago, their social evolution is inextricably bound to our own. A third of our global food supply depends on their pollination. Without their help, humankind would blink out in short order. These helpful insects live much as the ants do: a single egg-laying queen hatches an entourage of busy sterile female workers and a handful of disposable flying sperm. Each has a job to do. Together, the bees gather protein-rich pollen to feed the larvae and condense nectar into rich honey for the long winter. Their elegant honeycomb and beeswax hives are astonishingly efficient in both structure and material, matched by a sophisticated symbolic communication system of seventeen chemical words and twice as many body language modifiers—nearly as complex as the English alphabet.

Then there are the termites. These blind squirming things are only appealing if you're a chimpanzee or really hungry. Then they have a nice nutty flavor. The larvae are good toasted. They, too, have multi-level societies, and many maintain fungal gardens like the leafcutters. Some build towering mounds of perforated earth that serve as passive air conditioners, maintaining a precise and steady temperature in their underground world. Termites are unrelated to bees and ants; these are superorganism cockroaches that hit on the superorganism way of life quite independently. Termites are unique in another way: the royal chamber houses both king and queen. They are mated for life and may spend fifty years of marital bliss together—until the queen dies and the king shacks up with one of her daughters. The tender larvae come in both sexes, but all workers are sterile, and each has a job to do.

Ants, termites, honeybees, and social wasps spend their days building elaborate climate-controlled homes, growing and tending crops, or hunting and milking their domestic aphid and caterpillar herds. They work together in busy cities, and like most New Yorkers and Angelenos, they are often strangers. Nonetheless, they divide the labor among themselves, accomplishing remarkably complex things together. It's striking how similar our societies are.[5]

Besides the six-legged varieties, there are superorganism shrimp that live in marine sponges and superorganism aphids that live in plant galls. There are naked mole rats in Somalia, and Damarland mole rats in South Africa. All live in a strikingly ant-like way.

These are the traditionally accepted superorganisms. All of them. It's very rare, despite working so incredibly well. We'll get more into that surprising contradiction later. To me, there are other species legitimately vying for my superorganism vote: the toothed whales (dolphins, orcas, and sperm whales), elephants, and ourselves. In each case, there are whole classes of individuals that do not reproduce or even try to, and yet contribute to their group's collective success nonetheless. Childcare is communal, and grandmothers live long past reproductive age. Elephant and dolphin grannies even lactate! Some 5-20% of humans (depending which college town you're in) aren't remotely interested in mating with the opposite sex, and 75% of bottlenose dolphin males form long-term exclusive sexual bonds with other males—even including blowhole penetration, making this the only known example of nasal sex in the animal kingdom. Yeah, that happens. Elephant males often live apart from the general herd, in sexual companionships that last many years. All contribute to their society's successful future. I guess you could call this my "gays'n'grannies superorganism diagnostic." Which is why I don't have tenure. I could be totally wrong—tawk amongst yourselves. Our TeemLab Patreon offers a nice forum for discussion!

These species divide their labor in other ways as well. Individuals have distinct personalities, talents, and styles. Some dolphins act as highly influential social hubs, while other individuals perform aerial acrobatics to signal the beginning or end of travel for the pod. A few other odd species could reasonably argue their case as nascent super-organisms: the hamadryas baboons, dwarf mongooses, meerkats, marmosets, African wild dogs, crows, ravens, magpies, jays, and parrots. All these societies rely on helpers outside the immediate family to collectively raise the group's offspring. Some help out early in life, others assume that role later on. The same is true for humans, toothed whales, and elephants. To me, this just seems like an alternate way of accomplishing the same functionality ants and bees achieve through castes—which are also age-dependent.

Lastly, I point out the networked creatures—the slime molds and mycelial fungi. These to me are the ultimate superorganisms: dense networks of distinct individuals with different roles. Not everyone reproduces, but all contribute to the next generation's success just the same. Their collective intelligence rivals that of a creature with muscles and brains, allowing them to accomplish things an individual cell never could. The fungal networks are the most successful and ubiquitous organizations on earth, and their ability to sense conditions and adapt exceeds that of any other living thing.

Biological networks like these are powerfully flexible. Individuals don't need to be dazzling to achieve collective intelligence. Garish slime mold colonies are no more than oozing bags of gooey cytoplasm filled with individual nuclei—each with its own genes. This is the inspiration for that catchy horror classic, *The Blob*. Most of the time, each nucleus goes through the soil as a single-celled amoeba. When times get tough, however, a chemical alarm signals their fellow slime mates to congeal into the slug-like blob we know and love. The newly mobile protoplasmic party bus streams off to find a warm cozy spot to spore out the next generation.

The nuclei in the blob have no brains whatsoever, but together the slime has abilities you'd expect from an animal with muscles and a nervous system. A lurid yellow *Physarum* finds its way easily through a maze with food at the end. Like army ants, the amoebae branch out in a fanlike front as they search. If you place a single oat flake on each destination on a map and set the blob loose, they will fan out and find it, coalescing into the most efficient route—better than our own roadways and subway lines.

When resources are abundant and evenly spread, it's better to search alone—any New Yorker with out-of-town guests can tell you that. When resources are scarce, however, foraging together makes it more likely you will find them. This comes with a trade-off: larger groups need more food. You can't have it both ways unless you're everywhere at once. Which brings me to my favorite superorganism of all—the mycorrhizal fungi underground.

As the soil warms each spring, tiny, scattered, seed-like spores divide and grow into long threads called hyphae. When they meet, they chemically probe one another, asking, *are we compatible? Will you parasitize me?* If things seem kosher, the cell walls melt away and their bodies fuse into one. It isn't sex, exactly. It's more like a Vulcan mind meld, a two-heads-are-better-than-one kind of thing. A network of fine webby fuzz results—the mycelium, filled with individual nuclei with distinct DNA, all streaming through one shared mycelial body. These underground networks are so fine and dense that a single cubic inch of soil may contain 8 miles of cells stretched end to end, yet a single mycelium can sprawl across thousands of acres. This creature may sound impossibly alien and exotic, but it's actually comfortingly familiar. Mushrooms! Their fruit pop cozily from ground and damp logs, sporing out to seed their future generations for success.

No wonder mushroom experts love these beings. Paul Stamets[6] refers to them as nature's neurological networks, a kind of subterranean brain. These living patches of network constantly self-organize into new structures as the environment shifts around them. Where the soil is rich, hyphae branch often and grow slowly, maximizing their surface area to absorb as much as they can. In poor areas, they grow quickly and branch little, moving purposefully toward new ground. As the mycelium expands, the hyphae crisscross and interconnect in dense networks, shuttling resources to where they are needed.[7] Mycologist Allen Rayner referred to them as "diverse armies… equipped for different roles and in varying degrees of communication. With no commander besides the dictates of environmental circumstances, these troops organize themselves into a beautifully open-ended or indeterminate dynamic structure that continually responds to changing demands."[8]

That's exactly what we want in business.

Like slime molds, these fungal networks forage for moisture and decaying matter. But then things get interesting. They aren't just gathering it for themselves. They are trading these nutrients with nearly every land-dwelling plant on Earth in exchange for their photosynthetic sugar fuel. And that is not all that they do; oh no, that is not all. They also move that sugar from mother trees to their seedlings, transmitting signals between them like a switchboard operator. *Attention! Insects attacking in Sector Twelve. To arms!* The plants begin making chemical defense compounds in response. They are supporting these plants, bringing them irrigation, fertilizer, money transfers, cell phone service, much as we might fertilize and pollinate our own crops. In fact, you could reasonably argue the fungi are farmers. Why would the fungi do this for another species, in another kingdom of life? It's a promise—an act of delayed reciprocation between fungus and tree, allowing both their offspring to thrive.

Biological networks like a slime mold or mycelial patch are not just intelligent, they are resilient. The blob can't be stopped; resistance is futile against the Borg. Neurologists are regularly astonished at the brain's ability to rewire itself after injury. Similarly, mycorrhizal patches can get very large and old—a sprawling network like Oregon's 8,500-year-old, 16-football-field, humongous fungus will be fragmented by landslides, floods, falling trees, and digging bears over a lifetime, but the web remains resilient to these threats. Information and resources just flow seamlessly around them.

Occasionally, a mighty hub goes down—an ancient mother tree linking one patch of fungi to another. This is a major disturbance, but large, old patches span many such trees. The fungi simply digest and absorb the fallen, distributing their nutrients back through the network. Time marches on.

Over the ages, big fungal networks will acquire mutations here and there, and some bits become more adapted than others to a particular patch of soil—the network becomes exquisitely attuned to its local environment.

We know little about this subterranean world, but the fungi are everywhere, representing perhaps a quarter of all terrestrial biomass—far more than the ants or termites or all of us combined. These are the ultimate superorganisms, as close to immortal as living things get. They have much to teach us about growing wealth on our lovely little finite planet.

Chapter Four

The Sacred Desert Monkey

We are, indeed, unique primates, we humans, but we're simply not as different from the rest of the animal kingdom as we used to think.
—JANE GOODALL

Clifford Jolly is a brilliant, quietly understated sleeper cell in the world of physical anthropology—one of the old-school greats. In the 1960s and '70s, when other physical anthropologists were busy arguing over noble Man the Hunter or feisty Woman the Gatherer, Professor Jolly was writing about humble, squatting, shuffling seedeaters scrabbling around in the dirt.[1] He imagined our ancestors picking at roots and grains with a precise thumb and forefinger grasp, grinding the gritty stuff with a heavy jaw. His model for early humans was the odd gelada baboon, found only on the rainy Ethiopian mountain plains. Today, isotope studies of early human fossils suggest Cliff's vision was not far off.[2] We pretty much ate the same kinds of things geladas do now. These monkeys are a powerful model for early human social life.

Professor Jolly did most of his research in Ethiopia's Awash National Park, where the mighty Awash River pulls the tree-dotted forests and savannas of the Ethiopian highlands to the barren Danakil Depression—the edge of the Sahara Desert. In 1968, a group of Swiss primatologists[3] were surprised to discover that two very different "species" of baboon

64

met, mated, and produced viable offspring along this river. The Awash Baboon Hybrid Zone, as it became known, is an evolutionary crucible where new species and adaptations are born. It's especially exciting for anthropologists, because the Awash carves through the Rift Valley very close to the spot where the 3-million-year-old fossil protohuman known as Lucy was found. This is the cradle of humanity.

Several very distinct kinds of savanna baboons are found in Africa, and all live in large social troops that sleep in trees and forage together by day. Their social lives are shaped by dominance. When a male is old enough to mate, he leaves the group he was born into and joins a new one. There, he competes aggressively to be the top dog with first rights to the best mates and food. All males rank higher than all females, but each sex has its own hierarchy. Females stay where they're born, and know each other intimately; their politics are deeply entrenched. They inherit their rank from their mother, and the highest-ranked ladies receive the best food and grooming.

Hamadryas baboons are not this way. They live only in the stark deserts of Ethiopia and Eritrea, and natural selection has finely tuned them for life in these dry, treeless places. It's tough for any species to make a living here, and many—like the savanna baboons—throw in the towel and leave it to the specialists. Primates need a lot of water and trees, and there isn't much of either here. Only two have even tried to make a go of it: the hamadryas and ourselves.

Without trees to hide in, these monkeys cluster in huge troops at night, roosting on high vertical cliffs where the leopards can't get them. But food and water are scarce and patchy in the desert below, and they must split up during the day. How do they manage these conflicting requirements?

The hamadryas have altered their entire social structure, and mostly done away with the whole dominance hierarchy. Males have only two social strata: leaders with females and followers without. Females have no hierarchy at all. A leader male's glorious white mane, shocking pink face, and commanding presence (along with threats and neck bites) keeps a harem of females close. Males lacking females have only the scraggliest hint of a mane and remain celibate. They attach themselves to a harem, deferentially helping the leader safeguard his family.

The hamadryas have adopted a modular, multi-level, insect-like society: several harems hang together as a clan, and a handful of clans form a band. Leaders within a clan respect one another's female possessions and treat each other as equals. This is definitely a man's world. Several bands sleep together as a troop, but it's uncomfortable for them—their reproductive fitness is at risk if another male steals their females. It can't be helped, however. There just aren't enough sleeping spots to go around.

The Awash Baboon Hybrid Zone has probably existed for a million years, and you'll find every shade of in-between as genes flow across this non-existent "species barrier" from one population to the other. And yet, these populations remain distinct: some genes are pinned in place by the ecological and social environment.

In 1973, Professor Jolly had the genius of foresight to collect DNA from the baboons. He trapped, blow-darted, and sampled close to a thousand individuals over a 25-year period, from one side of the hybrid zone to the other. He and his former student, Dr. Jane Phillips-Conroy, detailed everything they could about every individual as they went along. Behavior, health indicators, physical descriptors, even palm prints. I remember seeing Cliff and Jane on Mutual of Omaha's *Wild Kingdom* as a child, in grainy black and white on our tiny TV.[4] I never missed that show! Cliff looked just the part, with his floppy hat and duct-taped ketamine spear gun, while Jane rocked her standard-issue safari hot pants. Marlon Perkins' assistant, Jim, even pretended to wrestle a baboon that was clearly deep in the K-hole.

The technology wasn't available in 1973, but Cliff knew that some-day a genetic analysis would let him see how their behavior, genetics, and social structure interact to drive revolutionary change. Twenty years later we had the tech. That's where I came in. I set out to figure out what all these monkey genes were up to.

Our team had been camping by the Awash for weeks, watching and trapping savanna baboons and hybrids. Now, with the river beginning to flood, it was time to pay a visit to their desert cousins. Our little Toyota pickup journeyed away from the grass-lined river, into the shimmering Martian landscape ahead. The trees shrank into bare shrubs, exploding with thorns. The warthogs and tiny dik-dik antelope disappeared along with the shade. We camped by a well frequented by the local Afar tribespeople, then hiked out to the monkeys' sleeping site as the night's hyena calls faded. The sun crept over the rocky escarpments, flooding us with an inescapable heat-lamp glare. We squinted up at the vertical cliffs, scanning for motion as the heat built unbearably—100°F, 105°F, 110°F and climbing. We arranged ourselves gingerly on the burning rocks, attempting to hide in a sliver of shade. Ants nipped angrily at us, lean bees and wasps homed in on our water bottles like missiles. A dung beetle rolled his golden treasure past my foot, while a miniature volcano puffed tiny dust clouds further off—naked mole rats toiling away below ground. Mad dogs and Englishmen go out in the noonday sun... Cliff was the latter.

We tossed handfuls of dry corn along the foot of the cliff, though it seemed unlikely that anything would come. Surely these rocks were too steep, this place too inhospitable? Our eyes struggled against the glare, gradually making out a few shaggy grey humps swarming high on the shale walls above. They were unlike any monkey I had ever seen. *Nedj djinjero*; the white monkey; sacred hamadryas of Egyptian lore, muse of scribes and scholars. Thoth, who weighs the souls of the dead. And here they came, launching themselves down the cliff with terrifying abandon, a seething mass of muscular creatures plunging directly for us.

Scree rained down, each reckless column headed by a flamboyant white-maned, long-haired, pink-faced male, followed tightly by a single file line of nervous, scraggly grey-brown females. A handful of joyful black infants clung to them, eyes twinkling brightly. In many families, a boyish and maneless grey male respectfully brought up the rear. These beasts were a cavalry in full charge, practiced, powerful, and confident—and a little terrifying! They hit the ground running, then fanned out along the sand, stuffing greedy handfuls of corn into their mouths, eyes darting suspiciously at us. The little females skittered just out of reach of their possessive husbands, but well away from us. A skirmish broke out here and there as the corn brought families a little close for comfort. *Can't you see the lady's with me?*

Then a monkey called out *Bahu! I see you, and I don't like you!* And the whole group commenced barking a sharp warning. Instantly, the males coalesced into a shield, blocking females and youngsters from view. Savanna baboons do nothing remotely like this; they do not bark for another baboon's problems, unless their own baby or a booty call is at stake. Certainly, there are no organized military maneuvers in savanna social life.

What was our transgression? We looked around and saw that three tall Afar tribesmen had silently joined our entourage. Neatly draped in rich red and crisp cobalt blue, their fiercely etched faces watched expressionless from a lacy patch of acacia, ancient Kalashnikovs dangling by their sides. Everyone in this land carries one, but bullets are harder to come by. Nonetheless, the Afar remain unconquered by government or Google translator, and are known for being inscrutable and unforgiving.[5] Just a month earlier, they had apparently shot and killed the Ethiopian minister of interior for honking at one of their camels in his Mercedes, and a few months after we left, the Afar commandeered a tank and turned it on the troops.

These baboons weren't taking chances. The corn frenzy we'd seen moments before broke apart into tiny units, each slipping into the bush. Fifty or so baboons evaporated without a trace, a crackerjack Navy SEAL drop at perfect ease in their element. They stormed the beach and melted into the desert before our eyes. How could they be so quick and precise, without orders, debate, or discussion? The key lay in their oddly egalitarian multi-level organization.

Analyzing the baboons' genes revealed many interesting things. Hamadryas bands are made of cousins, nieces, nephews and uncles. Nobody comes, and nobody goes. We learned that savanna males can't make it in hamadryas society—because they act like jerks. But savanna females love to hang out with hamadryas males, who protect them from bullies of their own kind. Still, savanna females never learn to follow hamadryas. They wander off at will, mating with whoever they like. The poor, harried fellows must resort to following them around with a worried look. We discovered that some genes flow like water between these populations—quite possibly all across Africa—while others are pinned in place by local conditions, the same way human skin pigmentation protects against UV radiation in the sunniest parts of the world.

Most importantly, we learned that social structure—who mates and associates with whom—can accelerate or suppress evolutionary change, creating conditions where cooperation is likely to thrive or fail. Mixing and clustering and structuring diverse populations is how novelty sparks and spreads. This is the source of evolutionary transformation.

Baboon evolution parallels our own in many ways. We are both children of the Pleistocene, an epoch of great tumult and uncertainty when immense glaciers slid repeatedly across the north from the Arctic, sealing Europe and North America like a lid on a cooler. Great land bridges melted, retreated, advanced, and submerged, stranding our ancestors in pockets. To the north, the ice was a mile thick at times, and many animals like mammoths, rhinos, bison, reindeer, and muskoxen acquired thick, woolly coats to blot out the piercing cold. Ancient hominids followed them right out of tropical Africa, borrowing their coats for the journey. Like ants and termites, wasps and honeybees, our ancestors changed their environment instead of letting it change them.

Some 20,000 years after these ancient humans expanded out of Africa, a sudden burst of innovation flourished across Europe. Why the delay? Perhaps they borrowed the ideas and genes of the other kinds of people they came across.[6] At the time, anthropologists were hotly debating whether our ancestors mated with Neanderthals, and if so, whether Neanderthal genes lived on within us. What kind of genetic signature would they have left behind? Today, we recognize the blue-eyed Neanderthal stamp on our human genome, and genes of another population, the Denisovans—and surprise! A third ancient human we didn't even know existed. Neanderthals and modern humans lived alongside each other for at least 30,000 years in Europe and Asia and some 2 to 4% of your genes are descended from them if you're among these populations. Features like blue eyes and tough skin and hair are probably Neanderthal in origin, but because humans migrated back and forth from Africa so many times, such genes are found across Africa as well. Meanwhile, Australian Aborigines and people from the South Pacific are about 6% Denisovan—contributing to features like a better sense of smell and adaptations to high altitude. The Denisovans themselves mixed with another early human, a mysterious ancient people who split off more than a million years earlier, quite possibly *Homo erectus* herself. No one knows the circumstances of all this mating and mingling, but it's safe to say we can welcome Neanderthals, Denisovans, and even *Homo erectus* into our human family.

It's important to understand that race does not exist in any biological sense and never did. We are not a melting pot, because there never were any races to melt. Rather, humanity is a network of many populations of intermingling genes. Some are locally adapted—genes for dark skin help us live beneath blazing sun, while pale skin helps us get sufficient vitamin D in gloomier parts of the world. These kinds of genes tend to be pinned in place by the environment. But most genes flow through the human soup like water and have done so for a very long time. As my friend Professor John Marks[7] says, "human evolution is strongly rhizotic,"[8] meaning our family tree is more like a tangled web of the ropy, rootlike structures mycelia form underground.

Imagine our collective ancestors and relatives—tiny, fragmented bands of humans making their way across the icy Northern Passage or in Polynesian rafts guided by the stars. Life was hard, but such innovators lived by their wits, flowering into many populations of clever people that swapped ideas and genes. These groups were diverse, filled with unique personalities and talents and even languages, all working intimately together as high-performing teams—just as the desert baboons do today. The legacy of earlier people lives on in us.

Collaboration is the secret to our success, just as it is for the hamadryas—and not just any kind of cooperation, not even the kind you see in wolves. Our radical human breakthrough was combining the political and problem-solving abilities of an ape with the tight-knit society of a social insect. In many ways, hamadryas and humans have more in common with ants and honeybees, slime molds and fungal networks than other primates. Hamadryas are ant-like monkeys, humans are ant-like apes. There's been a phase change and we are a different kind of animal entirely.

Chapter Five

All for One, and One for All

Ubuntu means literally "human nature," but is used in a more philosophical sense to mean "the belief in a universal bond of sharing that connects all humanity." Ubuntu asserts that society, not a transcendent being, gives human beings their humanity. Man is born formless, like a lump of clay, and it is up to the community to use the fire of experience and the wheel of social control to mold him into a pot that may be of use. Imperfections are borne by the community—it does not throw out its own. Not all clay is the same, and not all pots are of use. Likewise, not all people are the same, and not all people are fated to have the same function.
—FROM WIKIPEDIA ENTRY FOR UBUNTU, SOUTH AFRICAN TRIBAL CONCEPT

The human brain is the most complex structure on Earth—the ultimate biological network. Stimuli from the outside world (the things we see, touch, taste, here, or smell) travel through our neural networks like electrical pulses. Neurons are connected to one another by narrow fluid-filled synapse gaps—if a signal is strong enough, it jumps across the synapse to spark the next neuron. In this way, informative signals amplify, while noise is filtered out. The result is a structure capable of unparalleled pattern-recognition. We instantly recognize faces, understand language, and fill in the blanks with a degree of speed and subtlety no artificial system can rival.

Biological networks like the brain are designed by and for such sense-and-response, but we tend to reserve our notion of sentience for long-lived social mammals. The octopus, however, is neither. These cunning hunters live alone and die young, yet their intelligence is beyond dispute. They easily pop child-proof medicine bottles open and take apart Lego, and they can solve virtually any puzzle with a juicy crab at the end of it. Octopi[1] also intentionally seek specific tools and store them for later use, stashing suits of coconut armor and exact numbers of stones for their rocky den-doors (because apparently they can count).

Captive octopi need enrichment activities the same way bears in the zoo need food puzzles to stay out of trouble. The devil will find work for idle hands to do—*no bueno* when you're bored with eight arms. These midnight aquarium marauders are notorious for sneaking into other tanks at night, returning home sated with neighborly concern. And how about Inky, the captive New Zealand octopus who made his way across the room, shimmied down a tiny drainpipe, and headed back to sea? Before implementing this great escape, he visited all the other tanks. *So long, and thanks for all the fish!*

The octopus' cleverness is astounding, especially because its actual brain is pretty small. But 3/5 of his neurons are in his skin, along with taste buds and photoreceptors like the ones in our eyes. His whole body is an inside-out brain, coated in cameras and tongues. But there's more. The Indonesian mimic octopus imitates at least 15 different not-to-be-messed-with creatures in order to intimidate would-be predators. Enemies flee in terror before a deadly sea snake, venomous finned lionfish, cruising stingray, poisonous flatfish, or the bullet-fast claw of the mantis shrimp. The mimic shape-shifts into whatever psychological combat he thinks is called for. How does he know what his enemies are thinking, which version of himself he should use? How does he know what he is in relation to these creatures?

The octopus is self-aware.[2,3] He knows he exists and how he appears to others—the key diagnostic for sentience. He can imagine what others may be thinking, and therefore how he might plan or manipulate them. That's radical stuff very few animals can manage. How is it possible that a species not too distantly related to the brainless clam, with no prolonged lifetime of experience to lean on, can do this?

Octopus intelligence emerges from distributed actions of millions of neurons, producing the same kind of instant sense and response our own brains deliver, in just the same way. Natural selection has designed him for the quickest and most flexible response—exactly what we want in our companies.

Organizational design pioneer Peter Drucker[4] imagined companies as biological networks, much like a primitive brain or artificial octopus. Middle managers were like synapses, the empty space between neurons. Their role is to remove noise—to prevent random signals from traveling up the hierarchy unless a threshold of stimulus is crossed. Traditional corporations have whole layers of management who's main, if not only, function is to relay information—they are human boosters and filters for the faint, noisy signals that pass for communication in traditional, pre-information organizations. Today, digital neurons replace much of this extra wiring, resulting in less hierarchy and fewer jobs. Hierarchies amplify or suppress information. Flat networks distribute it. Our brains or the octopus' skin do both, and companies need to as well. The key is designing systems that use the right amount of each kind of structure to facilitate the desired speed and innovation required for a particular task. We'll talk about finding this sweet spot in Part Four.

But there is one major difference between octopuses and organizations. A company is not a collection of cloned cells. Our purposes overlap, but don't coincide exactly. Companies might wish it otherwise, and they try hard to standardize folks as best they can, but forcing diverse and independent people into the cloned model leaves so much of what we have on the table. We are superorganisms forced to leave much of our super at home.

Clone networks like brains and octopi are designed to amplify informative signals and filter out noise. Our hierarchical organizations are designed to do the same thing. Most companies actively disregard and filter out our creative diversity—they have to, if they are to scale up. The trouble is, that noise is the source of our collective intelligence and capacity for adapting to change. That's what makes superorganism super. We need that diverse independence. But how do we keep it while scaling our endeavors?

Tension between individuals and their groups is inherent. Some cells turn against us, and some people do too. Groups work best when members cooperate, but if, for example, a meerkat shrieks out a warning every time it spots a hawk, it is more likely to be eaten than its friends. Such kindness would not be expected to spread—selection should favor those who look out for *el numero uno*. But… meerkats do it anyway. They pop up and down constantly, squeaking warnings all over the place. How and why does such selflessness persist? There's clearly more to the story.

Darwin acknowledged the dilemma back in the 1860s, but he didn't see a problem.[5] The answer seemed obvious to him: competition must occur between groups as well as between individuals. Groups of meerkats with lots of warning-callers must do better than groups with the every-meerkat-for-himself strategy.

This isn't just a mathematical abstraction, it's reality. Some bacteria float around ponds in filmy mats, producing a plastic-like substance that keeps them afloat. This buoyancy is energetically expensive, though. Why not hold back and float by on the efforts of others? Logically, selection should favor such individuals, but it doesn't. Why not? Because when freeloaders proliferate, the whole mat sinks. The math has changed. If we cheat on our teams, they will sink with us in them.

This may seem intuitively obvious, but I can tell you brilliant minds have struggled with it. Not too long ago, scientists tossed the whole notion of competition between groups into the dustbin of history, along with flat Earth, plate tectonic naysayers, and climate change denial (all of which should stay there). The slightest whiff of group selectionism could render you academically unviable. Dawkins' Selfish Gene (and Trivers' sociobiology) ruled the day.[6]

Math errors aside, that's probably because many otherwise fine naturalists of a certain era said things like, "Lemmings commit mass suicide for the good of their species." Evolution just doesn't work like that, and good biologists knew it. Throughout the latter half of the 20th century genes were selfish, and that's all there was to it. Nobody did anything for the good of their species, or anyone else for that matter. But careful math by theoretical biologists and game theory experts showed that Darwin's group selection hypothesis was actually correct—but only under quite specific and narrow circumstances. It also showed that both sides were arguing different sides of the same equation. Today, group selectionists and superorganisms can poke our heads from the metaphorical naked mole rat burrow once more.

Here's what Darwin perceived: natural selection operates at every level. It chooses between genes in an ant, ants in a colony, and between colonies themselves. It can even operate in opposing directions at these levels. Cooperative groups may be favored even as cooperative individuals are handicapped, and selfish individuals may succeed even as selfish cells within them metastasize and kill them. The outcome in any particular case depends on the environment and who hangs out or mates with whom. Whenever competition between groups is stronger than it is within them, the line between groups and individuals is blurred, and selection bumps up a level. The math changes, and cooperation grows. That's how superorganisms form. But it's rare.

All superorganisms face the problem of integrating diverse individuals into a collaborative whole. They must succeed in this, because diversity is the source of their success. Individual ants, slime mold amoeba, and fungal hyphae are not clones, any more than the people in your organization. They *are* closely related—closer than sisters in many cases—but they are not clones. Their diversity is the source of their collective intelligence, and it reduces competition between them, allowing them to work together more closely. Integrating diversity is the most critical element to superorganism success, and the hardest to achieve. Diversity is what makes superorganisms super.

It's hard to wrap our heads around this contradictory tension. Superorganisms seek that chaotic sweet spot where unity and independence are optimal. It's a trade-off. Diversity is the basis for evolutionary change, but cooperation requires shared purpose and reciprocity. This tension is inherent in any team, and gets at the heart of why superorganisms evolve so rarely in the first place. How do these societies resolve their contradictory impulses? How do they maximize independence and diversity while increasing solidarity? And how can we?

Our organizational evolution requires that we transcend our network-of-clones workplaces, to encourage diverse creative individuals to contribute their special sauce. It's something we do naturally in smaller groups, but our challenge is to scale it. How can we achieve the kind of collective intelligence and innovation we require? How does the rest of nature do it? Let's find out.

Chapter Six

Our Magic Friendship Number

The bird a nest, the spider a web, man friendship.
—William Blake

British primatologist Robin Dunbar[1] has spent most of his life watching one of the oddest primates around. Geladas (with a soft g) are the only grass-grazing primate. These baboons shuffle around on their bottoms all day, picking seeds, grass, and corms on the rainswept Ethiopian mountain plains. There are no trees to hide in, and these monkeys are easy prey for leopards. Their solution is bunching together in huge groups. Humans (and the enormous secretive hordes of mandrills that slink through the jungles of West Africa) are the only primates more social.

Geladas are strange for another reason: their constant sing-song chatter to one another. Professor Dunbar, alone in the rain, kept turning around to see who was talking to him. Instead of checking into the asylum, he compared primates with different group sizes and discovered something interesting. As the average size of these groups expanded, so did the species' average brain size. The neocortex—center of executive planning, memory, and language—became especially enlarged. The biggest-brained species also spent the most time grooming and maneuvering for dominance... their politics were more complex. Gelada troops are huge, and their brains quite big. If they groomed one another as much as their group and brain size predicted, they would have no time to eat—they'd starve to death petting each other.

Dunbar wondered if the singing and chatting was their hyper-efficient workaround. Maybe the geladas doubled-up on friends by vocally grooming many at once, while keeping their hands free to find food.

This hypothesis would explain our own big brains and chatty ways pretty nicely. If you were a primatologist from Mars, and you read Dunbar's paper on brain and group size, you could simply measure the brain of the first human you stumbled across (after shooting it with your ketamine speargun) and immediately suspect that it likes to live in groups of 150. And you would be right! This magic friendship number turns up everywhere. Bands of hunter-gatherers average 150 members, Neolithic farming villages contained about 150 people, and military units have historically hovered around there. I once sent a Facebook friend request to Professor Dunbar, but he never answered my request: he already had 150 of them and I guess he knew his limit.

That same Martian primatologist would also guess that we never shut up. Maintaining 150 friends would require us to devote 40% of our time to grooming our buddies and love interests, leaving no time to eat or sleep. Instead, we speak 40,000 words a day—the equivalent of 4 to 6 hours of talking. And that's just the men.

Group-living mammals like us have large, complex brains, the same way our organizations have large and complex central management. Both are expensive to maintain, but social mammals need these central processing units to navigate the complex and exponential politics of dominance.

As apes, humans are predisposed to fall in line when intimidated (and intimidate those who fall in line). We are the most extreme example of the big brain trend. Our heads are as big as they can get without toppling us over or getting jammed in the birth canal. If a big brain is the only way to make teamwork succeed, you can stop reading right now, because we're maxed out. We would just have to hope the smartest among us can tell the rest of us what to do. If bigger brains are the only way, we are screwed. But such is not the case.

Social insects have taken a very different approach to managing cooperation. As their groups get bigger, their average brain size actually declines. They distribute the processing power among themselves, so each one needs less. Perhaps it's an evolutionary accident—they went one way, we went another. Or, perhaps, when a species crosses the superorganism threshold, a new strategy kicks in. It certainly seems that our intellectual edge is fading as we distribute the cost of thinking through our phones.

Vocal grooming is a clever workaround, but today we've surpassed even this exponential gain in connectivity. Now, we live in cities with millions of people, working in global companies employing tens of thousands. Our magic friendship number is woefully inadequate. I don't know about you, but I can't groom seven billion people with words. Bob Marley did as good a job as you could hope for, but mostly we depend on hierarchies to pick up the slack. It's a functional workaround, but an expensive and dangerous one. It requires lots of expensive maintenance for one thing (paying all those managers), and these hierarchies inevitably filter out our diverse intelligence, making it harder to perceive and respond to change.

Those who control information and resources are invested in maintaining the status quo; they will keep driving money and power to the top in a runaway loop until structures grow top-heavy and fall. It's ironic. Our ability to collaborate in big groups brought us global success, and now we've outgrown our ability to collaborate. It's the Peter Principle in action—we've been promoted to the level of our incompetence.[2]

Here's my own little "Just So" story about our ancient ancestors: bigger groups survived better for whatever reason, and groups who cooperated and divided the labor did best of all. Individuals with bigger brains were better at keeping score of complicated politics and relationships, so brain size expanded as well. Groups expanded further still, and we talked and sang together, vocally grooming our friends. At some point, we crossed the superorganism threshold. Breeding was left to the breeders, and we worked ant-like from there. This is the 2% phase change.

Ape society is strongly hierarchical, characterized by Machiavellian political machinations and brute force. There are friendships and touching moments, but chimp social life is no Quaker meeting. By contrast, most, if not all traditional foraging peoples are obsessively egalitarian. They insist on social equity. Nomadic tribes like the Afar people maintain flat networks of male-led clans, not too different from those of the hamadryas baboons. Foraging peoples have strong norms around sharing resources and work, and actively and collectively subvert any who dominate, hoard, boast, lie, cheat, steal, or shirk obligations. Such freeloaders are teased, ostracized, and occasionally even killed.[3]

Over time, people weeded out the most aggressive and acquisitive individuals—we tamed ourselves.[4] Today many of us live in huge cities and work in sprawling global organizations, but we are still superorganism apes yearning to live our human nature. Our brains are maxed out at 150 friends, but if we could just find a way to pet and chat up everyone at once, we could get our flat networks back and live and work the way we like best.

Cute cat videos are that solution.

Well, the connective technologies that allow us to make and spread them are. This new ultra-networked way of collaborating requires far less brain power than traditional hierarchies[5]—remember those amaze-ball slime molds? Even those blobs of brainless jelly can tap the power of collective wisdom and distributed leadership to achieve the kind of intelligence reserved for social mammals.

You may be thinking—*my coworkers are pretty tiny-brained already, thank you very much. I'll pass on this superorganism thing.*

But imagine what you could accomplish with the brains you've got if you worked this way more intentionally!

If we can understand what's going on in our social networks, and structure our organizations to align with this nature more consciously, I believe there is no limit to what we can do. This requires an expedition into the wilds of our humanity…my favorite thing. Let's go!

Chapter Seven

The Tao of Superchimp

Ubuntu [is] the essence of being human. . .
You can't be human all by yourself.
—DESMOND TUTU

I love the South African tribal concept of ubuntu. This is the birthplace of our earliest ancestors, and it seems fitting that today's inhabitants have articulated our superorganism nature so clearly. Some of the most respected biologists on the planet, including EO Wilson, view people as superorganisms. We can't survive on our own for long, any more than an ant can. Solitary confinement is one of the worst punishments we can devise, and given the choice, most people prefer to receive an electric shock than be alone.[1] Like ants, each of us excels at different tasks, and our personalities are unique. Even folks we don't care for can carve out a parasitic niche for themselves. Society permits and requires all kinds of people.

Termites and leafcutter ants split their work similarly. Some toil outdoors, herding aphids and caterpillars. Others patrol the territory, defending the nest and foraging for food or performing trash duty. Some work inside, making or tending babies, womaning the grow rooms, or maintaining the nest.

Women's hips are narrow, made for bipedal walking, but our babies' heads are big. Giving birth is not easy for us, and we rarely do it alone. We work around our physiology by giving birth early, letting our babies continue developing outside our bodies. That makes us and them vulnerable. We can't raise them alone, and it makes us crazy if we try. Let's start a Paleo movement around that! Globally, half our childcare is shared with other adults, many who are completely unrelated to us. Other great ape mamas do all their own childcare. That's a profound change. Shared childcare is so critical to us that one-third of a woman's life is spent as a post-reproductive grandmother. Menopause is a very rare thing—only elephants, dolphins, and orcas share it with us. It really does take a village.

Superorganisms are distinguished by their masterful communication. Chemical symbols emerge from an alphabet of pheromones, mixed in glands of different kinds. They even use syntax, modifying signals by changing the concentration or context, adding various tactile motions or vibrations. Chat revolves around foraging and childcare, nestmate and caste identification. There are alarm, attraction, recruitment, attack, and nest site signals. Fire ants have twenty different chemical words, and honeybees seventeen, with more than twice that many modifiers.

Toothed whales and dolphins mainly communicate with sound and dance, using complex and culturally-specific dialects of clicks and movement. They even have signature whistles as names. Elephants use a wide range of calls and signals to mobilize defense, warn others of danger, coordinate movements, reconcile conflict, attract mates, express their thoughts and feelings, and share social and ecological knowledge. Elephantologist Joyce Pool describes over 70 kinds of vocalizations and 160 visual and tactile signals, expressions, and gestures. Like the dolphins, each individual has a signature rumble and can recognize hundreds of other elephants from half a mile away. Much of their communication is at frequencies far below human hearing, and they can send and receive messages over long distances through these seismic vibrations.

Ravens and crows mimic sounds and memorize useful and intriguing noises, recombining them in novel ways. They have specific calls for different predators and types of food, and even use our own words to manipulate us. At England's Buckingham Palace, straying tourists are commanded to keep to the path, I'm pretty sure the crows around my house tried to push me over the edge of sanity raising three young boys alone, by calling *mama mama mama* every time they saw me.[2] Alex, an African grey parrot studied for his linguistic abilities for nearly 30 years,[3] had over 100 different words for abstract concepts like shape, color, texture, and quantity. He knew what they meant and could readily apply them to novel situations. He is also the only non-human to ask a question.[4]

None of this holds a candle to human communication, though we aren't much different from other primates in the content. Our chat revolves around the politics of dominance just as theirs does. Apes use hand gestures, facial expressions, noises, and body language, throwing sticks and stones and making faces to share their state of mind. Our ancestors surely did all this, adding chummy chatter, song and dance,[5] painting fantastically realistic animals on cave walls, drawing symbols on rocks, and shaping curvy female figurines. Imagining and expressing alternative realities is a very old activity indeed, though possibly those paintings and figures were just early porn.[6] Porn leads the way in all things techy.

At some point, we acquired individual names, allowing us to trade information, mates, food, and promises. We could now make plans, tell stories about things only old folks remember, and talk about other places and times—and most of all, other people.

As our societies grew larger, vocal grooming developed into hieroglyphs and smoke signals, paintings and the written word. The printing press, radio, television. Today we pelt a steady rain of digital packets at one another through a vast global network. The Internet is everyone singing and dancing all over the world at once. Actually, it's mostly porn and spam and cat videos.

Smartphones are now practically part of our bodies, our human antennae. How many of us check our devices before we get out of bed? Old folks may grumble, but people of all ages embrace cheap and ubiquitous contact with family and friends. Maybe this is how we'll scale our superorganisms.

The speed and strategic planning behind these innovations is nothing short of astonishing. In the 1960s, when our communication infrastructure was facing the imminent threat of nuclear war, Paul Baran of the Rand Corporation imagined a more resilient solution.

Baran proposed a web of electronic nodes, through which data broken into small redundant chunks could be sent. Any node could substitute for any other, and there would always be multiple routes around an obstruction. The communication could be reconstituted on the other end—any end. Such a network would even heal itself, adapting without plan or oversight.[7]

As far as I know, no one ever set out to mimic fungal networks. Nature just tends to hit on the best ideas again and again, as Welshman Donald Davies (who independently came up with the packet-switching concept) can attest. It was a simple case of convergence.

Fifty years later, the Internet and cell phones have completely reshaped the fabric of our lives. We have constant two-way communications, and our networks are dense and distributed on a global scale. We imagined the sense-and-response network our superorganism way of life requires, and we built it to order. This is evolution in overdrive, a spectacular display of human ingenuity and foresight.

Ants and bees have maintained their complex societies for some 150 million years, and the termites nearly twice that long. EO Wilson takes adorable delight imaging the dinosaurs bitten, stung, and sprayed by these insects so long ago. But the fungi have networked in the soil for a billion years or so. This approach works. Their organizations operate without plan or boss, consuming far less processing power than we do. They are everywhere, the very foundation of life's expanding potential.

Our own networks are laughably puny and ineffectual by comparison—but who knows, someday we might grow them, just as the fungi do now. We might even partner with them on it. You could say we are rookie superorganisms—we've only lived this way for a million years, and maybe only a tenth of that. Our digital communication networks are only five decades old, and we've only carted our antennae around with us for a couple of decades. I didn't even own a cell phone ten years ago, and look at me now, relentlessly text-tormenting my friends. We are fabulous apes to be sure—but Padawan learners in the superorganism Jedi Academy. Respect your elders, listen and watch. They have much to teach you.

Chapter Eight

The Maker Instinct

The maker instinct is key to making the future.
—BOB JOHANSEN

The urge to make things—what Bob Johansen refers to as maker instinct[1]—is innate. Humans have a strong drive to grow and build. Children at the beach sculpt tunnels and castles for the tides to wash away, but the joy of making remains. We imagine what we'd like to see and work backwards, testing, failing, and repeating until our visions come to pass. This collective desire to procreate is the glue that turns the work of one into the work of many. We can do so much more, and organizations have the deep potential to help us do it.

We are apes—political, selfish, affectionate, and clever. But also, we are like paper wasps driven by the urge to create; industrious ants moving earth; responsible honeybees filled with civic duty. Like them, we share resources and information. We nurture a collective commons, and strive to create something better for our collective children than what came before—after all, they will not be in the future alone.

What brings the ant and ape in us together for such runaway success? It's the same powerfully compelling purpose that drives every other living thing: to nurture the next generation and ensure its success.

But for superorganisms, the next generation is collectively important. The future belongs to us all.

We've been superorganisms for a while now, but doing it ant-scale is new. Getting there requires new models of leadership, teamwork, and production that leverage the mycelial nature of our networks as well as our human nature. These changes will be profound, altering the way we work, govern, learn, buy, and sell—but the shift is just beginning, and we still have a foot in both worlds. Corporations and governments, banks and political parties, unions, universities, and NGOs remain our dominant systems. With all their vertical layers, opacity, and filtering, they control the flow of resources and information. Wealth and power consolidate at the top, crushing the base beneath. As I write this, just fifty families gave 75% of all campaign contributions in the United States Presidential election, and just 1% of the people control 99% of the wealth.

You can't build tall when the base is weak, but information and resources are increasingly trickling the other way as well. Organizational monoliths are breaking and being broken into tiny packets, their flows passing through hundreds of thousands of nodes—us.

One-way consumption strengthens hierarchies; two-way communication flattens them. The printing press was an agent of revolution; TV an agent of brainwashing. Does anyone see your print ads? Who knows. The maker movement— from Pirate Radio to the Anarchist's Cookbook, garage computing and garage bands, fanzines and alternative comics, to 3D printing—is a revolution against one-way consumption. The more oddball consumers among us have pushed back for some time, and now it's a two-way world: our children are making videos with their phones and posting them on YouTube, while Friends like and share photos of their cats sitting in boxes. Anyone can create and disseminate content through their digital network and instantly find out what others think about it.

Centralized concentrations of wealth, knowledge, connections, and technology are increasingly breaking up—flowing through individuals in tiny bits. Many are poor and powerless, and the bits very small and insignificant—little more than marine snow drifting down to feed an entire unknown world at the bottom. But when the base is wide and the layers few, the structure is nearly unbreakable.

This sounds revolutionary, and it is. Is there even a place for institutions and powerful corporations in this vision? Yes, and an important one, as you will see. Sprawling fig trees in the Congo and Amazon explode with sweet fruit—attracting creatures of every kind. These are the mother trees, keystone providers, connecting a wide web of inhabitants in complex and interdependent ways. What you don't see as easily is the dense superhighway of fungal mycelium below the trees, shuttling nutrients and messages among their roots—billions of hyphae working together underground, soaking up impossibly diffuse scraps of value in the poor rain-leached soil to bring to the trees. Leaves high in the canopy, basking in sunshine, those mighty old trees feed them in return. Tree hubs and fungi thrive in this way, while feeding an entire ecosystem of interbeings. Abundance spreads, in widening spirals of diversity and complexity, compounding wealth in an otherwise finite world.

Organizations have this deep potential to bring us together around common purpose. Every organization, every government, every institution—every mighty tree—can take the lead in this transformation. It will be worth it.

Part Two
Collective Intelligence

Work is of two kinds: first, altering the position of matter at or near the earth's surface relative to other matter; second, telling other people to do so.

—BERTRAND RUSSELL

Chapter Nine

Build From the Bottom Up

Evolution is not just "chance caught on the wing." It is not just a tinkering of the ad hoc, of bricolage, of contraption. It is emergent order honored and honed by selection.
—STUART KAUFFMAN

The starlings of Venice flock with such machine-like precision that people long thought they must be orchestrated by telepathy. Tuna and sardine school the same way, synchronizing to appear as a single, fluid organism. We can only wish that our global organizations—with all our diverse personalities, talents, and viewpoints—worked with such unified direction. But people aren't that way.

Nature has other ways of coordinating teams. A colony of ants or termites may contain hundreds of thousands, if not tens of millions of genetically distinct individuals—most of whom are strangers. Yet they live and work in synchrony. How?

Their complex endeavors grow from the bottom up, with no top-down direction. Individuals sense and respond to their own slightly different perspectives on life, and apply their own unique tendencies and talents. Each contributes firsthand expertise, performing whatever tasks they select as they see fit. There is no top-down plan beyond a collection of DNA blueprints—themselves highly labile in response to the environment. No one gives the order, yet complex behaviors result.

Part Two focuses on the first five principles of teeming—how superorganisms work together to build infinite wealth from the bottom up, beginning with the ways they generate and maintain their collective intelligence on a day-to-day basis, and how we can use that in our own collaborative designs.

Pattern #1: Superorganisms cultivate collective intelligence.

Principle #1: Facilitate self-organized networks.

In superorganism societies, team performance emerges in real time—like a film reel of snapshots built from thousands of constantly updating pixels. These colonies break large complex problems into tiny bits of action requiring little computational power. Work builds, and various tipping points trigger sudden behavioral cascades. There are no forecasts, budgets, strategy meetings, or plans. There is no boss, and no one has the whole picture. The entire hierarchy exists within each small team, and strategy happens organically, all the time, everywhere. Decisions are frequent, small, and imperfect, constantly course-corrected in response to signals from others and the environment itself. This is how superorganisms adapt to change: at the edges, all the time, in little bits of work done by everyone.

Principle #2: Aggregate scattered scraps into something greater.

Superorganisms thrive in landscapes of scarcity that exclude most other species, by collecting tiny scraps of value that aren't worth the effort for others. The peer-to-peer economy naturally reimagines companies as platforms for collective value creation, nurtured by tiny, self-organizing contributions by many autonomous individuals. The network economy opens the door to act on shared purpose at scale.

Principle #3: Cultivate diversity and independence.

Like ants, we rely on collective intelligence to accomplish things together. Making our intelligence accurate requires many diverse and independent contributions. But we are apes, not ants, and like our closest relatives we fall in line when intimidated or intimidate those who fall in line. We are very good at imagining what others think—mostly about us—and we care deeply about it. Nonetheless, we require cooperation to thrive. For better or worse, this combination can easily lead to runaway conformity and a herd mentality. If workplaces don't actively insist on diversity, individuality, and creativity, then the human urge to conform will silence them. We'll get more of the same old clones. Our collective intelligence will fall short, and our superorganisms won't scale past a certain point.

Principle #4: Communicate through open, two-way, always-on conversations.

Very large superorganisms like leafcutter ants and termite colonies may contain tens of millions of individuals. Most never meet, but their individual contributions inform and influence the colony's collective activities regardless—by stimulating specific behaviors in others. This is called stigmergy: when one individual's action leave a physical trace that triggers a response in another. Nobody tells anyone what to do, but diverse individual actions can aggregate within smart, flexible, two-way, always-on communication arenas where behaviors are coordinated indirectly, in real time response to on-the-ground stimuli. Organizations require analogous structures, real or virtual—places where indirect conversations between huge numbers of people can happen without suppressing individual contributions. Organizations need "termite mounds."

Principle #5: Trigger tipping-point decisions with simple rules and feedback loops.

Superorganisms regulate their production through small and frequent interactions governed by simple rules and stimulus thresholds. Basically, this is a series of cascading on/off switches—highly complex, noisy, and irregular. Because everyone is following the same basic set of simple rules, surprisingly synchronized patterns emerge, like a starling murmuration or an air-conditioned termite mound. Bouts of coordinated behavior break out as individuals synchronize with nearby others in tiny ways. Once systems sync up, they tend to stay that way and the pattern spreads. Small world social networks like our own amplify or suppress signals especially well. A belief or behavior exhibited by a very low percentage of us—as little as 10% of a given population—can trigger systemic restructuring.

Chapter Ten

The Power of Self-Organization

Self-organization is not a startling new feature of the world.
It is the way the world has created itself for billions of years.
—MARGARET WHEATLEY AND MYRON KELLNER-ROGERS

The photosynthetic pathway is bizarrely and unnecessarily complicated. I had to memorize it in high school. *Nobody would design*
something like this on purpose, I thought.

I was confused. If evolution honed life to perfection, then why
were plants so woolly-headed about this? Suddenly lightning struck—
whatever worked and made more, survived and made more. End of
story. The DNA blueprints inside were the smoking gun as far as I was
concerned[1]—impossibly complex and messy, filled with useless junk.
Evolution was a drunk who somehow staggered home each day.

I imagined each life as a seed with its own size and shape, gathered
in a rainmaker—a tribal instrument with interior partitions and seeds. If
one happened to fall into a hole and fit, gravity pulled it through to the
next segment, striking the wood with a pleasant sound and maybe altering the seed just a bit. The path between partitions and segments could
be convoluted, I reasoned, because things just fell to the next possibility
if one was available. The plants had stumbled into photosynthesis. Life

was no more—or less—than seeds in a rainmaker, accidentally finding right-size holes to fall through. As simple and relentless as gravity, requiring nothing more than time and expanding possibilities.

The results were impossibly beautiful. A miracle. My "photosynthesis epiphany" had me wandering around in a religious daze for weeks. Why didn't everything just fall down dead? It seemed so improbable that such complexities could even function. After all, a carefully designed and tested toaster could be expected to break in a year. How could something that designed itself by accident possibly keep working? It turns out this redundant junk is what makes life so fiercely resilient. There is always a backup plan, or two or three. Self-organization is the *reason* we don't fall down dead.

Evolutionary biologist Stephen Jay Gould used to write about his collection of sandals made from automobile tires, each purchased in his travels around the world. I looked forward to wrestling with his maddening monthly essays in *Natural History* magazine for many years, and was saddened by his untimely death. His sandals were a metaphor for evolutionary innovation. Nature has to work with what's at hand. Evolution is a tinkerer, not an engineer—it doesn't start from scratch.

Adaptations aren't always the simplest or most obvious, or even the best. They are simply good enough—which is to say they are better at whatever they are trying to do than whatever else is around. Our bipedal foot and spine are hacked from our ancestors' tree-swinging body plan, and for the last 3 million years we've been plagued by herniated discs, ankle sprains, and plantar fasciitis. I'm certain an engineer starting from scratch could do better, but you gotta work with what your mama gave you.

It's the old "monkeys typing Shakespeare" bit. With enough time and monkeys, they will eventually write *A Midsummer Night's Dream*. But the monkeys never actually type Shakespeare, because each possibility precludes the others—and also because they are monkeys.[2] It's just not in their nature; this is a really terrible way to design something specific—like trying to drive to a fixed destination by just going which-ever way opens up. If you have four billion years you will certainly get somewhere, but almost certainly not where you wanted to go.

All living things are rigged contraptions of duct tape and paper clips. Only the best designs go on to the next round. The survivors are dazzling, but each is no more (and no less) than a vanishingly improbable accident.

That photosynthetic patchwork pathway thrilled me. The likelihood of being here as we are seemed so vanishingly slim.[3] By accident or design, here we are dreaming of the future, loving family and friends, making stone soup together. The whole photosynthesis epiphany epi-sode stuck with me, and I started liking people more—we're just ani-mals after all, and I had yet to meet an animal I didn't like. Sure, some were best viewed from a distance, and the wild ones needed their space. Even tame ones will bite when threatened, and some, like our pet cockatiel, were just plain neurotic. But all were doing their best, living out their nature as all creatures do. The seeds fall through the holes if they fit. Evolution isn't perfect, just good enough. As humans and as Earthlings, we are united by imperfect striving.

Did you ever see the *March of the Penguins*, that documentary nar-rated by Morgan Freeman? Life for the emperor penguins is impos-sibly hard. Males and females take turns scooting and waddling hun-dreds of miles across Antarctic ice until they reach the water's edge, where they gorge on fatty fish, fill their crop, and head back to regur-gitate it for their loyal mate who has been huddling in -40°F winds all this time. The pair undertakes this perilous effort in the desperate hopes of hatching a single precious egg and raising one tiny chick. Some make it, but most do not. A webbed foot drifts the tiniest bit to the left and the egg rolls away, freezing instantly, killing the tiny embryo inside. Sometimes a chick gets lost in the shuffling mass of bodies, crying out for their mother. She can't reach them through the crowd and the gulls soon take them away. These things happen in the space between heartbeats, despite the fact that you and your mate have conscientiously shuffled back and forth to the edge of the ice for many hard miles and months, standing in the howling wind on the frozen ground eating puked-up old fish while balancing an egg or a chick on your feet. Life isn't fair, and those things just aren't relevant to your infant's success. It doesn't stop the penguins from trying. The birds persist, taking their best shot at regenerating life. We are all little seeds falling randomly through holes as best we can.

Some people go to church, I watch *March of the Penguins*. It works for me. Life is a miracle, don't take it for granted. I think we can all agree on that.

So, I majored in Plant Science. That surprises a lot of people, because I don't have what you'd call a botanist's personality. But plants rarely lie, run away, or do anthropomorphic things that could easily be misconstrued. There is a lot less baggage to unpack. Nobody says "aww" for sprouts or shares videos of cute saplings. You can look a potato dead in the eye and see the raw naked truth—plants that work best make more. It's just easier to study life objectively when it's not looking at you.

A year into my studies, I went backpacking in Hawaii with the Sierra Institute, studying Island Biogeography with botanist Bill Lester, a beaten copy of MacArthur and Wilson's classic in my hand. Our little class trekked the wild, lava-strewn backcountry, discovering the many ways opportunity and constraint had shaped these inhabitants. After millions of years sifting through life's rainmaker, the seeds were going nuts. A riot of leaves and trunks, stems, fruits, and flowers had developed, each taking advantage of the opportunities available to them. Too much rain or too little, too much sunlight or not enough, salt spray, poor soil, herbivores, altitude—each had hit on a unique strategy and preferred conditions. Some flung their pollen and seeds to the wind, others dropped them straight into the soil below. Each had ancestors that floated or flew here—all survived the endless churn of the Pacific to find these shores.

These islands and every living thing in them are complex adaptive systems composed of many other such systems. Like molecules in a reaction, they attract and repel one another, catalyzing and suppressing other such reactions. Each acts opportunistically, accidentally, stumbling into opportunities as it goes along, becoming progressively more distinct and simultaneously more interdependent. Molecules reorganize to form proteins; neurons cluster into networks; populations interact within ecosystems; and people and ants cluster into superorganisms.

Principle #1: Facilitate self-organized networks.

Superorganisms—whether ants, hamadryas, orcas or elephants—work in networks of self-organizing teams. Individuals do their own thing with little or no top-down control, while their teams zip and unzip to deal with shifting conditions. Interactions are simple: one individual follows a trail left by another; a termite daubs sand next to a blob placed by someone else; a honeybee scout recruits her nest mates to harvest pollen and nectar until the bonanza fades away. The whole organization functions this way—in modular teams that form or disband around specific opportunities and threats as they arise. These simple interactions build into complex, intelligent, and even creative solutions.

You can think of them as a single being, exploded into individuals with their own roles, like diverse cells. Certainly none of them are "whole" on their own—like most cells in your body. The difference is that these individuals are not clones. Each is unique and distinct, and acts on their own free will, though they are bound tightly by their shared purpose because their futures are quite literally one.

This isn't to say they don't have hierarchies: dominant social wasps force subordinates to work so hard they are too starved to reproduce, and some leafcutter ants are forced to stay in the garbage dump, filled with dead bodies and parasitic microbes. Tending it is short-lived but sticking workers there does isolate the hazardous waste.

For the most part, these societies are broad-based and flat—a couple of levels, no more. Instead of a centralized brain, administrative functions are pushed out to teams on the frontlines. They distribute their neurons where the action happens, much like the octopus' skin. Strategy happens all the time, organically, everywhere, and brain power stays where it is needed at a moment's notice. Workers with nothing to do forage for work, and their nest-mates recruit them to join tasks requiring assistance. Roles shift within minutes, and decisions are frequent, small, imperfect, and local.

We work this way too, using simple rules to accomplish our daily tasks. Complex outcomes result: the noisy flow of Egyptian traffic, South African bands jamming in townships, women hawking spices and fruit in the markets of India or navigating the curving madness of ancient Venetian streets. Even crossing the streets of Manhattan, we synchronize and adjust in response to one another, while self-organized Alcoholics Anonymous groups have pulled a million people out of addiction. Self-organization is a powerful thing.

The Internet helps us self-organize at unprecedented scale. In the 1990s, the entire music industry was knocked off course when listeners began sharing music instead of purchasing it. Meanwhile, thousands of programmers volunteered to build the Linux operating system. Without even meeting each other, they were able to challenge Microsoft's monolithic software empire when no company could. Likewise, hundreds of volunteer strangers self-organized to produce Wikipedia, with open writable web pages that anyone can edit. Wikipedia is free, belongs to all, and reflects our lives in real time. Contrast that with the venerable *Encyclopedia Britannica* which costs a few million dollars a year to maintain and is always a little behind the curve.

Today, many companies are experimenting with self-organized value generation.[4] Some, like Amazon and Netflix, use it to generate evolving purchase suggestions based on what like-minded people are buying. Harrah's Casinos feeds frontline workers real-time digital information about who's playing, allowing them to deliver targeted perks to valued customers. British Petroleum self-organized around their environmental performance objectives, eschewing company-wide pollution targets and predetermined goals, allowing them to surpass those targets handily.

Other companies self-organize around specific functions. Over 300 Whole Foods utilize self-managed units; GE's top aircraft engines division self-organizes around a single objective: putting the next engine on the truck on time. SEMCO's Ricardo Semler's book *The Seven-Day Weekend: Changing the Way Work Works*[5] documents efforts to radically de-structure the workplace, eliminating organizational charts, job descriptions, and standard working hours. A few companies have moved their entire organization into self-managed teams—some are quite old and successful. The Orpheus Chamber Orchestra at New York's Carnegie Hall, widely regarded as one of the world's best, has been entirely self-managed since 1972. W. L. Gore pioneered self-management at Gore-Tex in the 1950s, and Zappos made the switch (with mixed reviews). Collaborative methodologies like Agile are helping to scale the power of self-organized teams, but self-management remains rare; only 3% of large companies rely on it exclusively. Frederic Laloux describes some of them in his fascinating book, *Reinventing Organizations*. Most of these examples are his.

How does self-management work? Action shifts from top-down decree to local team interactions. There is no fixed hierarchy, no one sets a course. The functions of management are pushed out to the teams and strategy happens organically, all the time, everywhere. Instead of following directions and rigid job descriptions, individuals take personal responsibility for planning and executing their own work—employees are guided by the organization's purpose and their own informed judgment. People do what they think is best in the moment, and decisions are frequent, small, and imperfect. Change is smooth, response is agile, because they adapt all the time, in little bits of work done by everyone.

Laloux gives some fascinating examples of self-management at work. Buurtzorg, a Dutch nonprofit in-home nursing care organization, serves patients through neighborhood teams. Each team of a dozen nurses does their own intake, planning, scheduling, and patient care—everything that would normally be centralized and siloed is done on the frontlines. Each team is like a mycorrhizal patch feeding its trees. Patients and nurses know each other well.

This model might seem charmingly quaint but unscalable—but in five short years, Buurtzorg exploded to 7,000 nurses. Patients and caregivers jumped ship from their traditional providers, as word grew of their "outrageously positive" results: 60% fewer visits to the ER, 40 fewer hours of care, stays cut in half, faster healing, and better outcomes. The Netherlands would save close to €2 billion a year if all home care was done this way. Scaled to the US population, that's a $49 billion savings each year—with personalized house calls and neighborhood care!

Buurtzorg is a stunning financial success, with double-digit surpluses, low overhead, and overwhelming productivity. But Buurtzorg is a nonprofit. Does self-management work in the for-profit sector?

Sun Hydraulics, a publicly traded Florida-based producer of hydraulic cartridge valves and manifolds, believes so. Their 900 employees consistently deliver gross margins around 35% and net around 15%—numbers more typical of a Silicon Valley software start-up. In 30 years, Sun has never taken a loss. Their reputation for quality and service is exemplary, and even in 2009, when revenues were cut in half by the Great Recession, they posted a profit for the 35th year in a row with no layoffs.

Sun is entirely self-managed, with no centralized quality control, purchasing departments, time clocks, or piece rates. Project teams form and disband as needed, and engineers work on whatever they think is most urgent or promising. Laloux describes it as Google's Exploration Friday expanded to fill the whole week.

FAVI is another self-managed success. This family-owned French industrial foundry primarily makes gearbox forks for the automotive industry. It's the last remaining producer in Europe, because the competition has all moved to China for cheaper labor. FAVI keeps their 500 employees' salaries high and has virtually no turnover, a common theme in self-managed organizations. Workers coalesce into mini-factories of 15 to 35 people, each dedicated to a customer. There is no middle management. HR, planning, scheduling, engineering, production, IT, and purchasing are all done by the teams. Issues are simply entered in a logbook as they arise throughout the day, to be claimed by team members with their initials. Product quality is mythic—not one order has been delivered late in over 25 years, and profit margins are exceptional.

Self-management scales, and this is the key to our superorganism success. These companies operate the same way no matter what size. Buurtzorg's 7,000 nurses work the same way they did when there were just a few hundred. Applied Energy Services (AES), a global energy provider headquartered in Virginia, ran a massive 40,000 employee organization for 20 years, entirely in self-managed teams of 15 to 20 workers. AES operated as Buurtzorg, FAVI, and Sun Hydraulics do: the teams handled all day-to-day operations, including budget, safety, scheduling, maintenance, hiring and firing decisions, training, evaluations and compensation, capital expenditures, purchasing, and quality control—even charitable giving and community relations. Millions of customers throughout the world received their energy from these self-governing teams, with only 100 administrators for 40,000 employees all over the world! Today, AES is traditionally managed. The board just got nervous. it seemed kind of weird to them.

Self-managed organizations don't need to restructure. They just fission or fuse, like dividing and multiplying cells. They are virtually meeting-free, and they trust collective intelligence the way the bees do. In a hierarchical organization, report lines converge; there are more meetings the higher you go. Senior leaders have to gather and integrate a bewildering set of global perspectives to make decisions—the process is highly prone to human error and bias. Dominance hierarchies make folks less transparent about what they really think as well—some are never asked or even seen. It's stressful for leaders too!

Contrast this with self-managed organizations, where there are no reports, approval delays, or meetings. Management, if it exists, is simply there to ask tough questions and give an opinion before moving on to the next question; the teams will do the work of integrating these perspectives—someone on the front lines who knows the details.

These skeletal administrative staffs lack decision-making authority. They are not deciders, they are facilitators. Buurtzorg's 7,000 nurses are supported by just thirty people, yet it is regularly named the best Dutch company to work for and receives 400 applications a month.

You may be thinking, *what kind of hippie-dippy nonsense is this? You're telling me people do whatever they want, and do the right thing? That might work in France, or at Ben & Jerry's... but come on now.*

It's a good question. Why don't people slack off? The answer is deeply biological and uniquely human: peer pressure, reputations, and caring for others. These teams work together closely, day in and day out, for years. It matters what their teammates think of them. Employees are accountable to each other all day long, not just when the boss is looking. Nobody wants to be the weak link in the chain, and free riders and bullies get cut out of the work. Laloux says these folks get uncomfortable or frustrated and leave. Good people, however, like being part of high-performance teams. They like working with competent, conscientious, self-motivated teammates, and they like being in charge of their own work. These workplaces are competitive to get into, and employees seldom leave. Self-management is a heavy responsibility for those conscientious people who are willing to take it on, and it is more rewarding for them as well.

Laloux notes that these self-managed employees seemed proud of their work, even if it was just moving tomatoes around. Their work provides jobs for their community, teammates, and families, a motivation far stronger than any sales target could give. At FAVI, teams are excited when orders are high. They talk about orders in terms of jobs provided. Nobody wants to let down their teammates' families and community. Perhaps surprisingly, few of these companies do sustainability reports—targets are irrelevant. They just do their best every day. Performance will be what it is.

These companies also lacked rigid job descriptions and titles. One exception that proves the rule is Morning Star, the company that produces most of America's canned tomatoes. These roles are carefully defined, because canning and shipping tomatoes is pretty cut and dried, with a ruthless margin. It's all about efficiency. Each employee selects 20 to 30 specific roles from a list, agreeing to perform them by signing a written contract with their upstream and downstream colleagues. Because these tasks are so itemized, it's easy to trade if you are sick or overwhelmed or just want to learn something new. At Holocracy One, a self-managed company that designs self-management modules, colleagues rate their roles yearly and swap them through an internal marketplace. If you don't like what you do, or the people you're doing it with, you vote with your feet. That's literally true at Valve, a 400-employee gaming company in Seattle, where the desks are on wheels. People just unplug and roll on to the next project. An intranet app helps them find each other.

These companies also lack promotions. Employees' roles grow as their peers grant them more responsibility. As they do, the pay goes up. At W.L. Gore, each employee rates the colleagues they work with once a year, noting how closely they work with them. Software crunches the numbers, placing everyone into one of just a few salary tiers.

These organizations don't operate by consensus or compromise, and they don't design by committee. Anyone can make any decision at these places—you are just required to ask those affected what they think about it first. As long as no one objects, the solution is adopted. When a better idea comes along, it's revised—just like the ants do. The bigger the decision, the wider the net that needs to be consulted. That can include the CEO and board of directors. Buurtzorg's CEO once had to apologize to all 7000 nurses for neglecting to ask about a decision. That kind of failure can get you fired, though you aren't bound to act on their advice. Disregard it at your peril, though, because the responsibility stays with you. It's a fast way to take action, and responsibility stays localized.

Zappos CEO Tony Hsieh adopted self-management in 2013, saying, "The one thing I am absolutely sure of is that the future is about self-management." Every time a city doubles in size, innovation and productivity per resident increases 15%, while in companies, innovation and productivity per employee generally go down. How could he structure Zappos more like a city, and less like a bureaucratic corporation? In cities, people and businesses self-organize. Hsieh felt traditional managers impeded progress toward his self-managed ideal, and in 2015 he ripped the Band-Aid off and asked everyone to commit or leave. There would be no more people managers at Zappos. 18% of his 1500 employees took buyouts, another 11% left with no package. That sounds traumatic. Certainly, it was a massive social experiment, filled with chaos and uncertainty. Jennifer Rheingold reports that it "created new winners and losers," and "sparked fresh ideas."[6] Introverts benefit from the expectation that everyone will speak, while younger and less experienced employees reported enjoying their jobs much more. Where a customer service specialist was once blocked from transferring to the culture team by his manager, he now "can't imagine going back to traditional hierarchy."

The switch to self-management is fraught with uncertainty, and you will likely get a great deal of pushback, as Hsieh discovered. But eventually all the slackers and bullies leave, as they get cut out of the work and their pay declines. This is a rare and telling glimpse behind the curtains of peer pressure, conformity, and politeness that mask dominance and politics in service of fairness. We use these curtains to suppress each other's desire to dominate, while hiding our own bullying and slacking—even from ourselves! The superorganism ethos is a double-edged sword that can only be wielded with transparency, reputations, and the freedom to move to more conscientious circles and exclude less conscientious folks. You have to be able to walk away and find better teammates, or band together to keep them out. That's the essence of the human mechanism for creating and maintaining adaptive superorganisms.

Chapter Eleven

Scattered Squandered Scraps

The journey of 1000 miles begins with one step.
—LAO TZU

M y parents were the best patrons a budding natural philosopher could have. They tirelessly transported me to midnight
grunion runs and bankrolled my little whale-watching expeditions
with unfailing cheer. The Scripps Institute of Oceanography, world's
oldest center for deep sea research, wasn't far away, and my dad took
me to the monthly lectures. One presentation in particular stands out
in my memory—a slideshow from the depths about "marine snow." I
remember my irritation—*I came to see grotesque pop-eyed oddities
of the deep, not floating specks of snot and feces!* This bland detritus
sifting slowly from the surface seemed unworthy of my notice—just
bits of yesterday's sunlight drifting down from another world. And
yet, here was the foundation of life in the blackness of the bathy-
sphere: tiny scraps feeding an enormous ecosystem we knew virtually nothing about.

Principle #2: Aggregate scattered scraps into something greater.

Superorganisms thrive in landscapes of scarcity in much the same way—by collecting tiny scraps of value that aren't worth the effort to anyone else, and converting them into something more valuable.

Harvester ants embody this principle. They gather tiny seeds, one by one, storing them for hard times. In South Africa, people rely on them to harvest scattered rooibos seeds for tea. One in ten plant species depend on ants to disperse their seeds, and in fire-prone grasslands the ants store them safely below ground.

A single termite's scraps of wood are negligible, but collectively, their bite-size specks can feed a cow-sized colony. Similarly, the mycelial fungi search for and absorb impossibly tiny molecules of water and nutrients—enough to feed a forest of trees. Honeybees gather specks of nectar, converting them into rich honey for the long winters.

But superorganisms can't convert these scraps into value without gathering them someplace first. Often, that requires partnering with other species to unlock the value contained in them. Termites and leaf-cutter ants can't just eat the wood and leaves they collect, because they can't digest plant fibers. Instead, they feed it as a compost to their carefully tended underground fungal gardens. The fungi break it down, yielding rich mushroom fruit for the larvae to eat.

Mycorrhizal networks act in a partnership with other organisms as well. They can't produce their own carbohydrates—only chloroplast-filled plant factories can do that. So, the mycelia concentrate diffuse molecules of fertilizer and water in the soil, trading them with trees for sugar. It's the partnership and the platform that unlocks this value.

It's easy to reimagine companies as aggregating conversion platforms for collective value, nurtured and cared for by tiny, distributed contributions from ordinary people. Many companies do this already—think of Google turning our clicks into a search engine, or Amazon using our product ratings and purchases to drive sales. At Facebook, Twitter, and

Instagram, volunteers create, gather and donate scraps of content for free.[1] Why do we do it? Because we are social animals, driven to connect, make, and share things with others. These companies provide the platform, we provide the scraps. NYU professor Clay Shirky refers to this as a "cognitive surplus" made possible by the Internet. Previously wasted scraps of time, talent, and energy can now be pulled into something of heft and weight. Our network economy becomes the emergent product of millions of diverse, independent, and connected minds.

Obviously, we can only cook this stone soup at scale with digital networks. Our connective technologies draw those who were previously shut out, giving them a means to engage in wealth-building transactions. Many are poor and powerless, and the bits are no more than insignificant drifts of marine snow. But those specks add up to feed an entire world at the bottom. Just as thousands of honeybees bring pollen to the hive, and millions of fungi pool molecules of fertilizer, peer-to-peer production offers new sources of value.

What kind of platform or partnership can your company offer? How can you help people collect and convert their previously wasted potential? If done well, people will bring you their scraps for free, because your company becomes both the pot that holds the soup and the fire that cooks it. This kind of wealth is virtually infinite. Put the pot on the fire, toss in a stone, and entice the willing contributions of the superorganism itself. Make yourself an irresistible platform for collecting and converting scraps of distributed value.

Emerging markets are a foundational piece of future growth, offering potential new customers. These "rising billions," as entrepreneur Peter Diamandis[2] calls them, have little to spend, but they represent "3 to 5 billion new customers who have never purchased anything, never uploaded anything and never invented and sold anything," and are about to come online. Their individual incomes are low, but when aggregated, represent tens of trillions of dollars in newly created wealth.

Ten billion people loom on Earth's horizon. We certainly do not lack human potential. But the 4 billion poorest of us have been cut out of humanity's collective imagination. Their hard-won ideas, unique perspectives, and scrappy DIY determination have a great deal to offer. Now, with cheap cell phones, global pay-per-job opportunities, and neighborhood microloans, the poorest can access jobs, training, information, and customers—and our collective intelligence gains access to them.

Diamandis' version of the rising billions is alluring, because even a billion pennies a day adds up. It's an exciting frontier, mostly unexplored. Beyond the teeming slums of India and Brazil lies Africa. Even in North America, the poor and disconnected are everywhere, just waiting for a chance to taste the soup. Everyone can find a few scraps to contribute and exchange for access to it.

I think of this as "lichen strategy." Lichens are a collaborative chimera of algae and fungus in which the fungus provides a safe harbor for the tender algae to do its work, and the minerals it digests from surrounding rocks provide essential nutrients for the plant. Meanwhile, the algae cook up the duo's photosynthetic fuel. Lichens don't need much to survive; they thrive in the forgotten cracks of the world. But slowly, imperceptibly, these hearty beings crumble bare rock into soil, opening the door for others. As soil builds, new life sprouts.

Obviously, this strategy requires that people everywhere become connected. That's happening.[3] Less than half the global population is online, but nine in 10 have a cell phone.[4] Only 70% have access to a toilet, but nearly all can get to a phone. There are "more phones than thrones" in the world. Many companies are stepping up to provide this connection. Facebook plans to provide Internet access to underserved countries with unmanned aircraft through its internet.org initiative. SpaceX is deploying some 700 small satellites, giving access to rural and developing areas. Google's Project Loon posits thousands of balloons at the edge of space, designed to fill coverage gaps and bring people back online after natural disasters. Meanwhile, Greg Wyler, with Sir Richard Branson of the Virgin Group and Paul Jacobs of QUALCOMM propose a constellation of 650 satellites.[5]

We can taste the first results. The microwork, microfinance, crowd-sourced information and resource revolution opens the door for us to act on shared purpose at unprecedented scale, while sparking real economic growth. Michael Joseph, founder and former CEO of Safari.com, the largest cell phone service provider in Kenya, believes half of all recent Kenyan GDP growth has resulted from this technology.

In 2007, Safari.com launched M-PESA, an East African mobile phone-based money transfer service created for microfinance borrowers to receive and repay loans. It was a hit, and customers soon reappropriated the system to send remittances and make payments. Today, M-PESA lets users deposit, withdraw, and transfer money through their mobile phone. By 2010, it was the most successful mobile phone-based financial service in the developing world, and by 2012, 17 million Kenyan accounts were registered. Soon, millions of people in Afghanistan, South Africa, India, and Eastern Europe had access to a formal financial system for the very first time.

This had the unexpected benefit of reducing corruption in these cash-based societies. When Afghan police began receiving their pay through a mobile payment system modeled on M-PESA,[6] they were surprised to receive a 30% raise. For the first time, their wages weren't skimmed by higher-ups!

The poor have largely been cut off from financial services. Banks won't give loans to those without assets, and fees are too high relative to the tiny amounts of money they need. Poor people try to save on their own, but neighborhoods and families are rife with addiction, violence, and theft. Community members, particularly women, lose a quarter of what they save on average—mostly to their own family members.[7] The poor need places to safely save their pennies and access them when they need it.

Microcredit pioneers like Muhammad Yunus[8] developed ways for women to get small loans and entrepreneurial skills. Today, the Grameen Bank serves 40 million poor Bangladeshis. Families served are less likely to pull children out of school and more likely to open small businesses and create jobs. Quality of life is higher as well, with three meals a day, a toilet and a rainproof house with clean drinking water.

One of the challenges with microcredit is managing tiny loans ($250 and a cell phone) affordably. The percentage overhead is much higher than it would be for a single large loan, despite the remarkably low default rates on these microloans. As a result, interest rates hover around 30%—usury by any standard. The industry is rife with parasites, and even member-owned and interest-free Grameen Bank clients fall victim to misinformation and predatory debt collectors. Sometimes groups lose their members' money, trapping them in a spiraling cycle of debt. Digital networks offer workarounds. Iqbal Kadir created Grameen Phone, giving Bangladeshi villagers cell phones and microloans, empowering them to grow small businesses, even in isolated places. Thanks to these efforts, millions of people have been able to pull themselves out of poverty. The phone/microloan combo helps folks access the pot and the fire, so to speak, allowing them to contribute their scraps of value to the soup. Richer communities result.

Web-based platforms connect lenders directly to these micro-entrepreneurs, eliminating opportunities for parasites. Peer-to-peer microlending platforms Desha and Kiva, both US-based nonprofits, link individual lenders and borrowers directly across international borders, cutting out any potentially corrupt local intermediaries.

Digital networks aggregate our smallest scraps in other ways. Crowdsourcing and microwork platforms break large projects into small tasks, allowing them to be completed by multiple individuals working independently through the Internet. Oracle and SAP fill their employment gaps through nonprofit Samasource, which gives trained remote people the opportunity to earn a living wage. Amazon's

Mechanical Turk is similar. Workers perform all kinds of paid tasks online, from writing algorithms, to labeling photos, tagging articles, writing product descriptions, and transcribing documents. Meanwhile, Uber and Airbnb connect users and providers.[9]

Distributed solutions like crowd-work, crowdsourcing, micro-lending and additive manufacturing are bottom-up, place-sourced technologies that facilitate local ingenuity. They work by harnessing the power of collective intelligence in service of human adaptability and resilience, ultimately energizing our industries and regenerating healthy systems.

The gig economy is maturing, though, and the shine has worn thin in spots. Social capital is the glue that holds our superorganisms together, but these upstarts don't always have much of it. Users, providers, and platforms may lack personal relationships—no one knows anyone else. That's partly why it works: we are Paul Baran's interchangeable nodes in a wide, resilient network. But people aren't interchangeable. In real life, natural selection sorts between us. If no one wants to mate with you, your genes die out. Currently, peer-to-peer partnerships aren't necessarily well vetted, and there aren't many options to choose from. Users and providers can't just move to other "good" collaborators, because there's nowhere to go just yet. Nor is it a fair exchange. Workers get all the responsibilities and few of the benefits. There is no safety net or backup plan for them. I believe there are superorganism-inspired solutions to these issues. Figuring out this collaborative math may ultimately feed us all.

Education is another value-aggregating conversion platform made possible by connection. School has always been difficult for the poor to attend, and studies show clearly that the primary factor for reducing population growth and increasing standards of living is education for girls, who are often excluded from it. Digital access has exploded for them. By 2019, half of all classes will be taught online, many free to those with Internet. Millions of people are using platforms like peer-to-peer Ubiversity or Coursera, without even leaving their homes. Khan Academy, a nonprofit educational site, offers thousands of free videos, in some 65 different languages. My children readily jump on the site for help with their homework—Khan is much better than I am. In my experience, virtual classes can offer a greater value than similar in-person classes, because the diversity of students is greater. Many are practicing professionals from all over the world, with wide experience and insight. Engagement and discussion tend to be high, rich with unexpected opportunities.

Free education, good jobs, loans, corruption-free money transfers—all this sounds great. But let's back up for a second. Right now, 9 in 10 of the people in the world can't count on reliable food, water, or shelter, let alone an education, training, or good Wi-Fi. Even lichens need something to live on. The gap between rich and poor is stark. That's nothing new, but now these inequities are glaringly visible. "It is one thing to be hungry and hopeless," says Bob Johansen,[10] "but it is quite another to be hungry, hopeless, and connected." A world filled with humiliated, desperate digital natives stuck in poverty is sure to be explosive.

Basic technologies around food, water, and energy are the necessary foundation of any bottom-of-the-pyramid strategy for growth. Policymakers struggle to improve these things, but like a termite colony rebuilding its mound in the wake of an aardvark attack, global problems fiercely resist our best efforts. A diverse network of entrepreneurs is stepping up to try.

Forty years ago, innovation, communication, and consumption were mostly one-way affairs, fed to people by large institutions, with decisions made at the top. *Need water? Here's a Coke. We diverted your water to make it.* But now, innovation increasingly percolates up from the bottom, fueled by cell phones and the maker instincts of many.

Singularity University, a Silicon Valley educational track and business incubator founded in 2008 by Ray Kurzweil and X prize founder Peter Diamandis, helps dedicated entrepreneurs tap fast-growing "exponential technologies" like artificial intelligence, distributed computing, water technologies, and synthetic biology to "improve the lives of one billion of the world's most vulnerable people." The program focuses on open source, locally relevant, user-driven solutions to global problems—helping local innovators develop better ways to deliver energy, provide clean water, financial infrastructure, and education.

Meanwhile, crowdfunding platforms like Kickstarter and Indiegogo have democratized innovation. Today, you can propose a creative project (this book was financed this way—thank you, Kickstarter supporters!), and potentially draw contributions from a multitude of patrons. Anyone with an Internet connection can become a lender, borrower, or patron. Kickstarter fundraising for the arts surpassed the NDA in 2011, and by 2012, 63,000 projects had received $250 million.

When you add distributed manufacture to the mix, the possibilities seem infinite. In 2011, a South African carpenter who had recently lost several fingers saw a YouTube video of a steampunk hand an American prop designer had made. The carpenter was curious—could the designer make a functioning hand for a real person? 10,000 miles apart, the strangers began swapping ideas and eventually designed and printed a customizable prosthetic hand. The carpenter displayed a prototype of their creation on Facebook, where a South African woman saw it. She asked if the two would make a hand for her little boy, Liam, who was born without fingers. The pair created a tiny hand for just $150. With donations from strangers following the saga online, the designer flew to meet the carpenter and the boy. They assembled the hand together, then uploaded the design for anyone who wanted it. Word spread, and soon, people around the globe were offering to print hands for those without a printer. Other folks tinkered with the design, and they gave the modifications away as well. Today, it is possible for anyone, anywhere in the world, to create their own working hand for just $150.

With a self-replicating rapid prototype printer, anyone with an Internet connection, power source, and feedstock can download an open-source design and print what they need. Nonprofit Field Ready brings these rep-raps to struggling regions like post-earthquake Haiti and trains local people to use them. The printers stay behind, allowing communities to print umbilical cord clamps, IV bag hooks, oxygen tank valves, and prosthetic limbs as needed.

The power often goes out after natural disasters, of course, and a quarter of the world's population have no electricity to begin with. These are exactly the communities needing local on-demand manufacture the most. In response, Joshua Pierce, an engineering professor at Michigan Tech Open Sustainability Technology Lab (MOST) developed a completely open source, solar powered, mobile rep-rap printer. Pierce provides free links to all technical files, schematics, and instructions, allowing anyone to build one for less than $1000. The printer packs into a duffel bag, easily toted to isolated rural communities. Pierce offers designs for wind turbines, hand cranked power generators, medical braces, breast pumps, prosthetic leg covers, waterspouts, and more—all open source and printable for the cost of the raw feedstock.

This raises an important question: what should we print with? A team of students at the University of Washington has one idea: recycling plastic waste into printer feedstock. The students harvest trash, printing composting toilets and rainwater barrels, sidestepping supply chains and radically reducing cost and environmental impact. Imagine turning river garbage into prosthetic hands. Of course, we'd need to make sure that plastic wasn't full of toxins first! We want to print with things other creatures will eat.

Science has traditionally been an exclusive activity requiring specialized degrees and privileged access to libraries and laboratories. Those walls are starting to come down, as a kind of "biocitizens movement" takes root—with DIY bio meetups, science hack days, bio-blitzes, and maker fairs. Bay Area social entrepreneur Eri Gentry founded Biocurious, "the world's first hacker space for biology" with a simple Kickstarter campaign. This volunteer-run nonprofit community lab offered shared lab space and equipment to anyone with an academic or professional background, along with classes and community support to help amateurs pursue their own scientific inquiry. Members could do their own genetic testing, explore synthetic biology, and seek correlations between various genetic markers and diseases. Another of her community organizations crowdsourced health experiments and clinical trials—ordinarily a prohibitively expensive undertaking that can only be done by organizations with big financial backing. This allowed members to simply propose a trial to the community, which then helped recruit participants, design the trial, and analyze the data. Subjects were members of the community, fully engaged in the research at every stage. Data were openly available, and trials virtually free.

Swarm creativity is revolutionizing other aspects of healthcare as well. The Institute for the Future's game-like foresight engine crowdsources ideas for multiple sclerosis treatments, while University of Washington's FolDIT is a massive online platform that allows people to fold proteins for fun—collective intelligence often cracks the code where the scientists cannot.

Global organizations increasingly see that American-style capitalism doesn't play everywhere. Rising entrepreneurs in places like India and China, Brazil, the Middle East, and even Europe are reworking it to suit their own values. Century-old Royal Dutch/Shell sought to combat the stifling effects of hierarchy and tradition. Leaders became more of a learning experience designer and guide, rather than an authority figure with the answers. Once folks at the grassroots realize they own the problem, they also discover they can help create the answers, and they get after it very quickly, aggressively, and creatively, with a lot more ideas than headquarters could ever have prescribed.

Companies can flip the equation by building platforms where people can self-organize to adapt, innovate, and regenerate value in ways that mesh with and support local purpose and values. They can create opportunities for people to design their own products based on their own needs, styles, and available resources. This is hard to do when consumers are far from corporate decision makers, but building local sense and response loops "right into the octopus' skin" by inviting consumers to become local entrepreneurs that create what their communities need, how and when they need it is a start.

Look for ways to make yourself indispensable to local people everywhere by providing platforms where they can build their own solutions. Imagine the brand loyalty and value that accrues when capitalism isn't done to people from afar, but by and for them.

Chapter Twelve

Think for Your Own Damn Self

Good work can be defined only in particularity, for it must be
defined a little differently for every one of the places and
every one of the workers on the earth.
—WENDELL BERRY

There comes a time in the life of a hive when they need to find a new home.[1] They are tense as they prepare for the move, gathering tightly on a nearby branch like itchy facial hair on a Portland Tinder profile. Most workers wait quietly, but the oldest most knowledgeable bees are busy scouting. Each sallies forth in search of a suitable spot for her swarm. She circles, inspecting. Is it dry? Safe from bears? She paces it out to measure whether it could store enough honey for the winter. She might spend forty minutes scoping it out. If it satisfies her exacting criteria, she will return to the swarm to do her waggle dance—a series of symbolic movements indicating its direction and distance. The more she likes it, the more waggly figure eights she will do. Other scouts follow along, and some will fly out to see for themselves. Good sites spark longer dances than mediocre ones, so more scouts see and decide to visit. They, too, return and dance. Good choices amplify while more lackluster options fade away. Meanwhile, the scout who discovered the site stops flying and joins the ranks of the waggle watchers. Maybe she'll check out someone else's site, or just wait and see. Few bees will visit more than one site, but none will vote for a site she hasn't seen. Fake news just doesn't fly in the honeybee world.

Once a site accumulates a threshold level of support, it's winner-take-all. The scouts shake their torpid hive-mates, stirring them into action. *Let's go!* The entire hive takes off *en masse* for their new home, with the scouts zipping valiantly through the swarm, leading the way with their beelines.

This decision-making process is messy and unpredictable—there are no leaders or committees, and the computing power is low and distributed. Scouts gather a diverse collection of possibilities, stage an honest competition of ideas, and unanimously converge on a single choice. Dr. Thomas Sealy's painstaking research shows they nearly always choose the best one. This "smart swarm honeybee democracy" distributes the problem-solving among members, building and synchronizing their simple interactions until a tipping point is reached and decisive action is triggered. By aggregating many diverse opinions, each conveyed by small, distributed actions in a single arena, the tiny creatures converge on the best answer to an extremely complex problem very quickly, with minimal computing power. This is collective intelligence at work.

Collective intelligence requires diversity and independence in its members' thoughts and actions: individual scouts first discover and share a wide range of home possibilities, expressing their diverse opinions through dance. The bees solicit agreement from others, but bees only vote for sites they have independently verified. This is a matter of life and death, not something to be trifled with. If gossip and dominance took root, the margin of error would compound instead of canceling out. A mistake could prove fatal.

Principle #3: Cultivate diversity and independence

Until recently, increasing the diversity in our organizations generally meant being politically correct and legally protected. The focus was on fairness and inclusion around gender, race, sexual identity, and ethnicity—and not getting sued. As you can see, though, diversity is even more important than this.[2] It is the very foundation of collective intelligence and future potential. Organizations must actively cultivate diversity and independence, because they cannot muster collective intelligence or swarm creativity without them.

Diversity affects a whole range of things. Some individuals are more resistant to disease than others. Honeybees are in catastrophic decline from "colony collapse disorder"—science for "we don't know." Essentially, the colony just ups and flies away, abandoning its queen. We do know that colonies with more variation are more likely to survive. It's worth adding that 10,000 years of human domestication has eliminated much of the bees' diversity. Their poor health may not be too different from that of many purebred dogs or the British monarchy in Victorian times. Ants, by contrast, have never gone in much for human work, and like coyotes, they are far more diverse.

Diverse groups perform better. Harvester ant colonies with greater genetic diversity grow faster, survive longer, and reproduce earlier than less diverse ones nearby. Some workers start forage early or end late; some are active and intrepid, others slow and cautious. Collectively, they achieve more.

Diversity helps maintain a healthy temperature in the hive as well: bees fan their wings or shiver and cluster to adjust the heat. More diverse hives enjoy smoother, more consistent, more gradual change, as stimuli thresholds are more spread out.

Honeybee colonies with greater diversity also seem to be less stressed. It's even possible the bees abandon their queen because they sense she isn't mated with sufficient diversity to support their efforts. Why bother? Life can't just create what it needs from thin air—it can only move into the adjacent possible, the next open door.[3] Without a variety of diverse options, these doors don't exist, and the population is easily trapped when conditions change.

Collective intelligence also rests on the independence of its members. Clay Shirky[4] writes about a group of Canadian students who were given this assignment: make a video, put it on YouTube, and get one hundred thousand views (this was 2012). The team produced what looks like a shaky, unedited phone grab of an eagle swooping down to take off with a baby. In reality, it was carefully constructed in Photoshop. The video went viral with more than 2 million hits. *Wildlife attacks child!*

Shirky points to this as an example of collective intelligence gone wrong—the worst of the ant and the ape coming together in us. We are extremely good at seeing patterns. As of this writing, our ability to recognize faces is still beyond the ability of a computer to replicate. We are so good at extrapolating meaning from the noisy chaos of life that we spot patterns when they aren't even there. That's the dark side of our pattern-seeking prowess—our tendency to stereotype, overgeneralize, and make snap judgments. We overvalue the first thing we hear and ignore facts that contradict what we think we know. We are notoriously prone to latching onto preconceptions that blind us to opportunity and risk. We look for meaning when there is none—and we find it.

As apes we have a long history of living in dominance hierarchies. Non-experts defer to experts, lower ranked folks defer to higher ones. We readily fall in line when intimidated or intimidate those who fall in line. We are skilled politicians, excelling at guessing what others think. That's the ape in us, constantly assessing, maneuvering, dominating. And yet we are superorganisms, doing our best to suppress all this through social conformity and peer pressure. We care what others think about us, and we generally try hard to fit in. The fallout is we don't always verify information from friends or authorities. And once a small percentage of us agree, the rest tend to go along.

In Asch's classic 1951 experiment, twelve students were shown a series of lines and asked to select one that matched a second card. The answer was quite obvious, but the first eleven people were plants, instructed to choose the wrong one. The real subject went last. More than a third of the time he (yes, all were men) went along with the rest.

The experiment is generally held up as proof of our mindless conformity, but the particulars are more revealing. 95% of the subjects defied the majority at least once, and only 5% went with the crowd every time. A quarter consistently defied the majority. When asked in follow-up interviews why they conformed, most said they knew the others were wrong but felt a sense of solidarity with them because they had volunteered their time for something important.

The herd effect is powerful. Strangers two or three degrees removed from us influence our behaviors without us being aware. The wave at a football game, standing ovations at the symphony—if someone stares at the sky, we do too. What do they know that I don't know? The herd mentality affects us all, whether we are voting, losing weight, or quitting smoking—which is why the stock market's invisible hand is not as rational as economists would like it to be. We care what others think too much, making our bets neither diverse nor independent. People are not as coldly calculating as Wall Street thinks we are—and they are subject to dominance and conformity like the rest of us. Honeybees could probably run a rational market okay, but people—anxious, moralizing, herd-like, image conscious, wildebeest stampeding across a croc-infested river—are the last species you'd want running the global economy. *"I'll go if you go!"*

The urge to conform is the root of our lack of independence and diversity, and it's the reason why our collective intelligence is often not so very. Being surrounded by others like themselves makes people feel safe. It's easier to trust and give if folks around you do too. Cooperation and the value it generates snowballs, and surrounding ourselves with cooperators protects us from parasites and mooches, but conformity hinders our collective intelligence and dampens our creative sparks. It's a paradox: we require diversity, independence, and cooperation to adapt, but conformity protects cooperators from being exploited.

This tension gets at the heart of why superorganisms evolve so rarely despite their success when they do. Only very specific conditions can push a population into the superorganism space. Once they cross that threshold, however, each member reaps the benefits of high-performance cooperation and supreme adaptability. Humans have crossed the threshold—we are superorganisms. The most cooperative (and protected) groups among us will ultimately succeed.

The "golden eagle snatches kid" hoax illustrates another thing. Far away from the makers of the video, in a tiny bedroom in Brazil, a teenager watched and noticed a jerky frame. *This is a fake.* He went through the clip frame by frame with some amateur video software and exposed the fraud with a countervideo. That went viral too, and the hoax faded from circulation in days. The takeaway? Diversity and independence, globally networked around shared purpose, yields the collective intelligence we need to counter forces that seek to obscure and distort the truth.

Chapter Thirteen

I Feel Like Making Stigmergy

Your move.
—GARRY KASPAROV

The Kalahari is the largest stretch of unbroken sand on the planet. Local people call it "Kgala"— the Great Thirst. It's not the easiest place to make a living, yet the bone-dry soil is dotted with towering cones of baked earth, each one teeming with life. These mounds are the handiwork of millions of tiny blind squirmy rice-like insects— the macrotermites. The termites don't actually live in these towers, though. That's just their air conditioner. The city itself is far below the mound; insects only come up for repairs and defense by day. At night, however, foragers emerge to search the desert for twigs and dry grass. If you like campfires you know that wood contains a lot of fuel—but the termites can't digest it themselves. Instead, they chew these scraps into a paste and bring it deep into the nest to deliver it to their fungal cone: a brain-coral structure that houses their mycelial gardens. The fungus thrives on this compost, and the termites thrive on the fungus. They've successfully outsourced their stomach.

The termites and their fungi are the metabolic equivalent of a cow. In fact, I often think of these mounds as half-buried cows. Even a buried cow needs to breathe, and so do the termites and fungi. During the day, tiny tunnels lining the exterior of the mound heat faster than the deeper channels within it. Warm air is pushed up, but has nowhere to go; it gets forced back down through a chimney in the center, then fans out to the exterior layer at the base of the mound, where tiny perforations suck in fresh air. The cow inhales! At night, the temperature drops. As the outer walls lose that heat, the current reverses and the lungs exhale the carbon dioxide waste into the night air.

As you know from superorganism Principle #1, termites don't need a plan or central management to create or maintain this structure. Instead, one termite lays down a grain of sand, cementing it in place with its pheromone-laden saliva. This attracts other termites, which deposit their own bits next to the first. All these spit wads of pheromone build, enticing more termites to join in. As the mound takes shape, the termites obey a set of simple, hardwired rules. A specific column height triggers the switch to arch-making. A hard angle triggers smoothing. If an aardvark destroys part of the mound, the termites immediately begin rebuilding it just as it was before, right up to the spire on top, which points to the sun's highest spot in the sky. Imagine millions of individuals, most of whom never meet, collectively informing each other through grains of sand and spit to produce a net zero building that breathes. Each contribution stimulates a specific action from someone else, and nobody tells anyone what to do. With little in the way of brains or management, the termites maintain a steady 30°C throughout the day and year, with precisely the right amount of carbon dioxide.

This process of individual actions stimulating responses in others is called *stigmergy*. Smart communication structures, whether a termite mound, a waggle dance floor, or a chessboard are *stigmergic arenas*. Games are a classic example. You do something, I respond. Follow the rules, take your turn, and don't cheat—we've created something where nothing was before. Stigmergy is everywhere in superorganism societies. In large colonies, most members never communicate directly, yet their experiences still collectively inform and influence one another. These are smart, flexible, two-way, always-on communication hubs that facilitate living, breathing conversations in constant real-time response to change.

All superorganisms use stigmergy, though not usually in ways as enduring and dramatic as the termites. Fire ant foragers returning to the nest with food drag their stingers on the ground to release a powerful pheromone. Other ants pick up the scent and follow. The better the food, the harder she presses, and the stronger her trail. If there is still food when they arrive, they too lay down a trail. The signal builds, drawing more ants to the scene. Soon the site is crowded, and workers are triggered to turn back. The pheromones fade.

The honeybees' waggly dance floor is another stigmergic example. Scouts come and go at will; it's a conversation with simple imperatives and rules. Anyone can speak their mind to everyone, any time, though each bee will decide for herself what should be done with that information.

Principle #4: Communicate through open, two-way, always-on conversations.

Large organizations need something analogous to a termite mound or honeybee waggle dance floor—structures that allow indirect conversation between huge numbers of people. Ken Thompson, a business coach inspired by honeybee and ant communication, identifies "always on, blanket communication" as a consistent feature of these societies. Ants broadcast information about opportunities and threats to the whole group at once, with short-burst chemical signals that require no confirmation or reply, but simply trigger relevant action in the receivers.

What would that look like in business? There are many forms it could take. In today's global organizations, workers span many locations and times zones—we are not all "on" at the same time. But with the Internet, our communications can continue. Online collaboration technologies like Slack are akin to a network of ant pheromone trails. When you need information, you know where to go. Slack eliminates one-on-one emails in favor of transparent systemic messages available to the whole team. Each member has the big picture and can decide for themselves how or whether to respond.

There are other kinds of collective intelligence hubs we can use as well. Prediction markets, like the stock market or any other betting pool, gather diverse and independent perspectives to arrive at an answer. Combining these opinions randomizes bad information, cancelling it out.[1]

Hewlett-Packard's quarterly sales division managers used to issue sales projections. They weren't very good. Instead, HP devised an internal prediction market, asking staff members to bet on future sales. This betting market is now a formal prediction game called BRAIN Behaviorally Robust Aggregation of INformation. BRAIN assesses each player's historic accuracy quotient—a combination of past performance and risk attitude—and weighs these individual opinions. Betting is anonymous, but participants must back their bets with actual money—they must have skin in the game. BRAIN consistently beats traditional forecasts.

A few years ago, Congress began enthusiastically considering a similar betting pool for predicting acts of terrorism and other crises. It probably would have worked. But betting is only accurate if participants are personally invested in being right. This was a case where having skin in the game didn't sit well, and the idea was quickly scuttled.

Wikipedia and LINUX open-source operating systems are another kind of stigmergic arena. They rely on input from a lot of people in order to learn and adapt and facilitate large-scale collaboration with no bosses. Before LINUX, programmers were challenged to work on the same piece of software without overwriting each other or creating incompatible instructions. Each programmer only had permission to change a single part of the code, after which they had to return it to the owner who then put the pieces back together. Linus Torvalds believed everyone should have access to all the code all the time, and devised GITHUB—distributed version control, allowing multiple programmers to "cooperate without coordinating" the same way termites do.[2]

Massively multiplayer games are another way to elicit and gather collective intelligence. These are tremendously appealing, of course, especially for younger workers who grew up playing alternate reality problem-solving games and jump readily between an array of media to do it. My kids amaze me with their simultaneous layers of information. They hang out in the same world with their friends, chatting by text and instant message, with an iPhone on speaker while playing a YouTube tutorial that one of them made on an iPad. Today, grown-up GenZers can apply these same skills to more significant efforts—like providing logistics for global disaster teams in far-off countries, right from their desktop.

UCLA's BioGames project is a massive online gaming system aggregating hundreds of freely given amateur malaria diagnoses for sub-Saharan Africans, with the same accuracy as a trained pathologist on-site. Players give their time and energy because they enjoy it; they like contributing to the greater human good while they play.

Quora is one of my favorite time-suck termite mounds. This platform solicits, rates, and ranks responses to user-posted questions. Highly ranked opinions and ideas rise to the top. The answers are endlessly fascinating and unexpected. Companies can use this same kind of platform to coalesce collective intelligence in employees and customers and other stakeholders, while revealing expert and passionate folks that can be tapped when needed.

These always-on conversations stimulate bottom-up connectivity, helping people and resources find each other, sparking creative collaboration. You might invite people to contribute to a blog, as subject matter experts or enthusiasts. Digital message boards cross-fertilize ideas and talents, coalescing nascent superorganisms like a pearl in an oyster. Personal interests—whether programming, 3D printing, arts and design, sustainability, music, health, the environment, community regeneration and education—can become exciting sources of innovation. Why not add a voting system to these project balloons, with a budget for the best ones? The more transparent, inclusive, and self-organized you can make these cognitive adventures, the better. You never know what might spark an idea or a movement or where it might go. Your stigmergic arena can help folks turn their half-baked notions into collective pie.

Forums like these build organizational identity and grow social capital you need to do big things. Jokes and mythologies grow, distinctive cultures emerge. It's a great way to onboard newcomers and get them familiar with your organization's values and codes of conduct. Sometimes, a chat forum can make unspoken frustrations and inequities visible so they may be openly addressed before they fester. Done right, these arenas become focal points for collective decision-making—convergence zones where thinking shifts from central headquarters to the locals.

Joe Edelman, an ordinary Joe frustrated by FEMA's poor response to Hurricane Katrina, created GroundCrew, a messaging app that helps communities mobilize local teams using GPS. The app proved highly effective in organizing community snow shoveling during Boston's recent Snowmageddon.

With the right kind of software, you could even run a government or create a national budget this way. Iceland recently crowdsourced its new constitution as an open digital project; citizens proposed new clauses, deliberated and voted on them. James Fishkin,[3] Director for the Center for Deliberative Democracy at Stanford, developed a deliberative polling process that allows private citizens to make policy decisions, and MIT's Center for Collective Intelligence offers Climate CoLab, an online forum where people around the world create, analyze, and select proposals for addressing climate change. Anyone anywhere can participate. Experts review and evaluate the ideas and generate simulations that project their environmental and economic outcomes. Community members select the winners. As of February 2016, more than 400,000 global citizens had visited the site, submitting over 1500 proposals. The 2015 winners came from places as diverse and far-flung as the US, India, Ghana, Austria, Chile, Kenya.

The difference between traditional governance and this distributed "mycelial way" was on stark display for me the other day, listening to NPR News (financed by us, the people). A Kenyan journalist was describing UShahidi, a nonprofit open-source platform where local citizens can collect and visualize information in interactive maps. The platform was created during Kenya's disputed 2007 election as a way for users to counter election violence during a government media blackout. Local citizens were encouraged to text outbreaks to a central database, allowing local police to combat tribal hate-baiting violence in minutes. Minutes later, there was another story. The two US political parties had yet again failed to agree on a budget, despite everyone claiming to want to avoid the arbitrary budget cuts that would be triggered by such a failure. I never heard of a termite colony giving up on their mound because they couldn't agree where the sand grains would go. They just do it. Not perfectly, and they tinker constantly, but the structure emerges and functions and adapts, nonetheless. If we created the budget the way termites build a mound, or UShahadi pools distributed data, each of us would simply contribute our two cents, adjust and react, averaging our opinions, knowledge, and experience to create a budget that works. It wouldn't be perfect, but it would function and represent the will of the people—at least those who chose to participate—and adapt to on the ground realities in real time.

There is some precedence for such distributed involvement in politics: in ancient Athens, every male citizen was required to participate directly. Folks were chosen at random to serve on various governing bodies that met every ten days, and if you didn't show up, you were fined, punished, or exiled—and you better know about the issues when you got there! I think this is a great system. You could even get really crazy and include women!

Today's issues are complex; there's simply no way a single person can make all the right decisions. Collective intelligence is essential. Yet we continue to outsource our citizenship to a professional class of politicians, aided by professional opinion-makers, enabled by big money interests. Do we really need to pay someone to ride their white horse to the capital to make decisions for us anymore? We have the technology to govern democratically in real time, so why do we persist with archaic political parties and superdelegates, gerrymandered political districts, whips, lobbyists, filibusters, and the electoral college? The answer is tradition and entrenched interests—complex systems fiercely resisting change. I'm pretty sure the next generation will have little patience for this kind of willful backwardness. GenZ isn't going to understand why they can't just log in to their voting booth from their phone. I don't think GenX or Y get that either. Younger generations strike older folks as entitled and self-absorbed, living in a virtual world where their shallow demands are instantly gratified. It's true they are addicted to their devices. Addicted, that is, if you think phones are dead objects they stare at like zombies. But the real reason they are so attached to that device is that it's their missing superorganism body part. That phone is their antenna, pheromone gland, and waggle dance all in one. You can even order pizza with it.

The shift to collective intelligence is a global one. Peer-to-peer political movements like Arab Spring, Occupy Wall Street, MoveOn.org, or flash mob protests in Turkey and around the world spring up spontaneously, mobilizing instant action that can effectively destabilize entrenched money and power. The same is true for headless terror networks.

Ordinary people have great ideas and want a better life for their children just like everyone else does, but so many of us are held back from contributing by nothing more than the circumstances of our birth. They are simply unable to access the resources they need to leverage their talents.

Even the White House caught the termite mound bug. "We the People" is an online petition website where citizens can float their suggestions. If an idea gathers 25,000 votes, it gets an official White House response. When a petition to spend "850 quadrillion taxpayer dollars to build a Death Star" succeeded in gathering the votes, the White House was compelled to respond. The answer was no; the project was too susceptible to attack by one-man starships.

It's one thing for corporations to build stigmergic mounds, or for us to do it in our personal lives through venues like Facebook or LinkedIn. But there's a need for termite mounds in our communities.

Next Door is great for this. The app verifies your address with the utility company, then welcomes you to the neighborhood. It's a virtual message board of the sort that might once have been provided by weekly Sunday post-church chat. One family posts they lost their turtle, another posts they found one. Mrs. Klein's fig tree is going crazy, she can't keep up; somebody offers to pick them. A neighborhood watch springs up over a series of car break-ins. A barking dog prompts neighbors to check on the elderly owner who is needing care. Nancy joined Weight Watchers, does anyone want to walk with her?

Chapter Fourteen

Simple Rules and Tipping Points

Rule A: Don't. Rule A1: Rule A doesn't exist. Rule A2:
Do not discuss the existence or non-existence of Rules A, A1 or A2.
—R. D. LAING

Ants use neat little sets of algorithms to allocate workers on given tasks, each honed over millions of years of running their little fortress-factories. Some of them aren't so little, either. Imagine if you had to operate a company with five million workers. How would you do it? You could go the mycelial way, with networked intelligence, simple rules of engagement, local sense and response, a constant and transparent data stream, and mechanisms for excluding parasites, or you could try Stalin's approach. Or you could just go all traffic-in-Mumbai on it and hope for the best. Probably that's the same thing as the first.

Principle #5: Trigger tipping-point decisions with simple rules and feedback loops.

This chapter focuses on the simple rules that superorganisms use to get things done.

Dawn begins the same each day for harvester ants. The patrollers leave the nest at first light, heading in the direction the last foragers came from the night before. They roam around a little to see if it's

139

safe. Their return stimulates the foragers. Each ventures out, returning with a seed. Dropping it on the floor triggers a nest worker to collect it and take it down to the storeroom. Meanwhile, the first forager waits for a critical mass of other foragers to return—or maybe for certain teammates—before going out again. If many foragers return quickly, it indicates a lot of food is available; some nest workers switch to foraging. These changes happen in minutes, without bosses or managers. The ants are tiny roaming forklifts, with a general set of targets, tasks, and cues that trigger various behaviors.

The queen and her drones are born to reproduce, and that's all they'll ever do. That much is set in stone. But the sterile workers aren't permanently assigned a position. There's a natural progression to their work. The youngest ants begin working in the nursery, where they hatch. Various stimuli draw them up and out of the nest, leading them into more rigorous rules as they age. Eventually they find themselves working near the entrance, then out in the world as foragers. Once an ant becomes an outside worker, she will never switch back. In this way, workers progressively gain experience and perform riskier tasks. Only the fiercest old grannies take the colony's most perilous assignments, as patrollers, soldiers, and containment handlers. As EO Wilson says, "Ants would never send their young men to war!"

In some cases, the best workers for a specific job do it, but performance is just good enough. Ants are definitely on the "D for diploma" track. Many just mill around waiting for work to come along. Are these lazy workers reserves, waiting to be called upon? Or mobile food storage units? That's possible—honeypot ants have a whole caste of sterile workers that swell up so fat on honeydew they can't walk. They just hang from the ceiling puking up sugar for busier ants. Maybe these sluggards are a buffer, dampening interactions that might trigger excessive behavioral shifts, like a sponge beneath a leaky ceiling or an overflow valve in the bathtub. Their sloth may have some mysterious function. But then again, sometimes an ant catches a whiff of her own trail and recruits other nestmates to spiral with her, circling in endless ant mills until all die from exhaustion. Things don't always happen for a reason; some seeds just don't fit through the holes.

Superorganisms use all kinds of simple rules to go about their day. Ants take a fairly straight path in their wanderings, but upon meeting another ant, they turn. The more crowded, the more twisted their paths become. This simple response emerges into a functional pattern: individuals in small colonies are less likely to meet. Their paths remain straight, letting them cover more ground and make frequent new discoveries. In big colonies, however, ants run into each other all the time, producing dense search patterns akin to the mycelial strategy below ground. They must scour the area for every scrap, because they have more mouths to feed.

Mackerel schools and starling murmurations mesmerize us mightily, but it's not telepathy holding them together. It's just a few simple rules: "keep a friend between you and the edge," "stay one wing away from your nearest friend." With just a few rules like these, a computer program can generate artificial murmurations that act just like the real thing. Natural selection is math embedded in our genes—algorithms honed over billions of years.

Simple interactions build into surprisingly complex patterns, and huge numbers of individuals can collaborate this way. A colony of leafcutters may harvest half a ton of leaves every year. Ants are algorithm geniuses, and many companies have mimicked them. Some airports use an ant-based routing system to assign gates to new arrivals; it proactively alerts airport staff to predict backups before they occur. Southwest, Unilever, FedEx, McGraw-Hill, Hewlett-Packard, and Capital One all use ant-inspired algorithms to improve their operations. Southwest cut their freight transfer rates 80% at some stations, reduced employee workload 20%, and began boarding their planes more efficiently. *Temnothorax* scouts provided FedEx with a simple rule for improving efficiency—always turn the same direction when exploring.

A quick search of recent journals reveals that ant-inspired algorithms are optimizing everything from natural gas pipeline routing, operating room air-conditioning, supply chains, search engines, and storage solutions. Slime molds helped London reroute its traffic snarls and suggest better subway routes and roads.[1] Encycle Inc used simple honeybee-inspired rules to cut energy use by 10% or more while reducing strain on the grid at peak times.

All superorganisms—even complex mammalian ones like naked mole rats—exhibit strangely regimented behaviors. Input x, out comes y. It's a program. Really, the difference between us and them is just that we have more neurons and rules. We have a natural talent for seeing these patterns. That's what humans do: we make mental templates acquired over years of experience. What kind of animal are we tracking? How are they likely to behave? Where do predators typically lurk? Who is honest, who suspicious? We recognize such complex and subtle patterns instantly.

Six Degrees of Kevin Bacon is a party game where any actor must be connected to Bacon in just six steps. Some people are highly connected. Because of them, any person in the world is just 6 degrees removed from any other on average. It *is* a small world after all.[2]

Most of us know a handful of other people, but some folks seem to know everyone. This combination of weak and strong links leads to outbreaks of coordinated behavior—flocks of birds and schools of fish. This *synchrony*, the tendency of rhythmic things to synchronize, is a little bizarre, but even nonliving things like molecules, markets, and traffic adjust themselves in tiny ways to sync into patterns. The more similar the components, the more easily a network will sync. Once it does, the pattern tends to spread. Beliefs and behaviors adopted by a very small proportion of the network can trigger sudden systemic cascades. That's how revolutions begin.

Often, there are tipping points that trigger cascading behavioral changes, reconfiguring a system the same way we make snap decisions based on our expertise. It was this, now it's that. When threatened or tempted, living things move toward this edge of chaos—testing and experimenting. Fringe variations can lead to outsized effects.

Organizations can design networks and triggers to activate specific behaviors and strategies in a self-organized way. No one needs to make the call or give the order. All kinds of data may be used to catalyze these shifts: metrics on risk, group size, network density, trust, role specialization and interaction, coordination, or clarity of information, for instance. When a threshold is crossed, simple rules set new behaviors in motion. Such systems offer real-time feedback to individual actors, allowing them to operate on their own information and judgment, toward a shared imperative.

Digitally delivered prompts can elicit targeted responses from workers or other stakeholders. A text might go out to a group of workers when thresholds are crossed around inventory, order volume, system bottlenecks, or supply chain vulnerabilities. These prompts could interact with GPS or radio-linked chips embedded in the landscapes and products around us. A swarm-moves model from the Florida Institute of Technology uses RFID technology to tell consumers what's selling, for instance—playing on the herd mentality.

When designing such triggers, think about critical variables and thresholds and the kind of systemic behavioral changes you'd like to see in response. Tipping points can exist across any kind of metric—cost, risk, time investment, goodwill. Which variables should you measure, what are the critical thresholds? Can you entice your stakeholders—customers, experts, volunteers and employees—to participate? What kind of simple rules might catalyze your network into a distributed synchronized brain?

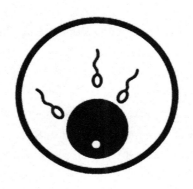

Part Three
The Urge to Procreate: Swarm Creativity

The world is full of magical things patiently waiting
for our wits to grow sharper.
—BERTRAND RUSSELL

Chapter Fifteen

Fairy Rings

Some see nature all ridicule and deformity…
And some scarce see nature at all. But to the eyes of the man
of imagination, nature is imagination itself.
—WILLIAM BLAKE

Part Three explores Principles #6 and #7: how superorganisms innovate for enduring value.

My favorite superorganisms—those underground fungal patches—grow in rings in the soil. Those familiar fairy rings! They move steadily outward, consuming nutrients. When a good rain falls, the mushrooms pop up and spore out, spreading innovative gene combinations on the wind. Eventually, nutrients and time replenish the bare centers, and they are ready to support new growth again. Spores land and a new inner ring begins. Spores constantly recombine to spark new circles and fine-tune old ones, and each thrives on its own particular patch of soil.

In his book, *Swarm Creativity*,[1] Peter Gloor discusses collaborative innovation networks—self-organized and nested groups existing in and around creative endeavors. He sees ideas as creative sparks, loci of innovation that diffuse outward like ripples from a stone in a pond. Creative visionaries are at the center of these rings, inspiring other innovators and networks to grow around them.

An initial innovation network contains only a handful of people. They work together intimately to nurture the idea. These visionaries are joined by developers, early adopters, and beta testers, forming an "interest network," a kind of incubator where the innovation is tested and refined (or rejected).

Soon, the idea spreads out into a broader "learning network" filled with enthusiasts who want to know what's going on at the cutting edge. These lurkers, learners, and listeners disseminate the innovation into the larger world. When the idea reaches critical mass, connectors step in—influential hubs who know everyone. Now the spores blow far and wide, recombining with new ideas far afield as they diffuse into the mainstream.

Like fungi, we pass information to our friends and neighbors and people all over the world. Our ideas transcend generations, borders, religions, and even species. We envision solutions and work backwards, using our voices and hands to make it so. When our island reaches carrying capacity, we build a boat—bring the pigs and coconuts. If winter cold punishes our tender topical skin, we sew animal skins, weave fibers, make fires, and build shelters. Our ability to innovate and teach what works is powerful. This is where deep principles of superorganism sharing come together with our clever ape heritage, driving forms of value not previously on this planet.

Our ape nature grants us extraordinary talents. We see complex cause and effect, solve difficult problems, imagine what others are thinking and therefore are likely to do. Meanwhile, the ant-like part of us shares the work and wealth by pooling our scraps and differences. The ant and the ape in us let us do pretty much anything we put our minds to. Fly a plane? Ride a bike? Go to Mars? Done. With that, let's set off on the next leg of our journey. Here's your roadmap to swarm creativity:

Pattern #2: Superorganisms nurture swarm creativity.

Principle #6: Align action around a compelling shared purpose: creating value for a collective future.

Nurturing the next generation and ensuring its success is every living thing's purpose. For superorganisms, however, the next generation is collectively important. The bolder and more ambitious our goals, the faster we get up in the morning, and the better we work together. We don't want to be the weak link in achieving it.

Every undertaking begins in the mind's eye, when we stop to ask, "What if things were different?" We imagine other futures and convince others to join us in making them happen. There is no shortage of big goals to focus on—poverty, famine, disease—and companies are uniquely positioned to tackle them. Doing important things together brings out the best in us. It's what gets us up in the morning, and the glue that integrates our work. How will the world be different from our actions? The bolder and more ambitious our collective goals, the greater our personal potential becomes.

Principle #7: Launch multiple low-investment experiments.

Many species specialize in finding ephemeral opportunities and windfalls. How do they maximize their chances of finding these rich open patches of bare earth? Every innovation begins with a mutant, a singular spark. Ant colonies and human organizations are comprised of unique individuals, each with their own ideas, styles, and talents. Anyone can make a difference, and the sum of these diverse strategies yields the collective intelligence we depend on. But there's a risk here as well—one mistake or bad apple can be catastrophic. That's why companies work hard to keep things standard and safe, and our hierarchies weed deviance out. But that isn't what ants do. Their solution is redundancy—massively parallel independent experiments. They support multiple solutions simultaneously, each a door to the adjacent possible. I think of this as "spore strategy": broadcast a profusion of diverse starts with little investment in any. Something will likely work. Life is a numbers game.

Principle #8: Tune the network to spread innovation or suppress it.

Evolutionary innovation results from mixing genes up sexually or copying them sloppily to generate mutations. Once something new arises, its spread depends on social structure: who mates and associates with whom. Superorganisms have unique social structures that help them adapt to change quickly with minimal processing power. Individuals cluster into distinct tribes on the proximal level, occasionally cross pollinating with other tribes, but there is rapid evolutionary change as well. This kind of structure is a recipe for accelerated evolution. Organizations can tune their own structures to accelerate change amplifying or suppressing transformation by dialing conditions conducive to innovation up or down just as other superorganisms do.

Chapter Sixteen

Shared Purpose

If you want to build a ship, don't gather people together to collect
wood and don't assign them tasks and work, but rather, teach them to
long for the endless immensity of the sea.
—ANTOINE DE SAINT EXUPÉRY

After settling on their new home, the bees must set out to reach it.
This is a risky moment, one of ultimate exposure and vulnerability. Everything they've worked on may be lost between one heartbeat
and the next. The scouts rouse their sister bees to flight. *This way!* The
queen travels alongside them, chaperoned by her doting entourage.
For whatever reason, however, she doesn't arrive.

Without their queen, the hive is dead. There is no point to working,
because they can no longer regenerate the future. The queen's daughters mill about anxiously, but she isn't coming. As her scent fades,
their unity evaporates, and the colony disbands. Each bee wanders off
to meet her own lonely and meaningless death.

Principle #6: Align action around a compelling shared purpose: creating value for a collective future.

All living things are driven by a powerful purpose: ensuring the
next generation's success. Natural selection has shaped every

living creature to do more than optimize return on investment or be sustainable. Nature does business by evolving regenerative systems that compound value for future descendants. Each of us has four billion years of ancestors that succeeded in this quest. We've all inherited the desire and the capacity to be good ancestors. It's baked into our DNA.

Superorganisms share this purpose as well, but for them, the next generation is *collectively* important. Each individual queen, drone, scout, soldier, or forager works to grow value for the colony's descendants. It's worth repeating: everyone has a job to do, but their purpose is the same: to collectively nurture the next generation.

Each hive has a signature scent—the queen's personal chemical body wax. Her attendants constantly gather it, hand-feeding it to their hive-mates. It's the scent of "us."

At some point, however, a queen's royal scent will begin to wane. Her daughters immediately start rearing her replacement. A handful of larvae will receive her royal jelly. As their mother's life fades, these new queens stir restlessly. The succession is swift. The first to emerge will quickly sting her rivals to death. Her sister bees converge on the old queen mum, "heat balling" her by buzzing ferociously and tightly around her until she overheats and dies. Divergence of purpose is deadly. The colony cannot waste a moment on it.

Most organisms don't try to convince others to share in a goal. There is no *"Hey I have an idea! Let's do this!"*[1] Individuals mostly work alone, like toddlers in a sandbox. They might be excited to play or hunt, and they may be attracted to do it close together, but for the most part this is parallel play.

Most creatures don't have much in the way of imagination either. Birdsong is lovely, but mainly ritualistic and imitative. They do change slowly over time, much as our languages, but the modifications are like molasses seeping slowly across space and time. They aren't jazzy, improvisational creations. Humpbacks don't imagine what could be and create it from whole cloth. But then again, we are still playing Bach to great effect.

Our undertakings begin in the mind's eye, when we step back to ask *what if...?* and imagine how things could be different. We tell stories, paint, sing, dance, and dream. To imagine other worlds and spiritual dimensions is fundamentally human. What if we put a man on the moon? Or put an end to polio and smallpox? What if cars ran on sunlight, or garbage was like fallen leaves, feeding tomorrow's insects and fungus while making more soil? What if we made things the way plants do, growing them from sunshine and water, with carbon pulled from the air? What if consuming things created more opportunities for more different kinds of living things? What if we made stone soup?

We make conceptual leaps about what the future might hold and consciously move toward our visions. What do we want for our children, and our children's children? What about the children of our very distant relatives, the ones with fur or wings or flippers? We have the ability to imagine new future possibilities and attract others to join us in bringing them about. We can blow the adjacent possible wide open, freeing us from accidentally falling through evolutionary holes one by one.

There are exceptions to these generalities, and they are found among the superorganisms. Humans are special but not that much. It's surprisingly difficult to isolate traits that are unique to us. We are animals, after all. Anthropology has mined the "humans are just smarter apes" vein for a long time. It makes sense to study them because they are our closest relatives. It's reasonable to suspect the roots of our nature will be found within them as well. And they are. Chimps certainly have imaginations. Washoe, the first chimp to learn American Sign Language, bathed and cared for a doll. Primatologist Richard Wrangham witnessed young wild chimpanzees caring for imaginary babies—cradling logs and tucking them into nests they built in the trees for them. Vicki, a chimp raised by humans (she had a four-word spoken vocabulary) dragged an imaginary toy around on an imaginary string, and even pretended to unhook it when it got stuck. They plan solutions to complex problems and use and make tools just as we do.

But they struggle to share their intentions. Their quest for dominance is pronounced, and they aren't all that interested in sharing unless forced to.

But humans have experienced a dramatic phase change since our last common ancestor walked the earth. Somewhere along the way, our ancestors crossed the inbreeding valley of death and became superorganisms. It is therefore useful to look at other superorganism societies. Social insects, toothed whales, elephants, hamadryas baboons, naked mole rats, parrots, and crows should receive a lot more attention from us, and studies on mycorrhizal fungal networks are some of the most interesting things going.

What about the other superorganisms? Do they share intentions, plan and make things together, coordinate in diversified teams? Ravens and crows mutter under their breath and copy sounds, recombining them for pleasure.[2] These creepy corvids seek revenge and bestow gifts—activities that require planning, imagination, a memory for past behavior, and an expectation of reciprocity. They are aware of what others may be thinking and therefore likely to do. Crows work together to purposefully chase sparrows and robins into glass windows to their death, and in the San Francisco Bay Area, they herd whole flocks of rock doves into traffic, then wait until rush-hour passes to enjoy the roadkill. In the American South, crows make clay catfish decoys to attract hawks, so they can eat the real thing in peace.

Elephants plan and reverse-engineer imaginative goals as well. Kandula, a young elephant bull at Washington's National Zoo, kicks a box until it's directly beneath the high branch he wishes to eat, then stands on the box to get it. If the box is out of sight, he will look for it. That isn't too different than when my dog sees me and goes looking for her ball. But if there's no box around, Kandula gathers boards around his enclosure and stacks them. That's like my dog making a ball and bringing it to me. Elephants live in extremely close-knit societies, and routinely work together on complex cognitive tasks. In captivity they readily cooperate to pull ropes that deliver food. Elephant ethnologist Cynthia Moss tells of an African elephant shot by poachers. The other elephants chased them off, then two members walked to either side of the injured elephant, leaning in to hold her up. Eventually, the elephant fell to the ground and died, but the two managed to get her to a sitting position. Other elephants came and put grass in her mouth. Eventually, they gave up trying to lift her and began throwing leaves over her body, standing vigil all night. They are the only animals besides ourselves, Neanderthals, and magpies known to have funeral rituals. Elephants even point their trunks to get another's attention for a task requiring cooperation—something only humans and crows are known to do. This is shared intention. Like them, we imagine things that don't yet exist, and work together to make them come about.

Poverty, famine, disease, habitat destruction, the climate crisis—there is no shortage of big challenges to focus on, and companies are uniquely positioned to tackle them. Doing important things together brings out the best in our teams. "Purpose," says Linda Hill[3] in her book, *Collective Genius,* "is the glue that integrates the work of one into the work of many… it's what creates and animates a community…and makes people willing to do the hard tasks of innovation together and work through the inevitable conflict and tension."

Purpose is what gets us up in the morning. How will the world be different because of our actions? The bolder and more ambitious our purpose, the fuller our lives become, and the greater our potential in the world. Sadly, most of us don't get this kind of reward from our work. It's just a paycheck, a way to feed ourselves and our families. Ultimately, we are hired help for someone else's purpose, and most of our waking hours are rented out to the shareholders. If companies are superorganisms, then workers are all too often their tame, wingless aphids.

That's not so terrible, I guess. Workers are often shareholders in other companies. Most workers have a stake in someone's aphid-farm. But our daily tasks are still not that compelling. I think it's safe to say most of us would prefer to spend our days doing something that matters in the world. When do we get to "procreate" what matters to us—future generations? The work we do often wastes our inherently creative and uniquely special natures. We have so much more to give.

Organizations could do far more to bring us together around big dreams. Most of us would love to leave something of lasting value in the course of our daily work. When it's more than a paycheck, your commitment to the team and each other grows. We trust each other more, because we know we share a collective purpose and set of values. That trust gives us the courage to try and fail in front of each other as many times as we need to succeed.

Most enterprises have a mission statement—usually some bland up-with-people bromide about "our greatest assets." I doubt anyone at the top ever reads it, because those assets are the first things to get tossed overboard when the economy goes south. That's okay, though. Everyone knows the mission statement isn't really the mission. Leadership is duty-bound to maximize value for the shareholders—their real purpose is to boost growth and quarterly share price. Theoretically, shareholders can even sue if the company puts any other mission before this! Shareholders come first, and the mission statement is most likely icing at best, smoke and mirrors at worst. Serve other stakeholders all you want, but only to the extent it doesn't detract from the bottom line.

Many companies serve deeper purposes anyway. Nobel laureate Muhammad Yunus' social businesses aim to serve society by alleviating poverty and human suffering. Profit sustains such ventures, but their real worth is measured in quality of lives. Profits are seen as a byproduct of this primary value. Other legal frameworks, like California's Social Purpose Corporations and B Corporations have emerged to legally protect desires to put other purposes first.

Traditional corporations like Procter and Gamble, General Electric, and Unilever do serve shareholders first, but they also strive to align with a greater opportunity: regenerating potential *future* growth. P&G's stated mission is to bring prosperity to communities by improving global access to sanitation and nutrition. GE pulled their sprawling global community together around "ecomagination"—innovations addressing the global climate crisis. Unilever's ten-year sustainable living plan promised to double revenues while halving environmental impact. The company had to reformulate many products and overhaul their entire supply chain, which impacted short-term profits and put the plan in jeopardy. In response, CEO Polman abandoned quarterly earnings guidance so he could keep his eye on the real bottom line—future potential. A regenerative approach to long-term business prospects works to bring essential products and services like nutrition, sanitation, and future infrastructure to underserved communities, empowering customers and employees in the process. You can't buy shampoo if you don't have water. These profitable ventures keep shareholders happy and provide wider value, while building capacity for future growth. C.K. Prahalad[4] refers to this as the bottom-of-the-pyramid strategy for growth. I think of it as "lichen strategy." Lichens thrive in the forgotten, difficult places of the world. Exposed on bare rocks or wedged in hard cracks, they slowly crumble unforgiving rock into fertile soil, creating opportunity for other plants to sink their roots into.

Reinventing organizations to "do good while doing well" is a welcome trend, at least in the business to consumer sector. P&G speaks of "corporate social opportunity," echoing Drucker's statement that "every single social and global issue of our day is a business opportunity in disguise, just waiting for the innovation, the pragmatism, and the strategic capacity of great companies to aim higher." Companies have tremendous power to create value with regenerative capitalism. Look at the gains in wealth and life expectancy over the last two centuries—an extra twenty years of life expectancy in the United States,

90% reduced infant mortality, and 99% fewer maternal deaths, mostly due to corporate efforts. Devastating diseases like polio, leprosy, and smallpox have nearly been eliminated, even in the poorest countries. Organizations have lifted millions of people out of poverty while connecting us globally. Capitalism has created global citizens where diplomacy could not.

Employees want to do big things, and companies need to if they want to keep growing. Google suggests "Do no evil," which seems like a modest start. Doctors pledge to do no harm and lawyers are bound to serve their clients. Why shouldn't executives swear to an ethical code? Though this one seems a little halfhearted, and I'm not really sure what doing evil entails.

Which stakeholders should you listen to first?[5] Customers, employees, shareholders, supply chain vendors, environmentalists, social activists, the communities that host your business? We can probably agree that all these opinions matter, but their definitions of evil may differ wildly. Deciding whose opinions come first is tricky.

Choosing employees is wise, as competition for up-and-coming talent can be intense. Debate Gen Y flaws and features all you want, but they do insist on purpose in their work. A third of North American college graduates said that corporate social responsibility was the deciding factor in whether they were interested in joining an organization—more important than salary. 70% said they wouldn't even apply for a job with a company they found socially irresponsible. Gen Y is globally informed and technologically empowered, with a fierce sense of fairness. They mostly find central authority irrelevant, incompetent, and an obstacle to progress. They feel entitled to more than a paycheck with their one true life. Why shouldn't they? Why shouldn't any of us?

Or maybe you will choose your customers. In that case, you will want to create more open platforms, and invite them to play and co-create with you. We'll get into this more in Part Four. As one-way consumption gives way to two-way co-production, customers increasingly want a custom, even DIY experience. They might not do what you want them to do, but you might want to embrace that reality before they make you irrelevant.

Regardless of what your big thing is, build it from the bottom up. Shared purpose is what's called in mathematical circles an "attractor"—a variable that pulls many disparate nodes together. In regular-people terms, shared purpose is what makes us stop acting like chimpanzees in a tree or toddlers in a sandbox and think about what we can make together for a richer future. Everyone must be committed to this purpose if your superorganism is going to hang together. When a fast ant works with a slow ant, both adjust their speed to make the team work better as a whole. They synchronize their actions for better performance. Human synchrony and collaboration snowball the same way, as our goals become more attainable. When the soup begins to smell delicious, more people want to make and eat it. Monkey see, monkey do.

What if you're just canning tomatoes, or building gearboxes for cars? How can you find a compelling purpose in that? FAVI and Morningstar did it. Their sense of purpose is something quite simple: each employee does their best for the team and the company, because its success feeds their community's families. The work they do together directly affects their next generation—a purpose that transcends politics. Feeding each other's families, supporting our communities, and having our teammates' backs are fundamentally human activities that give our work meaning.

Chapter Seventeen

Toss It Up and See What Sticks

To have a great idea, have lots of them.
—Thomas Edison

My first job out of college was living on a fishing boat as a marine biologist in the wild Alaskan Bering Sea. 2000 meters below these waves, in absolute blackness and cold, I wasn't the only one looking for whales. In the absence of plants and sunlight, every bit of energy and nutrition has to come from somewhere else. A sparse but steady rain of debris showers down from the upper world, to be snapped up quickly by an assortment of abyssal grotesqueries. Once in a while, this marine snow brings a great feast: a dead whale. A host of mobile scavengers converge on the carcass as it slips to the seafloor. Crabs, sleeper sharks, and hagfish tear at the windfall. An *Osedax*[1] (Latin for bone devourer) zombie worm larva drifts by. Its parents have launched millions of opportunities just like it in the deep-water current. Their expectations are low—each receives minimal investment. They are blind and sexless, lacking even a mouth or anus—or any digestive tract at all. But fortune has shone on this particular individual—it has the vanishingly slim good fortune of landing on a dead whale! Quickly, the larva transforms. Now she is female. She roots for nutrients deep in the bone, her feathery red plume absorbing oxygen from the water. Symbiotic bacteria in her "roots" do the work of digestion. *Oh, and here comes another sexless larva!* This one has the even more remarkable luck of landing on top of the first! Impaled on a needle in a vast ocean haystack. It hastily atrophies into a tiny dwarf male and crawls right up her oviduct. Together, the unlikely couple will pump millions of cheap larvae into the blackness. Maybe one will stumble on the next whale.

The zombie worms don't know when or where the whale will fall, of course, so control, planning, and centralized decision-making are of no use to them. Instead, the spoils go to aimless drifters, guided by a heaping dose of luck. "Intelligence"—if we can use that word for a brainless, gutless, sexless worm—is distributed among these millions of tiny starts. When one happens upon a bonanza, it explodes into activity—a hotspot of growth and regeneration. The vast majority fail: this is a numbers game. Put out as many possibilities as you can, invest minimally in each—just the bare minimum to get them started if luck should happen to favor them. The lucky larvae grow quickly, scrambling up new gene combinations as fast as possible, sending them off to seek the next opportunity. If you try enough combinations, something is bound to work. The important thing is maximizing your chances of being in the right place when opportunity knocks—or the whale falls. Then, first mover advantage is yours. You own the space.

I realize that zombie worms aren't the most appealing life form, sexless and gutless and blind as they are. But I mention them now because I thought they might remind you of someone you work with and make you feel more at home. Sometimes biology gets a little weird. It's nice to have some familiar comforts along the way.

The bone devourers are the poster children for innovation culture. What would their opportunistic innovation strategy look like in an organization? If it takes one million zombie worm larvae to yield a single colony of worms, then one thousand ideas are needed to launch a dozen innovations. To overcome odds like that, you need swarms of low-risk experiments. Most will fail, but each success lets you launch a thousand more.

Principle #7: Launch multiple low investment experiments.

Trial-and-error is a basic evolutionary tenet. Every species relies on it. Superorganisms are no different—they are masters of failing forward. I think of this as "spore strategy," but zombie worm apocalypse works too—that's ZWA for you acronym fans. Slime molds and mushrooms broadcast millions of spores far and wide on the wind, just put as many possibilities out there as you can.

When one of these experiments stumbles onto a new opportunity—an island, new niche, or novel adaptation—it gets first mover advantage. The world is their oyster. These castaways wash ashore on a wide blue ocean[2] of opportunity, and spread quickly on bare ground, exploring without competition.

Eventually, resources tighten up, and individuals diversify to avoid wasting effort. The original innovation radiates into many local variations. 60 million years ago a handful of lemurs, perhaps pitched from trees during big storms or tsunamis, drifted on rafts of vegetation to the giant island of Madagascar. Today, one hundred species of lemur are found in every shape and size and habit. Only two thousand years ago, a lemur the size of a silverback gorilla munched his way through these forests! Birds took flight and exploded into thousands of ways of life, using their wings in a multitude of ways.

Adaptive radiations often follow mass extinctions as well. When the dinosaurs disappeared at the end of the Cretaceous, they left their niches behind. Tiny furtive mammals and flighty birds expanded to claim them. What kind of creatures will fill the niches of the species we wipe out? Hopefully not robots and teams of human specialists.

There is always a certain amount of luck involved in stumbling on blue ocean—or a blue whale—but a predisposition vastly increases your chances. Island colonizers have to float or fly to their endless Hawaiian summer, for instance. Birds and plants with wind or sea-borne seeds made it, but no snakes. The only mammals to arrive in prehuman times were two species of bats and a seal.

Every habitat has an optimal amount of error. A bias towards discovery is a good idea in a rapidly shifting environment. The honey-bees' waggle-dance says there's a patch of flowers over there, but the directions are a hazy wave over yonder. Some bees will accidentally stumble on new patches trying to find it.

Opportunists build a certain amount of randomness into their experiments. Some African tribes spin a stick to decide where to hunt, giving prey time to recover. Companies can use this fuzzy logic as well, by sharing minimal standards and guidelines, deeply rooted in purpose and values but loose enough to allow people to use their own judgment in getting there. I have personally turned this fuzzy approach to rules into an art form. They just mean head over there to me. I want to know what you are trying to accomplish, and that is what guides me.

Rigid plans work against innovation and resilience. If you need these, I suggest you simply share a vision and some simple rules with employees, nurture diverse experimentation, and trust the wisdom of the crowd. Provide a setting where emergent strategy thrives—by empowering frontline workers to self-organize and respond to local conditions in real time.

Scientists, engineers, artists, and designers—all thrive on accidents.[3] Some of our greatest discoveries and innovations were unplanned. If you've ever been on a Transatlantic flight with a two- year-old, you know how vital Silly Putty is. This accidental discovery was made while looking for an alternative to natural rubber. Radio waves were discovered during a Victorian magic trick. The rule works beyond the confines of our planet as well. On Mars, the Spirit Rover's front wheel jammed, scratching away a layer of Martian soil to reveal a patch of rock that looks exactly like places on Earth where water and hot volcanic rocks have come into contact.

The best scientists are curious when their data look wrong. Instead of assuming they screwed up, they wonder what they stumbled upon. The guy who ate his moldy rye bread for instance. Eureka! LSD.

Purely emergent strategies are as rare as purely intentional ones, in nature or the board room. The balance between them must be tuned to match the environment. Top-down intention brings focus and control—the ants use it to go directly to their aphid hunting grounds. They use bottom-up strategies to increase the likelihood of finding whatever's out there. Ant scouts wander, and junebugs blunder, because they don't know what they don't know. The trick is to devise feedback loops that trigger the right amount of focused intention or opportunistic emergence when and where it is needed.

Nonprofit Engineers Without Borders Canada recognized their need to deliver results for donors was preventing them from taking creative risks. They began publishing a *Failure Report* to celebrate things people had tried. Today, appearing in the report is a coveted honor, and the organization uses it to attract folks who aren't afraid to try new things. The concept gives permission to try (and fail at) new things and ensures that every failure yields its full value as a teachable moment.

Amazon employees are expected to dive right in and learn from hands-on experience as they go. Bezos encourages employees to "go down blind alleys and experiment... If we can get processes decentralized so that we can do a lot of experiments without it being very costly, we'll get a lot more innovation." Yes, Bezos is amassing the troops of the zombie apocalypse as we speak!

One of Procter and Gamble's mottos is "fail early, fail often, fail cheaply!" In Silicon Valley, if you haven't failed, it means that you haven't tried. IDEO operates on a rapid prototype model—every product team is expected to generate a failed prototype by the end of the first day.

What does spore strategy look like in action? Dave Whitwam, former chairman of Whirlpool, could tell you. Worried about Whirlpool's drying innovation pipeline, he decided to put 10,000 of his 65,000 employees through a series of innovation-training workshops. They generated over 7,000 ideas, 300 of which matured into small-scale experiments, generating a stream of new products and businesses. Today, Whirlpool actively tracks a broad pipeline of ideas, experiments, and major initiatives with an internal innovation dashboard. Their CEO instantly knows how many ideas are moving through the pipeline and what their future impact might be.

My favorite spore strategist is probably Vineet Nayar, the author-philanthropist who ran HCL Technologies from 2007 to 2013. When he arrived, the company struggled with rampant disengagement. Under his leadership, revenues grew from $743 million to $4.7 billion, including a 25% increase following the global recession of 2009. How did he spark this dramatic turnaround? First, he put his frontline employees above all other stakeholders—even customers, prompting Fortune to name HCL the most democratic workplace in the world.

Next, he vastly expanded the company intranet, encouraging online interest communities to develop around everything from art, music, and sustainability, to technology, customer experience, and big dream projects. Everything was voluntary, self-selected, and totally outside the formal hierarchy.

Nayar then added a brainstorm site, where employees could point out problems and propose solutions. They generated huge numbers of ideas. He initiated an internal online help center, inviting employees to ask leadership anything. He personally answered hundreds of questions each week and ran weekly polls to find out what workers were thinking. Then, he started a portal where employees could answer his own questions. Each employee accrued an ongoing rating from other employees—how good were their answers? Experts who were previously invisible emerged, to be tapped for future projects.

Nayar saw that many people were uncomfortable being creative—they had never had permission and didn't know how. He wanted everyone to believe they were creative and impactful. He created an innovation group whose only role was to increase employee ideas. The group seeded 2,500 "innovation igniters" across HCL's Indian locations. Their job was to spark innovation through flash stand-up comedy. They would just walk into a work area, draw a crowd, and go to work like a carnival busker. Thousands of employees learned to let their creative juices flow through these improvised spectacles. The actual value of every employee's innovations was deposited in a virtual innovation bank account, allowing them (and their peers) to see the impact their ideas had made. It became competitive—everyone wanted to be seen contributing.

Now engagement was high and Nayar kicked a radical transparency campaign into gear. Performance score cards were kept for managers of every project and made completely visible to everyone. Some managers didn't care for that and left, but managers who stayed began posting strategies openly, inviting internally crowd-sourced review. The quality of the plans skyrocketed.

Today, Nayar is regenerating the future. He gave up his business role and went to work on his passion—the Sampark Foundation, a nonprofit that creates tools and training methods for Punjabi elementary school teachers—spore strategy at its best!

Cultures like Nayar's HCL and Whitwam's Whirlpool are eager to try new things and they aren't afraid to fail. Fail faster—find that whale!

Chapter Eighteen

It's Sexy Time!

*If you watch animals objectively for any length of time, you're driven
to the conclusion that their main aim in life is to pass on
their genes to the next generation.*
—DAVID ATTENBOROUGH

In San Diego County where I live, tiny ephemeral pools appear
briefly on the clay pan mesas after a winter rain. These oases
explode with feverish activity, and dry quickly. Creatures that live
here have to move fast. Fairy shrimp—a tiny freshwater crusta-
cean—flourish with a special strategy for capitalizing on the short-
lived bonanzas.

In dry times, the shrimps' tiny eggs lie in the dust—sometimes for
many long years. When the rains finally come, the cysts hatch into
female fairy shrimp, and get to work eating. They will clone themselves as fast as they can, making more little females exactly like
themselves. Why fix it if it ain't broke? Why waste time looking for
a mate? As soon as the pool starts to dry, however, the water warms
and oxygen dwindles. Suddenly, bam! The shrimp switches to sex.
Like magic, the sex ratio shifts toward males and mating begins. But
instead of making baby shrimp, they scramble up new combinations
of genes, making winter eggs that will lie dormant until the next rain.

Their strategy shifts from imitation to experimentation. The shrimp are regenerating their future.

Let's talk about sex. It's an old and widespread practice, which suggests it must be good for something. Fossilized evidence of multicellular sex is at least a billion years old—talk about getting caught in the act. Sex does a lot of useful things.[1] It's a good way to break up bad genetic combinations—mixing cool new mutations into different combos gives it a better chance of working.

Mixing genes this way also confuses parasites. It's harder for them to hit a moving target. In a population of snails where some are sexual mixers and others are asexual cloners, infection spreads rapidly among the clones, which eventually blink out and disappear. It's also possible the asexual ones just hated their lives and gave up without a fight. The ones getting busy continually upgraded their defenses, and dodged infection easily. There's a lesson in here, but I'm not sure what it is.

Sex is also nature's best source of innovation. Some poor species are deprived of it, but our planet's asexual cloners still get a nice dash of novelty here and there, because copying DNA is sloppy business no matter what. Small errors—mutations—will slowly accumulate. Some variants work better than others, and the population shifts that way. The process is slower and more random than sex (in my limited personal experience) and most mutations are harmful or do nothing at all. Still, they do introduce variation. The doors to the adjacent possible creak open a little wider. Different branches of the evolutionary tree mutate at different rates, too, by the way. Each has been tuned to hit the opportunity lotto where it lives.

Diversity is particularly high in places where one habitat transitions into another. These "ecotones" are rich with life, because the variety of forage and shelter is greater here. Many species are drawn to the possibility of expanding their niche a little. Remember Bambi's mother, urging him out into the meadow from the safety of the woods? Exciting stuff can happen on the margins—Bambi even met his future doe there. Edges are hotbeds of innovation—alchemical cauldrons where genes and habitats collide. Population geneticists love these natural experiments.

Natural selection is exceptionally strong in ecotones, because there are many variants and habitat combinations for nature to choose among. Sometimes, new species and adaptations can emerge here—in the Awash Baboon Hybrid Zone, for instance, or in our own simmering soup, enriched with Neanderthal, Denisovan, and *Homo erectus* DNA. Evolution accelerates around the edges.

Cultural ecotones, where different people and ideas bump up against one another, are full of ideas as well.[2] Marco Polo traveled from the Roman Empire to China along the Silk Road, bringing back postal systems, noodles, paper money, and gun powder. Like a coyote with burrs stuck in its fur, Polo carried the seeds of Eastern culture to fertile new ground—where a lush Renaissance jungle of cultural expressions soon flowered.

Principle #8: Tune social networks to spread innovation or suppress it.

In the West, we tend to think of creativity as something special people are born with. Lightning strikes Ben Franklin's kite, the Holy Ghost whispers in Mary's ear, man is born whole from the head of Zeus. *Eureka!* Ideas come to them unbidden.

Initial sparks do come from individuals, but identical twin studies suggest our genes only account for a third of our creative differences. People are not born innovators. Anyone can be creative, as Vineet Nayar showed. What do creative people do differently? They spend a lot of time looking for patterns, experimenting, and looking for diverse perspectives on what they think they know. Above all, they excel in Einstein's "combinatorial play"—the process of connecting previously unconnected things in unusual ways—just like sexy fairy shrimp. Hopefully this book will do that for you. If not, you should try Burning Man.

Ideas are "a surprising emergent property of networks," says writer Stephen Johnson, "thousands of neurons firing together that never fired together before." This explains why they come to us so often in our dreams: neurons synchronously fire in random combinations while we sleep. The more diverse our daily experiences, the more active our night neurons, and the more likely new ideas to spark. "Creativity is connecting things," as Steve Jobs liked to say. The looser and funkier those associations, the more creative ideas seem to get—until they degenerate into nonsense or madness. Some of the most brilliant people I know seem to walk this fine line.

Just as dreams bring new neural connections to life, diverse people can generate fresh ideas. Innovators are always seeking the edges of their discipline, looking for novel ways to think about what they know. These cross-disciplinary idea ecotones provoke inquiry and fresh ways of thinking.

At Larry Smarr's California Institute for Telecommunications and Information Technology (CALIT2) at UC San Diego, scientists and engineers come together with artists and designers to explore big challenges. Taking ideas from lab to marketplace requires creativity and broad expertise—schools like the Rhode Island School of Design are preparing students for the future through a STEAM (science, technology, engineering, arts, and math) approach to learning.

Artists are natural loose-associators—pattern-seekers well outside the constraints of "good science" and traditional approaches. They can more freely connect the dots to generate new understandings with the power to disrupt things we think we know—bare ground for something new to take root.

The Biomimicry Center at Arizona State University is another exciting ecotone where diverse ways of knowing collide. The center, founded by Dayna Baumeister of consulting firm Biomimicry 3.8, bridges the School of Life Sciences with the Schools of Design, Sustainability, Business, and Engineering. Ultimately, all our endeavors are biological—but designers and engineers are the ones who actually make the future reflect this. If biologists are at the table, solutions are more likely to align with the way life actually works, yielding more enduring value in the long run.

Companies can do more to encourage creativity. What if ideas were posted internally by anyone, for other workers to see? What if employees could upvote and comment on those ideas, as we saw Nayar's team do? What if employees accrued innovation or expertise ratings based on their input? Could teams have small budgets for investing in parallel experiments? Perhaps a bonus could go to teams whose ideas produced bigger returns or savings, allowing them to fund more experiments.

It's sexy time!

Chapter Nineteen

The Inbreeding Valley of Death

While every innovation can be traced back to individuals,
it is collaboration among creators that brings disruptive
innovations over the tipping point.
—PETER GLOOR

Naked mole rats are just what they sound like: hairless, burrowing rodents, nearly blind and ugly as sin. Sand puppies, as they're locally known, have a host of other bodily oddities as well. They are cold-blooded like a reptile—the only mammals physiologically incapable of regulating their temperature. Lacking fat, they can't shiver to warm themselves, but instead must huddle in the shallow, sun-warmed parts of their burrows or retreat to deeper, cooler tunnels. Their entire lives are spent underground, digging with their huge teeth, which protrude from tightly sealed lips to avoid a mouth of dirt. They need very little oxygen—tiny lungs and specialized blood snap up every stray molecule, and they use it extremely efficiently, needing 2/3 that of a much tinier mouse—and they can cut back another 25% in a pinch. These overgrown "sabertooth sausages" lack pain receptors, are resistant to cancer, and live up to 31 years in captivity—longer than any other rodent.

If all that isn't weird enough for you, they also have the distinction of being the only vertebrates with a truly eusocial superorganism society. They live just as ants and honeybees do: an enormous breeding queen pumps out naked baby mole rats for the nursery workers to care for. She and a handful of males are the only reproductives; the rest are sterile. Like ants, the smallest workers gather food and maintain the nest, while the largest soldiers defend it.

Nursery workers keep the pups safe and warm, and feed them feces to inoculate their tiny tummies with the bacteria they will need for a lifetime digesting fibrous roots.

How did this bizarre set of traits come together? It is partly due to inbreeding—naked mole rats rarely leave the nest they are born into, because it's just too dangerous out in the open desert. The chances of finding a mate and new burrow are slim to none. Better to stay home and raise the siblings. Colony members are highly inbred as a result—the genetic equivalent of cousins. This, along with the strong selection pressures of underground desert living, has transformed both their bodies and behavior.

Hamadryas, humans, and naked mole rats all transformed their appearance and behavior rapidly and dramatically (for evolution anyway, which is like watching paint dry). The conditions that led to this accelerated evolution are relevant to any organization asking how to transform quickly.

As usual I ask, how is the rest of nature doing it? Evolutionary adaptation happens in several ways—most obviously when some extreme environmental swing suddenly removes under-performers. But there are other factors as well. Sometimes, it's luck of the draw—whoever makes it to the island, or stumbles across the whale carcass wins the day. But there are social factors at play as well. Unless you are a clam broadcasting your eggs and sperm willy-nilly on the seabed, you're more likely to mate with some individuals than others. This has huge consequences for your functional rate of change. When similar individuals cluster, innovations hit critical mass faster, and groups become more distinct—ideal conditions for cooperation to grow and transformation to occur.

Clusters like the naked mole rats and hamadryas lack diversity, which limits their capacity for genetic transformation. Well-mixed populations like the Awash baboons contain plenty of diversity, but new genes are always flowing in, blurring local distinctions. That has the effect of reducing cooperation within populations, and makes it harder to protect collective value from parasites—but it also lets fringe innovations seep across populations rapidly. These variables—clustering, migration, mixing—can all be tuned to increase novelty, spread, or suppress it.

Diverse biological networks are more resilient. That's true for our bodies as well, which is why creatures prefer not to mate with relatives if they can help it. Their offspring will be healthier if they shack up with someone more distant. In most species, males or females (or both) leave their birth group when they're ready to mate. But sometimes, that just isn't possible.

Superorganism colonies are generally surrounded by inhospitable territory and heavily defended from intruders or usurpers. Naked mole rats will fight ferociously to protect their desert fortress, as will wasps and bees, and those angry Southern fire ants I mentioned earlier. The hamadryas baboons are ready to defend their sleeping cliffs and watering holes from other troops, and toothed whales won't even talk to strangers, so shacking up with them is out of the question. It isn't easy for superorganisms to leave home—unrelated mates are hard to come by. You are your own grandpa and that's how it's gonna be.

Inbreeding has powerful consequences. You have two copies of most genes in your body—one from each of your parents. If one has a harmful mutation, it's generally okay if the other copy is all right. Sometimes this is even adaptive. But inbreeding increases the likelihood of having two copies of the same mutation, so many more individuals are unhealthy. These populations are very likely to blink out—another twig pruned from the tree of life. This is the inbreeding valley of death. Evolution accelerates until the population's diversity is used up and either the harmful variants disappear or the population does.

If the population can hang on, those harmful variants are eliminated. Helpful variants double up more often too, and spread quickly. Who makes it through the valley of death? It's mostly a matter of luck. But isolated groups tend to acquire distinctive features from other groups. Now, selection is pushed up a level: groups begin to compete against each other more than individuals within them do. The most cooperative groups thrive and spread, as more selfish ones dwindle and fail.

As cooperation increases, individuals take on different roles—*you do this, and I'll do that*. Value increases dramatically. This is Adam Smith's *Wealth of Nations*. Eventually, the division of labor extends to reproduction and some individuals dedicate themselves to breeding, while others refrain entirely, helping others raise their offspring instead. Once the threshold is crossed, hivemates are forever entwined. Any groups that revert to an everyone-for-themselves way of life will do worse and fade out as more cooperative groups overtake them. From this point on, cooperation is required.

After making it through this inbreeding valley of death, the population needs whatever diversity it can attract, because the colony's collective intelligence depends on it. Baboons and people sneak off with tall, dark strangers. They welcome immigrants, and the occasional fringe oddball, while honeybee queens gather sperm like it's going out of style.

This is how superorganisms occur: similar individuals cluster into groups. Groups become more distinctive, and cooperation grows. Individuals take on distinct roles, and share the fruits of their labor. Add diversity and a compelling shared purpose, and dramatic things happen quickly.

If you're wondering why all species don't become superorganisms, now you know. They have to cross the inbreeding valley of death to get there. If you're wondering how this might help you accelerate transformation and grow cooperation in your organization, the next chapter will show you how.

Chapter Twenty

Going Viral

Innovation happens in organizations that nurture a culture for [it],
based on meritocracy, consistency, and transparency.
The determinants of this culture . . . are self-organization and swarm
creativity, operation by an ethical code, and communication
in small worlds networks by hubs of trust.
—Peter Gloor

Naked mole rat colonies are close-knit and inbred. No one comes and no one goes. it's just too dangerous out there in the blinding sun. Every now and then a good rain falls, however, and the abundant vegetation and water offer a fleeting opportunity to spread their genes. A few individuals appear that look quite different from other colony members. These fat little mobile gonad princesses are easy to pick out—and they can't wait to leave the nest. Like flying ant queens and drones, these influencers connect one colony to another.

Social structures like these are referred to as "tribal networks," in which some individuals are highly connected, and others less so. Evolutionary biologists have long observed that new species tend to emerge on the fringes, in isolated places like islands. Rare traits may become common.

New ideas may need nurturing in isolation as well. EBay Germany offers one example. This small, independent, and creative company was acquired by eBay,[1] and steamrolled by the larger culture. Yet, they knew their ideas—like Buy it Now—were good ones. The team opted to fly under the corporate radar, using local servers and outside developers to avoid detection of their experimental microprojects. "We felt this had to grow like a little plant," said one team member. "Once we were sure that it was a strong plant, then we could go out and socialize it." When the CEO Meg Whitman stumbled on their hidden microproject culture, she loved it. Many of this group's experiments were subsequently adapted platform-wide. Today, eBay has a well-established microproject strategy based on this experimental culture. Sometimes an idea needs to gather critical mass to pass through that inbreeding valley of death.

Tribal networks are novelty nurseries.[2] Other kinds of networks have other characteristics. Hierarchies repress and control change—biological systems use them exactly this way. When cells grow cancerous in us, a nested hierarchy of defenses usually prevents them. The same approach works in organizations: at Google, workers spend 20% of their time pursuing personal projects, allowing innovation to spark and grow in a self-organized way. At some point, good projects need resources, and a go or no-go decision is required. The hierarchy can squash it. Similarly, Wikipedia volunteers can change an entry at any time, but a small group of regulars can turn off editing if the entry grows cancerous.

Each network structure yields a different outcome, and these can be combined and fine-tuned at different levels of the organization to dial innovation up or down. How big should your teams be? How much "migration and mating" should go on between them? Do teams need to swap ideas with outside consultants or cross-fertilize in the ecotone for a little diversity?

Social networks spread innovation:[3] animals pick up behaviors from individuals they spend more time with, especially if they are highly connected. We tend to copy the popular crowd, and they tend to be exposed to more novelties. Innovations spread from these influential hubs until they cross a tipping point to become norms and traditions—things we do without thinking.

You've probably heard the haunting song of the male humpback whale. All of them sing the same song, but it slowly changes over time. Humpbacks, like elephants, have deep, lasting social memories, and can communicate over long distances at very low frequencies. Winter songs off the coast of Mexico change in lockstep with those sung 3000 miles away near Hawaii, and it turns out the songs map directly onto the whale's personal relationships. Friends copy friends, even across the ocean!

"Bubblenetting" humpbacks have a special hunting technique: they swim beneath schooling fish while blowing clouds of bubbles, which panics them into tight clusters. Then, they swim up open-mouthed through the swirling ball, netting these fish in their enormous ballooning mouth before pushing the seawater through giant sieves of baleen and mopping the tiny fish up with their huge tongues. This is a cultural phenomenon. Forty years ago, whale watchers witnessed a whale slapping the water with its tail before blowing its net. It turned out this one wasn't eating the usual herring, but another little fish that didn't panic as easily. Adding the tail smack did the trick. Friends and family picked up the practice, and a decade later more than half the whales were tail smackers.

Malcolm Gladwell contends in his book, *The Tipping Point*,[4] that trends are triggered and spread by a few charismatic, connected social alphas. He points to sociologist Stanley Milgram's classic "six degrees of separation" study, in which 160 Nebraskans received a letter, with instructions to try and get them to a particular Bostonian. The catch was each could only send the letter to someone they actually knew on a first name basis. On average, it took six links to deliver the letters, but half were delivered by the same three people. Gladwell dubbed them "connectors" —social hubs with an outsized effect on idea flow. Marketers embraced the concept, and they work hard to identify and reach such people.

There's more to the story, however. Most of the letters weren't delivered at all. If you repeat the experiment with hundreds of *completed* deliveries, a different picture emerges. It still takes six exchanges to get a letter to its destination, but it doesn't depend on the connectors. It depends on the network: members must be *ready* to receive and share the information. It doesn't matter who generates the trend as much as how susceptible society is to it. If they are ready to embrace it, then almost anyone can start it. If it isn't, almost no one can. Connectors don't govern person-to-person communication—we all do.

A population geneticist would say that both connectors and the network are essential to the spread of innovation. In the Awash Hybrid Zone, genes occasionally cross from one population to the other via a few "tall, dark strangers." Savanna baboon females love trysting with visiting hamadryas, because they act as bodyguards, allowing the females to eat better food, unmolested. These are the connectors. By the same token, hamadryas troops want nothing to do with an itinerant savanna male. We watched one fellow desperately try to gain entry into hamadryas society. His life was a sorry affair. Constantly and cluelessly violating the rules of female possession and male politeness, he was regularly beaten by both leaders and followers. Females avoided him like the plague because they were beaten as well. This guy came off as an oafish bully. He was thoroughly friendless and punished. We wondered why he stayed. Connectors succeed when society is susceptible to them, but they will get no traction in a resistant one.

The key to triggering transformation may not be looking for magical connectors so much as cultivating susceptible networks. "It's not the nodes, but the network that creates disruption," says Greg Satell.[5] Phenomena as diverse as obesity, smoking, and even happiness, spread in our social networks like epidemics. Your chances of becoming obese skyrocket 60% if you have an overweight friend. Generosity and cooperation are contagious the same way.

Seek those who relate to your innovation most strongly and empower them to find other people to share it with. Think of Mary Kay Cosmetics or Tupperware. Reps self-organize to leverage their own circles of trust and identity. Harley-Davidson and eBay thrive because of users' strong bonds with each other and the brand. That critical mass attracts more resistant outsiders to invest.

Peter Gloor uses social network tracking software to identify informal networks in our organizations so they can be more consciously nurtured. Feed any communication log into the software to get a dynamic snapshot of exchanges. The most active communicators appear in the center, and primary creators, collaborators, and communicators grow out from there. It's easy to see who does what kind and how much work—who are the innovators, influencers, and supporters. The results may surprise you. Many valuable people work below the radar and may be overlooked, while the loudest bluster comes from those who mainly just breathe your air. The software shows who is socially peripheral, who is marginalized, and who dominates conversations. Drill down into activity hotspots to see where innovation is brewing. Maybe you'll discover a bottleneck or an idea sink—a place where good ideas go to die—or a struggling interpersonal relationship in need of a little help.

This sounds plug-and-play, but our interactions are rarely so simple. Even so, there are abundant possibilities for applying superorganism-inspired algorithms and network visualizations to support our team dynamics. Combine these kinds of insights with big data, feedback dashboards, instant messaging, reputation fingerprints, and style assessments like StrengthsFinder to empower the organization and your team.

Mentoring is another way of spreading innovation. Superorganisms rely heavily on it. Meerkats—adorable little mongoose-like creatures—live on the South African salt pans in close-knit families. They love to eat scorpions, a dangerous and difficult prey item. Older helpers teach the pups how to eat them. First, the helper kills the scorpion, allowing the youngster to explore it safely. Gradually, live prey with stingers removed are introduced. That's fun! Finally, the youngsters graduate to live, intact, fully stabbing scorpions. The older siblings stay with the pups throughout the process, correcting them as they go. Soon, pups can safely catch and dismember scorpions on their own.

In Argentina, orca whales hurl themselves onto the beach to catch seals. Mothers and older adults nudge youngsters onto the shore at just the right moment, teaching them to time their incursions with the waves. In Antarctica, pod elders catch seals and put them back on the ice so the young can have a go.

It may surprise you to learn that some ants teach others too! European wood ants maintain an extensive network of foraging trails. Most ants do not survive the long winter hibernation, however. A few OG elders emerge in the spring—wise ones that will lead the young on last year's trails, teaching them the way. They can persist as cultural traditions for decades.

Tiny *Temnothorax* ants must move frequently, because their twig and acorn nests make unstable homes. Scouts are always searching for a suitable spot. If one finds something she likes, she recruits other ants to follow her there, a process called tandem-running. Once an ant follows a scout, she'll explore a bit before finding a follower of her own. Following stimulates exploration that might lead to a better site. Each run gets straighter and more direct, and when a critical mass of individuals arrives, the decision to move is triggered: the scouts carry the laggards to the nest. Combining imitation with innovation allows populations to adapt with blinding speed.

Chapter Twenty-One

Brewtopia

If you and I swap a dollar, we each still have a dollar.
If we swap an idea, we both have two.
—PETER GLOOR

Hundreds of millions of years ago, a few intrepid plants ventured from the sea, struggling along the primordial shore. With the feeblest of roots, they survived in only the narrowest window of conditions. This was a marginal existence. But roving bands of fungi soon discovered these photosynthetic fuel factories, and snuggled up close to cadge a little sugar love. Over time, the fungi fused into fine netlike webs of fuzz, fully integrated with the plants' meager roots, gathering impossibly diffuse molecules of water and nitrogen and phosphorus fertilizer to exchange with their hosts. Together, they unlocked the terrestrial niche.

Green living things now carpet the land, capturing and transforming sunlight into perpetual golden sugar that powers us all, while puffing endless breaths of oxygen where there was none. By opening their photosynthetic platform, plants and fungi exploded future value.

Cooperation is older than life itself.[1] Even in the beginning, Earth's primordial soup was an ecosystem of molecules bubbling away. Some catalyzed the reactions of others while others consumed the chemistry those reactions required. One molecule affected the formation of another—the molecules of pre-life "ate" one another. It's fractals, baby—the same patterns repeat at every level of the cosmos. From molecules to cells, individuals to populations, and populations to eco-systems, partnerships are the agents of evolutionary change.

Today, we call such intimate collaborations *symbiosis*. Our very cells have evolved from such ancient intimacy: billions of years ago, some free-living cells traded chemical energy for a safe home inside another cell. The associations became so tight the little creatures took up permanent residence together. Today, nearly every cell in every creature on Earth contains either these tiny mitochondrial energy fac-tories, or photosynthetic chloroplasts—each with a vestigial genome of their own.

As soon as ancient plants crawled onto the shore, everyone wanted a piece of the sugar action. But animals can't digest most of what the plants make. Only bacteria and fungi can take on this fibrous stuff. Termites and leafcutter ants cleverly leveraged this microbial talent. Today, the insects care lovingly for their fungal gardens, plying them with scraps of wood, grass, and leaves, consuming their rich fruit in return. Termites host a multitude of bacterial species in their bellies, forming an army of mobile, distributed bioreactors.

Innovation prospers when ideas are free to recombine, but for the last two centuries, we've pursued the opposite strategy: building walls around it, with intellectual property, trade secrets, proprietary technol-ogy, and top-secret R&D labs. We do this in the assumption that inno-vation will increase if you make its use exclusive, because creators will reap large financial rewards for their efforts, enticing innovators to work harder. The problem with this model, as author Steven John-son reminds us, is "they make the adjacent possible harder to explore." They reduce the network of minds that can engage with an idea, damp-ening the number of unplanned collisions from different fields and effectively hamstringing solutions.

Like suspicious villagers, companies struggle to share information—debating whether to keep that old carrot for themselves or contribute it to the soup for an bowl down the road. Scarcity drives competition, but cooperation multiplies resources for the future. Companies can explode their future value by opening their platforms to distributed users.[2] Hoarding ideas is wasteful in today's fast-moving environment—their only value is what we can wring from them before they become obsolete. As Judge Alex Kozinski once said, "intellectual property rights are like children: cling to them too closely and you may lose them forever." Sharing innovations maximizes their value. This allows swarm creativity to go to work—openly sharing ideas, information, and credit, to create enduring opportunity and value.

Today, distributed production networks are driving innovation in every industry. Knowledge collectives like Wikipedia leverage them for learning, while Apache and Linux use them to design new software. Idea platforms like Inocentes and YourEncore help solution-seekers freely find one another. Talent platforms like Mechanical Turk help individuals find paper-task work, while sharing platforms like Airbnb, Etsy, Uber, and Craigslist rely on social networks to self-organize the exchange of goods and services. Flickr, Instagram, and Facebook use them to acquire free content, and eBay and Amazon leverage them by sharing accumulated user ratings and feedback. These innovations rely on open-source logic—they are transparent, accessible, public and hackable—available for collaborative innovation to go to work on them.[3] This is what Marina Gorbis[4] refers to as "maker instinct amplified by connectivity, a future in which networks of makers self-organize to do all kinds of things." That future is already here.

Manufacturers traditionally develop products and services in a closed process, relying on patents, copyrights, and other protections to prevent others from participating and freeriding on their innovation coattails. The users' role is simply to have needs which manufacturers identify and fill by designing and producing new products. Economist Eric von Hippel[5] sees the future of production quite differently. He points out in his book *Democratizing Innovation* that manufacturer designed products are typically generic, meeting a wide range of needs for a wide range of people. Inevitably, some users hack the product, adjusting it to meet their specific needs.

Inviting people to break in and play with your stuff is a little foreign to most companies. You can't open it if you don't own it. Generally, we don't and we can't, because it voids the warranty. Hacking used to be a negative term and is still a little subversive. Hackers break corporate systems to rebuild them their way. Corporations typically repress this kind of maker instinct by suing it. When artists started making Mentos and Coke fizz displays, the companies came down on them hard. Eventually, they dropped the lawsuits and sponsored the artists instead. The publicity added fizz to both brands.

Hacking and user driven innovation can be a little scary for traditional companies, because things aren't under their control anymore. But you can expect the public to claim squatters' rights on your logos, ads, and slogans, and remake them in ways you may not like. Resistance is futile and you may as well embrace it, because the network may commandeer you if you don't. When Microsoft unveiled the Kinnect motion-driven interface in December 2010, an army of hackers immediately designed their own applications. Microsoft threatened to sue, but the hackers defied them by putting up kinecthacks.com, a site inviting people to display what they made, with a prize for the best hack! The next day Microsoft opened the platform to them. There was no way to keep people out, so the company got in on the free maker-added value instead. After all, the fungi are hackers too. Their plants are hacked into the partnership, as the fungi override the host by injecting a protein that neutralizes the plants' immune defenses. If you don't step up to share your platform, users may take it from you or create their own. You may as well be proactive. Invite customers to open your products and systems and make things with you the way they want to. You might even be able to outsource your R&D and production to billions of users and contributors for free, while staying ahead of the innovation curve and earning enthusiastic user goodwill.

Manufacturers can elicit user innovation on purpose, outsourcing tasks that take much time and effort to an eager army of skilled volunteers. LSI Logic did this by creating a software design tool for customers to design their own circuits, making them a major player in the custom circuit market. Their competitors soon followed suit.

Lead users are often delighted to freely share their insights and innovations because they want their needs met. Manufacturers can help them by providing innovation tool kits—user-friendly, modular design tools that let users prototype their own solutions. Little Bits is one example—fun, modular, open-source electronics snap together with tiny magnets to facilitate tinkering, thus democratizing hardware so anyone can invent what they need. Users can even add Internet connectivity to their designs with a Wi-Fi module: now you can build that remote control toaster!

Pedro Oliveira and other scientists surveyed 500 rare disease patients and caregivers and discovered 8% had developed their own novel treatments. Why shouldn't these patients be tapped for their ideas? 3M began actively pursuing user-driven innovation twenty years ago, generating eight times more sales from these product ideas—to the tune of $125 million per year. The projects yielded entirely new product lines, where traditional research tended to produce incremental improvements to existing products. As a result, 3M divisions that relied on user-driven innovation generated more major product lines than they had in 50 years.

Gloor describes the chaos in Daimler Chrysler's procurement process when they merged. E3, the electronically extended enterprise they developed to manage their sprawling supply chain began internally, but eventually snowballed into a joint effort with competitors Ford, GM, Renault, and Nissan. It ultimately became its own company.

Part Four

The Sweet Spot Between Order and Chaos: Distributed Leadership

If biologists have ignored self-organization, it is not because self-ordering is not pervasive and profound. It is because we biologists have yet to understand how to think about systems governed simultaneously by two sources of order. Yet who seeing the snowflake, who seeing simple lipid molecules cast adrift in water forming themselves into cell-like hollow lipid vesicles, who seeing the potential for the crystallization of life in swarms of reacting molecules, who seeing the stunning order for free in networks linking tens upon tens of thousands of variables, can fail to entertain a central thought: if ever we are to attain a final theory in biology, we will surely, surely have to understand the commingling of self-organization and selection. We will have to see that we are the natural expressions of a deeper order. Ultimately, we will discover in our creation myth that we are expected after all.

—STUART KAUFFMAN

Chapter Twenty-Two

We Meet in the Middle

*Living systems exist in the solid regime near the edge of chaos,
and natural selection achieves and sustains such a poised state.*
—STUART KAUFFMAN

Many years ago, in a faraway land, seven blind men groped an elephant. "It's a column," said one. "No way. It's clearly a snake." said another. "A snake? Are you mad? It can only be a fan!" said a third. "You are all wrong. It's a flyswatter!" They argued like this for some time, until finally a passerby overheard them. He shouted and waved his arms. "You idiots! Are you blind or stupid! Anyone can see it's an elephant!" And he was right. But his commotion spooked the creature, which turned on him and charged. At least he knew what hit him.

Despite the observer's superior knowledge of the big picture, he knew nothing of the animal's power and heavy, fearful breathing. He hadn't felt its dry, wrinkled skin or thick, muscular trunk and breezy ears, or inhaled the sharp scent of dung. By sharing their diverse perceptions, these eight men ultimately expanded their collective understanding of what elephants are all about. Obviously, a great deal more than the sum of its parts. Here is the difference between local description, gathered from the bottom up, and global vision, imagined from the top. There is a sweet spot in the middle, and finding it is a challenge all superorganisms face. It is also the source of their success.

Where does the sweet spot lie? It depends on the degree of complexity and adaptability that specific environment requires. If things change faster than your teams can sense and respond to them, you have the wrong structure in place. It's like "trying to drive your car by shifting the passengers because your steering wheel is broken." You lack control because these actions should be occurring on the front line. The opposite problem comes from having too much structure—if you were to try to pre-program your car to drive through a herd of stampeding wildebeest for instance.

To paraphrase Bryan Robertson at Holacracy's description:[2]

Imagine if we rode a bicycle like we try to manage companies... We'd have a big committee meeting where we all plan ahead and try to predict exactly where the bicycle is going to be when... We make our plans, have our project managers, our Gantt charts, and we put in place controls to make sure this all goes according to plan. Then we get on the bicycle, close our eyes, hold the handlebar at the angle we calculated upfront and try to steer according to plan. If the bicycle falls over somewhere, Well, first: who is to blame? Let's find them, fire them, get them out of here. And then:...We obviously missed something. We need more upfront predictions. We need more controls to make sure things go according to plan.

Part Four focuses on Principles #8, #9, and #10: how superorganisms link top-down vision with bottom-up production to find the sweet spot in-between. Local information increases uncertainty, but also specificity and responsiveness. Top-down vision counteracts chaos, but whitewashes vital local details. Superorganisms integrate both in just the right amounts, allowing them to surf the sweet spot between order and chaos.

At the beach near my house I frequently see pelicans surfing the air, rising effortlessly over the swells in their prehistoric formations. Who sets the direction? Who bears the brunt of the wind? It turns out the birds have no permanent leader. Everyone takes a turn at the helm, falling back when tired or uncertain. The birds are aligned in their purpose, and the lead is filled by desire and ability, not age or dominance or who they know. Switching off is triggered naturally by cycles of flagging energy. Leadership is shared, and the burden of accountability spread among them.

Every superorganism society accomplishes this balancing act through the same deep principles, but each has their own unique ways of implementing them. Our organizations can do that as well.

Pattern #3: Superorganisms rely on distributed leadership.

Principle #9: Zip modular teams together as needed.

When conditions change frequently, flexibility is critical. Species like grizzly bears and coyotes are highly flexible "generalists"—they do a little of whatever it takes to survive. In predictable habitats, the winning strategy is specializing in something until you do it better than anyone else, like aardvarks.

Both approaches work, but specializing is risky. If conditions change, the specialist may be left high and dry, unable to shift into a new niche. Superorganisms sidestep this issue by specializing in opportunism, using modular teams of diverse specialists to zip or unzip into right-sized working groups to match whatever opportunities or threats arise. Each team has a generalist "leader"—one who constantly gathers information, distilling and disseminating it to specialist workers and other teams they encounter. These individuals knit the organization's bottom-up activities into a bigger picture.

Principle #10: Integrate local specifics with global vision.

Superorganism leaders are quite different than our traditional corporate conception of one. There are far more of them in these societies, for one thing. A third of the bees and ants that work outside the nest "lead," despite giving no orders of any kind. They function as bridges between local information and global vision, sampling local perceptions, distilling them into patterns, and disseminating these chunks across the organization. These leaders have other important functions as well, including actively spreading unity of purpose and identity. Their role is not to command and control, it is to bridge the gap between local information and the bigger picture, knitting diverse local expertise and action into a cohesive and purposeful whole.

Chapter Twenty-Three
Surfing the Edge

Leaders are to a social system what a properly shaped lens is to light.
They focus intention and do so for better or for worse.
If adaptive intention is required, the social system must be
disturbed in a profound and prolonged fashion.
—RICHARD PASCALE

Researcher Dr. Olga Bogatyreva spent two decades on her hands and knees tracking individually marked ants on the steppes of Kazakhstan.[1] She's an ant's worst nightmare—no doubt the aging queens still threaten the young larvae to behave by telling tales about her—like the time she transported an entire colony of carpenter ants to a faraway glade, miles away, after making them spend a tawdry night in her hotel bathtub. Their awakening that morning is a terrifying tale straight from the *Iliad*.

The poor ants awoke in shock, reeling in abject terror as they stumbled onto the windswept steppe. Gradually, they struggled back to the nest in traumatized twos and threes—only to be set upon by a vengeful colony of black ants. For hours, the beleaguered carpenters fought their attackers, as a blood-lusting audience of steppe ants ogled from nearby blades of grass. Hundreds of black ants lost their lives that day, and eventually the invaders fell back.

At first light of dawn, small clusters ventured out, exploring the new land in curiously rigid paths—a few short, neat triangular or square circuits. The ants were counting their steps. Finally, a new strategy emerged. A handful of very active and social ants went out and discovered a patch of aphids, then returned to rally other workers. A series of small teams began forming. A new rhythm of life slowly emerged, and the colony went back to work.

During her 20 years with these ants, a dozen different species felt the wrath of Dr. Bogatyreva's hand. In each scenario, Dr. B. daubed paint on individual ants and recorded their behavior. Besides her house-falling-in-Munchkinland experiment, she also tinkered with their social lives.

Some colonies awoke to find hundreds of larvae mysteriously added to their nurseries overnight. The ants faced this internal crisis by again relying on their teams: several groups of three joined together, forming a brigade of nursery workers. The specialists got to work, and leaders followed along. They raised the larvae as fast as possible, making more nursery workers. With all these extra workers, the chaos stabilized, but soon the colony was overcrowded and confused. Again, leaders stepped up, leading their teams away from the mass to hunt more distant grounds.

In each scenario, Dr. Bogatyreva observed the ants working in teams of three: one hyperactive leader wandered around exploring, while two specialist workers plugged away. In an external crisis—like waking up to find you're not in Kansas anymore—these active leaders discovered new hunting grounds, while being touched by every ant they passed on the way—that's why they call them feelers. I can just imagine these exchanges. *Hey lady! What's shaking? No freaking idea what's going on! Aphids at two o'clock, FYI. Catch you later!* All in ant-Russian, of course. In each case, the ants resolved their local instabilities without restructuring. They simply zipped or unzipped their modular teams as needed to take on whatever roles needed filling.

Researchers have long known that ants and bees leave the nest in bursts, but only by marking them individually could Dr. Bogatyreva see the clusters were semi-permanent teams. Many species of ants and honeybees seem to rely on these loose trios, zipping and unzipping as opportunities and threats arise. Thirty ants can quickly form a brigade this way, and bumblebees zip their triple units into teams of twenty-one—nimbly claiming opportunities on the wing.

Principle #9: Zip modular specialist teams together as needed.

Dr. B. began seeing trios everywhere, and now I do too. I used to think killing an ant was no worse than grazing my knee. What's a few cells? But now I wonder where the other two are, and quite often I see them. It seems each ant is a uniquely creative individual with its own personality and talents, just as we are.

Chapter Twenty-Four

Are You a Grizzly or an Aardvark?

Nothing can substitute for depth of analysis, and there's proven value in specialization . . . but generalism is a secret talent . . . it is increasingly important to have generalists around to make sense of it all, of the big picture.
—STEVE HARDY

Most individual ants specialize in one kind of work at any one time in their development. Leaders are the synthesists, stitching them all together into a single adaptive fabric. In most species, everyone makes a living doing roughly the same stuff—a grizzly is a grizzly, aardvarks are aardvarks. Yes, they have distinctive personalities and preferences, and they do differ locally, but at the end of the day, each individual must feed and protect themselves and their own offspring. Nobody will do your mating for you. They don't take on different *roles* for the most part. Grizzlies deal with this by being highly flexible generalists. They can make themselves at home just about anywhere—on the beaches (not my beach), forests, mountains, the frozen tundra, even in semi-desert. The secret is their omnivorous habit—"omni" meaning all. They will eat it all, and they are clever about acquiring it. In Yellowstone, half the bears' yearly calories come from moths and pine nuts (not peanut butter and jelly), while in British Columbia, salmon is the thing. Alaskan bears dig for razor clams, adding a heaping side of sedge-grass and berries, and will even scavenge whales. Mammals large and small are always tasty, as are ladybugs and bees. Roots, shoots, and mushrooms; nuts, grubs, and garbage. And honey, of course.

Grizzlies are so versatile that some of their ancestors ventured into the extreme life of the Arctic. In just a million short years (the blink of an eye in evolutionary time) their descendants became polar bears—fearless creatures that won't hesitate to swim across miles of open ocean or jump on a narwhal's back. Yes, these former grizzlies now ride the unicorns of the sea. The occasional hook-up still happens—pizzlies and growler bears are the stuff of meth and legend. Isn't evolution magical?

Grizzlies are amazing.[1] But generalizing isn't the only way to make a living. Some creatures take the opposite tack, doing one thing better than everyone else. Like aardvarks. Each night, this solitary pig-like animal zigzags through miles of African desert, sniffing out termite mounds with its powerful nose. A colony is a cow's worth of meat, a nice bit of protein if you can get it. But termites aren't worth the effort of catching one by one. You could starve to death trying. Aardvarks have solved this problem by eating them where they gather—right in their nests.

This is easier said than done. The mound is a mix of iron-rich soil and glassy sand, all cemented with spider silk saliva. It is rock hard—but the aardvark is one of the few animals that can pierce it. He's the ultimate specialist, eating only three things: ants, termites, and the bizarre aardvark cucumber, from which he derives all his water. He breaks in with scimitar claws, digging like mad with powerful forelegs, his rabbity ears alert to big cats and wild dogs in the night. His eyes and nose are tightly seated against the flying dust, his thick skin repels the tiny outraged soldiers' attacks, until he eventually reaches the nest, far below the mound, and begins hoovering masses of panicked insects with his foot-long tongue. He is as ruthless as he is toothless, inhaling 50,000 termites at a sitting, but never destroys the nest completely and avoids the royal chamber entirely. The mound will be safe for several weeks while the insects rebuild. Regeneration is built into this system.

Different conditions require different strategies. In predictable habitats, even a harsh one, the winning strategy is the aardvark's: specialize in something and do it better than anyone else. When you need flexibility, however, victory goes to grizzly opportunism.

Superorganisms meet this dilemma with a network of self-organizing modular teams that can readily specialize in whatever possibility comes along. The colony and its members reap the benefits of both strategies. It's hard to compete against it: honeybees gather nectar and pollen from over a hundred different flowers, but any given team will specialize in whatever patch is blowing up at that moment. Species that specialize on one blossom all the time are forced to scramble, expanding their ranges and extending foraging hours. Competing becomes energetically untenable for them, and the superorganisms slowly push them out, taking over territory like a big box store in Manhattan. Any niche is fair game. The specialized team puts the specialist out of business.

Chapter Twenty-Five

Lead Like a Superorganism

*As a leader . . . I have always endeavored to listen to what each and
every person in a discussion had to say before venturing my own
opinion. Oftentimes, my own opinion will simply represent a consensus
of what I heard in the discussion. I always remember the axiom: a
leader is like a shepherd. He stays behind the flock, letting the most
nimble go out ahead, whereupon the others follow, not realizing that
all along they are being directed from behind.*
—NELSON MANDELA

The moon rises full and pale over the Rift Valley escarpments as
twilight descends. A handsome baboon leads a string of rangy
females in tight single file to their cliffside roost for the night, the
wind playfully ruffling his white mane. A warning bark and flash of
eyelids commands his females' attention, alerting any who stray. A
deferential and maneless grey brings up the rear, toting a tiny black
youngster on his back.

These harems are a little hard for a modern fearless female field
worker to accept,[1] but it's taken a lifetime of dedication for these
males to acquire their harems. These grey ladies represent his whole
shot at success. His evolutionary fitness depends on preventing other
males from stealing them.

Things aren't quite as they seem, however. His threats keep the entourage obedient and close, but a stolen female won't be kept against her will for long. She'll find her way back to her favorite harem, filled with friends and a favorite cousin—the humble fellow who followed her harem as a baby. He is the leader male's nephew,[2] a trusted ally that helps him guard the family from predators and competitors. As a follower, he's taken a vow of celibacy for now, politely refraining from challenging his uncle or shacking up with his women. He's also a fabulous babysitter. Hamadryas males are softies—gruff would-be tyrants that love to tote youngsters around. This sort of thing would never be permitted in savanna baboon society. The aunties and grannies would scream bloody murder. But these young fellows have put in their time. Someday they will inherit the little females, and one of the little males may babysit his own children.

The shadow of the future looms large here.

At first light of dawn, several harems disappear into the bush to forage as a clan. You can easily tell which fellows belong together because their faces match: there's the Pink Clan, Purple Clan, Lavender Clan—and of course the elegant Dusty Rose Clan. They are brothers, sons, fathers, nephews, and cousins. They share a bond of trust. It's like Braveheart but with bright red buttocks. They can safely bring their women together.

Like ants, bees, orcas, and humans, the hamadryas' modular network of teams can zip or unzip to handle whatever the desert throws at them. If food is scarce, harems forage alone. When conditions improve, they move as a clan. A dominance hierarchy does exist—followers are deferential to leaders, and females don't have much say. But leaders are equals, and the network is pretty flat—three layers, no more. The savanna baboon's hierarchy is mostly missing, as it is among foraging peoples today. Our ancestral societies likely functioned similarly, with small, modular family units networked into clans and larger bands.

This society has taken on a distinctly insect-like structure, with cooperation, classes of celibate individuals, and differentiated individual roles. How did these primates, whose ancestors lived in dominance hierarchies for millions of years, acquire this more egalitarian social structure? You can see how they accomplish it day to day—by suppressing the urge to dominate with constant ritualized appeasement gestures the same way we do. They present their rumps in a twerkishly fetching way—the equivalent of a smile. *Excuse me, pardon me, I'm so sorry, after you.*

The monkeys must travel away from the safety of their sleeping sites each day in order to forage through the open desert in search of food and water. Who decides which way to go? Which waterhole should they meet at for the midday siesta?

As among ants and honeybees, orcas and elephants, it's the grannies who take the lead. These are the scouts, now afforded greater freedom than their closely watched sister-wives. These elders keep a constant eye on opportunity—sampling the plants, seeing what will be going to seed this week. Where will the best nuts and berries be found? When will the termites fly? Who are we likely to encounter on the way? These intrepid grannies know where food and water is to be found in a pinch, and they remember where crafty predators hide.

An elaborate dance takes place at dawn each day. The leader moves with studied nonchalance in one direction, then waits to see his clanmates' response. It is clearly stressful for him. He wipes his nose and yawns, moving casually here and there, as if to say, *I really don't care. How about this?*

Eventually, the females find one of his suggestions suitable, and get up and go ahead of him.

Despite their *de facto* ecological leadership, there is still a hierarchy to be honored. Their white maned leader must look like the decider. I'm sure you can relate to this. But try and see it from this fellow's perspective. What if his team doesn't follow? What if they lose confidence in his ability to lead and slip off with one of his rivals? There is always someone looking for a hot new acquisition. He must be sure consensus is squarely behind him before staking his leadership on an opinion.

Compare this dance to gorilla society, where the silverback just goes where he likes, and the harem follows along. Or savanna baboons, where folks just follow their friends, relatives, and booty calls while looking out for *el numero uno*.

Principle #10: Integrate local specifics with global vision.

We've seen the ants' triple-unit leaders and the honeybee scouts— buzzing out into the world to look for homesites and flower patches. Arguably these represent a kind of leader class, but not the way we are used to thinking about it. What's the difference? There are far more leaders in these societies. For one thing, 30% of outside workers "lead," exploring, observing local realities, distilling them into larger patterns, and disseminating that vision back down and across the colony. They don't command or control—they look for patterns, using them to knit their modular teams into an integrated system.

Early European explorers and anthropologists were mystified by their encounters with foraging societies.[3] Their directives to "take me to your leader" were mostly met with obfuscation or a visit with whoever was most irritating, half-witted, or expendable. It wasn't clear whether leaders even existed. But they did, and still do. The ideal conception of a leader looks similar in foraging societies worldwide: they should be generous, kind, and respectful, and completely absent of temper, greed, or bias. Honest, patient, humble, couching opinions as suggestions. Gifted at sensing what others want, skilled at facilitating consensus—they should be last to speak up and least opinionated, like a hamadryas leader male. Foraging societies don't have a set number of leaders either, any more than ants and bees do. Anyone with the right temperament can step into the role. The more the better, in fact, as more diverse and independent voices make greater collective intelligence. Each of us has an important role to play in our collective future, and the more who step forward to fill it, the better for all of us.

Superorganism leaders perform several vital functions, none of which look quite like our chiefly executive job descriptions. They spread social unity and shared purpose, distill and disseminate the big picture, and cultivate diverse possibilities—potential.

I like Peter Gloor's summation:[4]

The trick is to distribute control among the contributors, granting them a broad ability to make their own decisions, select their own tasks and methodologies, without sacrificing strategic direction and coordination. Allow those with highest stakes or firsthand knowledge to assume temporary leadership around that context. Engage the community of contributors in designing their own rules, ones that match their values and objectives. Ad hoc groups form around specific short-term goals, membership is fluid and self-selected, and temporary leadership forms around moving targets.

Chapter Twenty-Six

Freaks, Geeks, and Folks Like Me

*Never underestimate the power of a few committed people to
change the world. Indeed, it is the only thing that ever has.*
—MARGARET MEADE

Remember my colleague Dr. Bogatyreva, fearlessly tracking individual ants through the wilds of Siberia? Before long, she found she could identify individual ants by their behavior, without even consulting the colored dots on their backs.[1] *Hey, there goes Kropotkin! What's got Stalin so worked up over there?* It was remarkable—the ants were "creative little creatures with their own social attitudes." Some were conscientious, bringing lots of food to the nest. Others wandered in circles, making no attempt to do anything useful. Some were nervous, stopping constantly to look around, while others ran fast, touching every ant they passed. Dr. B describes one particular ant that "regularly hid for hours in the shadow of a stone or blade of grass, before spotting another ant with food, grabbing it, and taking it home!" No two were alike in behavioral style or time budget, and statistical clustering proved impossible; every ant was unique. Individuals contributed their own unique personal creativity, expertise, and awareness.

Once Dr. B observed a team of ants discover an enormous locust wedged beneath a twig. After having no success in dislodging it, they "left the prey and started to wander around." She thought they had given up and gone on to find other prey. But ten minutes later, one of the ants came back with a straw. She put one end of it under the branch and the ants used it to lever the locust out.

I am personally stunned by this: not only does it look like creative problem-solving and tool use,[2] but ants are not the clone army we often think of. Being part of a superorganism does not mean assimilation by the Borg. We cherish free will and individuality, and it seems other superorganisms do too in their way. For them, adaptability stems from creative local actions of diverse and independent teams. Individual decisions have dramatic effects in this world, and anyone may lead when called upon.

Spread Social Unity and Shared Purpose

The queen literally creates the hive's entire workforce from her own blood, sweat, and tears. Social wasp queens even eat their first eggs, gathering strength to make the first workers, who will eat her next eggs. Every action is focused intently on the generations to come. This is their shared purpose, and workers are unified tightly around it. Their whole aim is to help the queen lay more eggs; raise their sisters to feed the colony and raise more eggs and cultivate new queens to go forth and launch more colonies that succeed in the future. All evolved to bear out what vaccine pioneer Jonas Salk called "our greatest responsibility"—being good ancestors. Every individual—organism or superorganism—is focused on nurturing the next generation and growing value for future descendants.

The queen is the heart and soul—gonad really—of every social insect society. The colony can't survive without her. She issues no orders, however, and once she enters the hive, she will never leave it again. The other bees fuss over her, attending to every need. She is helpless to feed or groom herself and cannot survive without her caretakers. She is literally the workers' creation, formed by their decision to feed her royal jelly as a larva. In truth, she serves them, just as they serve her. Together they strive to regenerate their collective future just as your gonads serve your drive to regenerate the cells that are you.

Sometimes, beekeepers try to impose a queen on the colony, but it's a flip of the coin whether the bees will accept her. She has to be introduced in a protective cage so the hive will acclimate to her scent, but if she's already mated, she is more desirable to them. Now she has something to offer: diversity.

Her very first job is to gather as much of it as she can. A light rain tempts nearby drones and virgin queens to take to the air for their nuptial flight. They converge on a certain spot and get busy. The queen will meet with as many males as she can—more than a dozen if possible. It might take her several days to score this perfect sperm kaleidoscope, but she will keep at it until she does. She'll sock away some six million sperm to release one by one, fertilizing eggs for the rest of her career. A diverse colony is a healthy one, and she will work hard to achieve it.

Distill and Disseminate the Big Picture

Organizational cultures start at the top. The queen cements colony social identity with a special pheromone-laden chemical fingerprint that her attendants gather and spread among the workers. Leaders set the tone, and much of the time we march to their rules of engagement and purpose. But unique cultural characteristics inevitably bubble up from the bottom. Cultures have lives of their own, and leaders walk a fine line between channeling and guidance. Too many rules and excessive planning stifle initiative, risk-taking, and adaptability. It's better to provide a minimal structure that supports the group's purpose and values. That said, rules should be clear, fixed, and enforced at every level of the organization, with escalating rewards and sanctions, ideally determined and enforced by the workers themselves. Leaders can take the first sanctions to show how it's done—with grace, humor, humility, and contrition. Scaling requires not just insisting the rules are upheld, but walking the talk and insisting others do, too, even when the boss isn't looking.

No leader can know everything in this complex and changing world—leadership isn't generally about visionary genius. The more uncertain the future, the less any single vision is likely to be right. A leader's role is to provoke and facilitate conversations, strive to understand values and opinions, distill and articulate patterns back to the team and to other teams. Collective intelligence doesn't come from the top, it emerges in dialogue from the bottom. Ask and listen to stakeholders, try to understand what they want and need, and clarify and articulate it with them in an iterative feedback loop. Leadership gives voice to what followers want to do. Without a leader who listens, they may not even know what that is.

Cultivate Potential

Nature doesn't solve problems so much as move towards what's working—the next open door. Usually, there are many, and it is impossible to know where they will lead. In real life, you want to hold options open as long as possible, increasing the range of possibilities available to you down the road. But without strong purpose, shared identity, and transparency, asking people to "forgo rapid simplification" is confusing and stressful. Does this superorganism even have a queen, or are we stuck in an endlessly circling antmill, chasing our own pheromone trails?

Leaders know that in the absence of information and personal choice, certainty is comforting. Most try to eliminate options quickly—simplify things and move on. But it's all too easy to seduce those uncomfortable with complexity. Turn a dilemma into a polarized problem or a blame game, and watch people flock to the illusion of righteousness. Stereotypes, assumptions, and rushed certainty are the province of parasites—those who know how to prey on us by painting things black-and-white, good and evil. But these are oversimplifications, not deep patterns—deceptive pheromones fed to us by those who want to control or profit from us, like *Cordyceps*-infected zombie ants, compelled to climb blades of grass and hang over the colony, spreading the infection until the colony is sucked dry.

Good leaders resist the either-or choice, embrace fifty shades of grey, and allow ambiguity to persist—but they have to keep attention focused on the big purpose while feeding our sense of belonging to a special team that can achieve it. They remind us that our mission is ambitious, important, and attainable, and that each member has a specific, unique, and irreplaceable role in our collective success.

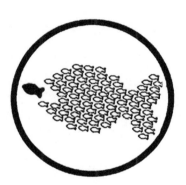

Part Five

The 2% Difference:
Trust and Transparency

The human brain is a poor thing on its own,
an inarticulate, undifferentiated beast like any other.
But joined to a community of its fellows, it has this remarkable
capacity to create a community of mind.
—RICHERSON AND BOYD

Chapter Twenty-Seven
Please Don't Eat Me

Culture eats strategy for breakfast.
—PETER DRUCKER

Fresh out of college, I made a beeline for the cultural Mecca of Seattle. My artist boyfriend and I lived with three other guys in a brick-walled loft beneath the Pike Place Market, above the original Starbucks roasting warehouse. We were poor, and my boyfriend and I shared a bunk under the loft bed of author Jonathan Evison,[1] best known then for his stint with the punk band March of Crimes (which later split and morphed into more famous bands like Soundgarden and Pearl Jam), his monthly Johnny Seattle column in the free weekly *Mullet Rapper*, illustrating a book with one foot, and inexplicable prowess with women. Our loft ceiling was high but not nearly high enough.

It was peak Grunge Era, and everyone we knew was an artist or musician or writer of some kind when they weren't pulling espresso, throwing fish, or delivering packages on their bikes. Cafés and messenger companies seemed to be the only ones hiring, and these interviews were humiliating cattle calls. A bunch of shaggy, hair farming musicians and their girlfriends usually showed up, each more plaid than the last, ready for an interview with some guy they grew up with on the island across the Sound. The manager would say something like "What'd you study in college again?" And go around the room. "Art? Your interview is at four. Anthropology? Cool, me too, bro. 4:30. You? A little community college, right? Did you catch that band last night? 5 p.m. And... you with the glasses. BOTANY???" Blank stares. Dorky science girls need not apply.

Finally, I saw an ad in the Seattle *Post-Intelligencer*: WANTED: Biologists for marine mammal observation at sea. I was excited. All I had to do was spend three months in the Bering Sea on a fishing boat documenting whale sightings for the government while monitoring the fish catch to be sure they were complying with federal quotas. In exchange, I would receive $100 a day, paid by the fishermen off the top of their haul on my return. I could scarcely imagine this kind of wealth. It just seemed too easy.

I went for the interview and was hired on the spot—on the condition of passing a drug test. I sat in the empty waiting room for what seemed an eternity, my bladder full of water (and vinegar). When was my turn? The receptionist kept staring at me, jerking her head. Was it Tourette's? Finally, I couldn't hold my urine any longer. I had to use the restroom. She pointed down the hall, and there on the copy machine was my form—signed and stamped! I picked it up, and the receptionist chirped *"Have a nice day,"* closed her window, and went to lunch. I was a certified drug-free marine biologist. All I had to do was live on a fishing boat with a crew of fish-smeared guys in the Bering Sea and look for whales. *Exceptional!*

The three-week training at Sand Point required a ten-mile bike ride, somehow uphill both ways and always in the rain. The sessions were long and fussy. They drilled us on fish identification and cetacean spout and fluke patterns. We were tested *ad nauseam* on sampling techniques, bycatch regulations, and documentation procedures. Last, we had to be able to zip ourselves into a bright orange watertight survival suit in two minutes flat, then pitch ourselves into the Sound. This was supposed to simulate abandoning a sinking ship. I hadn't considered that possibility. Hushed horror stories were whispered in class—one observer had thrown herself off in the night to escape her male crew. She floated at sea for days, until a giant trawler happened upon her. She spent the rest of her contract shell-shocked in their jacuzzi. *A jacuzzi! That didn't sound so bad.* I wondered if my boat would have one.

I got myself a little butch hairdo, a pair of black Chucks, some standard issue steel-toe rain boots and a heavy-duty yellow rain slicker and pants. A thrift store yielded a wool sweater and warm woolen cap, along with the requisite flannel shirts. As an afterthought, I added a folding knife with a fake mother-of-pearl handle. I had $5 left and I was ready for anything.

Off we flew—from Seattle to Anchorage, and then, in a little prop plane, to Dutch Harbor, a craggy little dot far out on the Aleutian Chain on the weather-beaten island of Unalaska. The pilot handed each of us a pair of earplugs as we boarded, the fishermen's knees pressed tight against the seat backs. Our Cessna banked hard as we approached and began circling through dense cloud cover. Down we went, threading the toothy crags that suddenly materialized in the gloom, then climbed laboriously back up, blind in the heavy fog. Over and over we tried, each time buffeted by the wind like a potato chip tossed to a dog at a breezy picnic. The engines roared and our knuckles were white. Round and round the pilot went, plunging down into the swirling mist, then hiccuping slowly back up to try again.

"We can't land, folks. We have to turn back." But now we lacked the fuel to return to Anchorage, and we'd have to fly to an island nearby. We'd stay the night, fuel up, and try again the next day. I hadn't considered this possibility either. I had a few dollars on me—enough for some leaden fries and a bitter cup of coffee from the dirty bar. I curled up in a chair and tried to make myself comfortable for the night. There were a few other people—an older Native American couple having a night out at the only bar in town, and a handful of rough fishermen from my plane. They were ordering shots, including me in each round. The glasses piled up and the men grew insistent.

They were rowdy and competitive, cheering and razzing the ball game, muscling each other at the bar and bumping into my chair. The air was thick with smoke. "Hey, can't you see the lady's with me?" said one guy, wearing a hooded Unalaska sweatshirt smeared with what had to be fish guts. This was going to be a long night. I felt something soft on my shoulder and looked up into the Native American woman's round face. Her eyes were wrinkled in a smile, but her mouth didn't show it. "These guys are no good" she whispered at me. "You come home with us and have dinner, and we'll bring you back in the morning." I nodded with relief and snatched up my duffel.

Joe pushed rusty tools and assorted fishing gear aside to make room for me in the dog hair-coated backseat of their wood-sided Chevette.

"Does your mother know you're here?" he asked softly as he rattled down the perimeter road, long since pounded into gravel by the endless winters. The dull grey sea heaved to our left. I explained about the job, and he shook his head sadly and was silent. Finally, he spoke.

"I don't like it. If you were my daughter, I'd say no way. But best thing I can tell you is to pick the biggest guys and make friends with them, but not too good, you know. Tell them you have a boyfriend back home. And tell them you don't give a damn about their fish, you're just a kooky kid who likes whales! If they leave you alone, you leave them alone, right? If they give you any trouble, get 'em mad at each other and get out of the way. Guys are dumb like that, right, Pearl?" He laughed.

Pearl nodded. "You got a knife, honey? That's good. Keep it under your pillow and don't sleep too hard!" She patted my arm. "You'll be OK." She sounded doubtful. Then she added "Don't go to the Elbow Room!"

"What's that?" I asked.

"You know *Playboy* magazine?" said Joe. Pearl poked him in the ribs. "Hey! I only read it for the articles! There was a story in there. The

Elbow Room is the most dangerous bar in America! Right in Unalaska!"
He was bursting with local pride. "It's the only bar on the island!"

Their place was a dark World War II-era shack, a single room with
heavy windows well-sealed against the savage winters with many layers of peeling caulk. An old wood stove stood in the corner, and a
once-black grizzled lab stood shakily to greet them, tail happy as a
puppy's. Dinner was hot and welcome—Salisbury Steak TV dinner
like my mom made when she worked nights.

Then Joe leaned back in his chair and rolled an American Spirit.
"Me and Pearl are Eskimo, you know. Aleut. That's kind of insult-
ing to you guys because it means 'the people'—like you're not
people. We say Eskimo not to hurt your feelings." He was laughing
off something deeper and quickly moved on. "We don't live that
old way no more, but my uncles told me how it was. There's still
a lot of whales around here: you know them sea wolves? Killer
whales?" I nodded. "My uncle told me a good story about them. It
was a long time ago, on an island like this one. Before the people
came. There was a pack of wolves, and they were excellent hunters. All the other animals were scared of them. Every day, the pack
swam out into the waves and killed a big whale for dinner. They
were spoiled by all that meat, and they only ate the tongue, the
same way killer whales do today. The *muktaq*—you call it blubber—they left to stink up the beach. Pretty soon, the other animals
couldn't stand it anymore, and they begged the creator to do something about it. So off he went to pay a visit. He turned himself into
a raven and perched on a rock to see. Sure enough, the stinking
blubber lay all around, reddening the sea foam with its blood. He
gagged on the stench and cursed the wolves' careless waste. He
waited for them to swim out to kill again, then called up a great
swirling fog to blanket the shore.

The wolves were frightened. They couldn't see which way to go.
"Help us!!" they howled. "We will drown!" But the Creator's heart

was set hard against them. Still, he was sorry to let these good hunters die. Finally, relenting, he turned them into whales, painting their shame upon them in great black stripes so no one would ever forget. Now they are sea wolves, hunting and howling to each other below the waves."

Pearl poured more tea, and Joe lit his cigarette. I was surprised by his dramatic flair! I told them how scientists knew each of the orca from their uniquely scarred backs and dorsals, and how different pods spoke different languages and couldn't understand one another. I asked Joe what he knew about that.

"I don't know, I never talked to them!" he laughed long and hard, dabbing his crinkly eyes. "But I'll tell you what. They are not good people. If you look one in the eye, you feel that Arctic chill right down your spine. They don't never attack people no more, but my uncles told me how in the old days they might swamp your kayak and knock a guy in, or grab your dogs. I guess they quit doing that sometime back. Men always want revenge. Now we leave each other alone."

My Alaskan expedition taught me a great deal about the layers of politics and psychology that vertebrate superorganisms like orca and people have to navigate in order to maintain their collaborations. Orca pods are stable and lasting, containing several generations of females, including a respected grandmother or two, plus their offspring and mates. Several of these pods keep in contact as a clan, with their own dialect of clicks, whistles, and squeaks, and an assortment of proprietary hunting techniques. The North Atlantic clan takes turns stunning herring with loud tail slaps. In Antarctic waters, the pods generate carefully timed waves to knock seals and penguins off the ice into the water. Along the Pacific Coast, teeth are often worn to the gums from chewing sandpapery sharks, while whales in Argentine waters hurl themselves onto the beaches to grab seals, timing their incursions with the tides and swells so as not to get stranded. Any of these orcas could mate with any other if they chose, but they do not. They don't like foreigners.

Like these whales, our own cultures share sets of norms, values, and rules. Many of these have explicit ecological and social functions, but others are somewhat arbitrary historical accidents that serve as markers cementing our identities. It's just who we are. These beliefs and behaviors bind us together, making clear who is us and who is them. The first rule of intergroup competition is to know who's on which team.

When groups compete, more cooperative groups outperform. But in order for them to work as teams, individual competition has to be suppressed. Ants and bees do this using chemical signals and pheromones that block reproduction by any but the queen. This is easier to do when members are close relatives, because helping your nestmates also spreads your own genes—many are identical by descent. But orcas and people are mammals with long histories of living in dominance hierarchies—and we aren't nearly as closely related to one another as hive-mates. It's harder for us to align our goals. Our answer is to suppress and subvert our urge to dominate with smiles, politeness, and collectively enforced norms of behavior. Suppressing dominance is necessary, because superorganisms have to share the work and wealth in ways that benefit everyone—not necessarily equally, but equitably enough for the evolutionary math to pencil out. Superorganisms cannot evolve unless these dynamics are met, and once they do, they stay that way or blink out. Groups that cannot achieve it are soon outcompeted by those that do.

Social insects go about their days using simple rules—if x, then y—and so do we. Our equitable superorganism nature rests uneasily on an inherited substrate of dominance and competition, however. Our rules are more complex, and everything has to be negotiated. We've acquired some functional workarounds over the millennia, including peer accountability, expectations of honesty and fairness, and ritualized politeness. Here I offer a navel-gazing tour of the fourth Old World ape and how it achieves its superorganisms.

You can easily see the creativity and talent for political maneuvering we share with our chimp and bonobo cousins. 98% of our DNA is identical, and our physical likeness undeniable. But that remaining 2% is something quite other. It represents, among other things, our superorganism strategies for equity, fairness, and cooperation. The genetic specifics don't matter much for us here—despite the poetic simplifications, we aren't chimps with good manners any more than you can wipe the superorganism shine off an ant and see the ancient solitary wasp underneath. Culture is not a thin veneer of civilization lacquered onto a wild animal. These things can't be teased apart in the least. We are human all the way down.

I am often asked what we would be like scrubbed clean of culture: what is our instinctive nature when stripped free of cultural baggage? But most anthropologists favor something like Clifford Geertz'[2] observation that "there is no such thing as human nature independent of culture. Men without culture…would be unworkable monstrosities with very few useful instincts, fewer recognizable sentiments, and no intellect: mental basket-cases." Certainly, they wouldn't be chimpanzees. I think it's more useful to look at everything we do, make, think, and say, in every culture and subculture, as our human nature. Smart phones, video games, plastic water bottles, air conditioners—everything. This is our human potential, not the universal common denominators we share. Finding the bits we have in common is not very informative, because we are much more than the sum of our parts. *Ubuntu*—you can't be human alone.

The differences between people and other apes are profound, but figuring out how we got here is a tricky task. Each species of ape has traveled its own evolutionary path for the past five to ten million years or more, and most of the apes' once-bushy tree is now extinct, extinguished by time and the natural replacement of forest by open grasslands. Those that remain are highly-derived oddities—knuckle-walkers, fist-walkers, and bipedalists! A bunch of freaks. It's hard to reconstruct an ancestral way of life with so little to go on.

Our cultural differences make it even more difficult. There is no single way to be a chimp or bonobo, let alone a human being. Every culture and subculture is unique.

This isn't generally the province of evolutionary biology; in fact, it can be uncomfortable to even talk about evolution in an anthropology department. There's a good reason for this tension: the legacy of eugenics. With a basic understanding of population genetics and natural selection, some scientists made a conceptual leap: we selectively breed chickens and corn for desirable characteristics, so why not people? Why not just remove the people we like less? A century of forced sterilizations later, we know how this plays out: those who get to choose will find everyone else's genes undesirable.[3]

When a select group is in charge of choosing the genes and ideas other people ought to have, it's a toxic recipe for human suffering. Apart from the basic moral repugnance and the systemic blindness that comes with the arrogance of presuming that your people are the ones who know where everyone else's future should go, the evolutionary fallout is devastating. That diversity represents our potential to adapt to different futures. We cannot realize collective intelligence without it.

This is where efficiency thinking has led us.

Anthropology has never really recovered from the biologists among it, but it's still essential to understand the nature of the human animal if we want to design the future with any intention. If we do not, those who profit most will do it for us.

In Part Five, we will delve into the hidden politics of the human superorganism: how we ant-like apes suppress and subvert bullying, mooching, avarice, and sloth to grow the collective intelligence we depend upon. Collectively upholding moral communities of fairness and sharing is a uniquely human activity—the key to our superorganism success. These dynamics are at play whenever we work together.

A disclaimer before we dive in further: peeking behind the curtains of human superorganisms is fraught with booby traps. I will probably step in some of them. It's not polite to look at the inner workings too directly. But I like to walk alone in the dark cougar-filled desert at night, probably a poor choice if you're a juicy little thing like me. But the stars are exploding overhead in endless shimmering galaxies, and the sage blows sweet and dry on the wind. It's just too lovely and miraculous to ignore. And anyway, adventure is what happens when things go wrong.[4] I'll carry a big branch over my head, walk tall, stay alert, and hope for the best. Please don't eat me.

Chapter Twenty-Eight
The Ant-like Ape

It is even harder for the average ape to believe that
he has descended from man.
—H. L. Mencken

The day I stumbled into Dr. Trivers' lecture hall I knew I'd found my passion. From there, I followed various odd paper trails for several years, trying to put it together. From coconuts and ohia trees to redwoods and cetacean communication, I tracked human nature—until finally, with my great Alaskan whaling expedition on the high seas with 25 desperately-troubled fishermen (hilarious hijinks ensue), I got to primate cognitive evolution and the endlessly fascinating nature of primitive man himself.

Imagine my thrill upon receiving a phone call from Professor Clifford Jolly himself, telling me I had just received a six-year full-ride scholarship from the New York Consortium for Evolutionary Primatology, including a comfortable travel and living stipend—more than three times what I was eking out in Seattle (obviously I knew nothing about the cost of living in Manhattan). I'd be studying human origins and primate evolution with the most incredible minds at the American Museum of Natural History, Columbia, New York University, City University New York, and the Bronx Zoo. I had just died and gone to geek heaven.

225

What I learned in my years there, and in my fieldwork, is that it's much harder to say what human nature is than you might think. All the living apes—including *Homo sapiens*—are unique and strange. Not only that, but each of these species inhabits locally distinct cultures—there is no single way to be a chimp, bonobo, or human. It is difficult to reconstruct what a last common ancestor might have been like.

Cultural anthropologists threw up their hands long ago in the search for a single human nature. Nearly all of us today have been touched by Hollywood, Coca-Cola, and the acts of a handful of agriculture-fueled explorers and prophets, but human cultures remain extreme in their variety.

Recent times have homogenized us like milk from a corporate dairy, but our cultural diversity must have been very great indeed in the not-too-distant past. Certainly there was never one Paleo diet or ancestral human condition or god—even less than there is one way to eat, dress, or pray today. The more you look, the more you see that the beauty of our lives and loves lies in their intimate details—the things only we can know and share. Even then, things are rarely what they seem. Everything we do must be carefully negotiated with those around us—and fairness is a moving target.

Not many researchers are willing to explore these kinds of human social dynamics from an evolutionary perspective. You're asking to get your head bitten off. But a few courageous souls have made a career of it nonetheless. Cultural anthropologist Chris Boehm followed his fieldwork in the mountains of Montenegro talking family-politics with Serbians with a season at Gombe with wild chimpanzees. His books *Moral Origins* and *Hierarchy in the Forest* articulate his thoughts on the nature of politics. Animal behaviorist Frans de Waal is deservedly well-known for his careful experimental research and deep firsthand knowledge of a wide range of ape behavior, as well as his thoughtful books like *The Bonobo and the Atheist*. Developmental psychologist Michael Tomasello's fascinating empirical research comparing chimpanzees and human toddlers in his book *Cooperation* is another surprising source of insight. This section is largely inspired by these researchers' observations and syntheses, though there is so much fascinating research and writing in this realm, and I apologize for all I have left out.

Chapter Twenty-Nine
Now We're Cooking Soup

You can't be a real country unless you have a beer and an airline.
It helps if you have some kind of a football team, or some nuclear
weapons, but at the very least you need a beer.
—FRANK ZAPPA

A century ago, tens of thousands of free-foraging societies lived all over the world. Far fewer exist today, as all face encroachment by settling peoples and their diseases. Most have been marginalized or confined to poor hunting grounds, devastated by the continued aggressive expansion of agrarian cultures. Ultimately, however, all our ancestors lived this way for tens of thousands of generations—it's a proven social strategy for us.

Foraging bands and pastoral tribes like the Utica, Navajo, Pintupi and the San still persist, and their ways of living can give us some idea of our ancestors' social environments—or at least dissuade us of our assumptions and ground us in more diverse possibilities.

Despite vast differences among these far-flung peoples, there are some commonalities. All oblige one another to help the injured or unlucky and share their good fortune with others. Everyone pays it forward, sharing work and wealth, and everyone eats the soup. On average, three-quarters of the food foraging peoples eat has been acquired by someone outside their immediate family. The Wapa tribe of New Guinea distributes their wealth through gambling—and quitting when you're ahead isn't permitted. Of course, sharing the wealth in superorganism societies also extends to their reproductive success: some South American tribes practice "partible paternity," in which a growing fetus is "nourished" by the semen of all the men the woman sleeps with. All are the father, and all support the child.

With such enormous personal investment in collective fortunes, it follows that foraging peoples are preoccupied with keeping things equitable and free. When the Kalahari bushmen make a big kill, credit goes to the owner of the first arrow that hits the animal—but the men trade arrows constantly and the owner doesn't even have to be on the hunt, let alone take the shot. It's his job to distribute the meat, regardless. It's a clever way to randomize credit and responsibilities so no one gets a big head or an unfair share.

In many foraging cultures, acts of theft, lying, stinginess, or laziness are unforgivable (and mostly unheard of), as is bossing others around. People talk quietly about these personal failures, tallying our grudges until a pattern and critical mass of discontent accrues. Suddenly you aren't just merely lying, you're a liar. You aren't just stealing, you're a thief. Now we band together and shut you out. These are the profoundly superorganismic norms, values, and rules that protect us from thieves and free-riders.

All human cultures collectively suppress greed, moochery, deception, and domination; with strictures against taking more than our share or being less generous than we "ought" to be—stealing and hoarding are generally frowned upon. Shirking our share of the work is a serious offense, and lazy mooches are quickly identified and mercilessly teased. We insist on transparency—lying is not okay and liars are shunned. And lastly, we cherish and defend our right to equal treatment, freedom, and independent thought. When any of these are violated, we resent it—it isn't right. That person can't be trusted.

"All men seek to rule," says anthropologist David Schneider. "But if they cannot rule, they prefer to be equal."

Chapter Thirty
Might Versus Right

Social status among humans is not extorted by brute force.
It emerges from others' willingness to establish social bonds with us.
—JEAN-LOUIS DESSALLES

My friend Paul and his girlfriend, Patricia Reed, now his veterinarian wife, were fresh out of college when they went off to Sierra Leone, a couple of animal technicians looking for adventure. By the time they escaped, they had slashed through impenetrable bureaucracy, battled malaria and river blindness, and witnessed a depraved civil war. The journey was heavy, and Paul jokes that maybe he personally crushed the carbon in his favorite monkey-watching perch into one of the world's biggest diamonds, discovered some years later. But Paul and Trish's dogged fieldwork ultimately produced something more valuable.

It was 1991, and their boss at the Aaron Diamond AIDS research center suspected that HIV had primate origins. He hired them to sample blood from pet monkeys in the region. The villagers were highly suspicious. What kind of black magic needed monkey blood? But eventually, a pet green monkey[1] tested positive for the simian version of the virus, which led Paul and Trish to a troop in the bush.

Paul is part bulldog, part bloodhound: he never lets go of his quarry once he's on the scent. Failing to trap an entire troop of wild,

231

SIV-infected monkeys deep in the jungle because of a civil war was not an option for him. They were on a mission—to catch and sample those monkeys without getting bitten, scratched, or shot. And they did. They got the precious samples out of the country and found they had identified the source of the virus. They almost failed to extract themselves, but the last flight out brought them to New York, which is where we met.

Paul can handle a monkey with eyes closed and hands behind his back. I once saw him jump headlong into the murky Awash River, teeming with sly Nile crocodiles and river blindness, to rescue a sleepy baboon that had fallen in while shaking off her sedative. Imagine grabbing a terrified baboon in your bare arms, canines inches from your face, while treading water in a fast-moving disease-infested river with 15-foot crocs sliding off the banks to investigate. Paul never thought twice.

He's less keen on chimpanzees, though, and how that came to be is an interesting story.

Back in the States, the Research Center had been analyzing their samples. Paul, now in Gabon, got a call from them. The human virus had mutated in some unexpected ways, and primatologists had recently discovered wild chimpanzees hunting monkeys. Perhaps some had eaten infected monkeys, allowing the virus to recombine in the chimps, thus becoming the fatal human variety. Sick chimps had been seen staggering around nearby villages—poachers found them easy targets. Bushmeat is a regular part of many rural West African diets. The Center wanted Paul and Trish to go and shop the deep forest bazaars to get samples from any chimp meat or pets they encountered.

Paul accepted with gusto. He heard of a French family living deep in the Gabonese jungle with a pet chimpanzee. Maybe he could get a blood sample and then look in the local markets. So off he went—five days slow journey on a rained-out muddy track, much of it spent pushing the truck, then several days by canoe, and finally hacking through the bush with a machete to emerge at a neatly white-washed French cottage. The couple came out to greet him, all smiles. Marc the chimpanzee was family. He was out back waiting. They brought Paul through the house and into a manicured garden, lush with ornamental flowers. And there, chained by his neck to a sprawling tree, was Uncle Marc.

Marc was the biggest chimp Paul had ever seen. He was uncharacteristically shaken and declined to take the sample he'd come so far to get. The family was disappointed. *But Marc receives vaccinations all the time! He will stick his arm out for the blood draw, you will see.* But Paul was firm. *Non, merci.*

He would, however, stay for lunch. Out came all kinds of French delicacies, each imported at great expense. Cheeses, crackers, patés, jams. And here was their daughter, skipping down the path, proudly showing the gap where her front tooth had been before. She hugged Marc and passed him a can of sardines, which he opened with a practiced hand—pulling the tab and winding back the foil—and offered graciously to Paul.

"Merci, Marc," said Paul, bowing his head with the fulgent grace of a Renaissance courtier, reaching for the tin. Screaming and baring full canines, Marc crunched down, removing the better part of Paul's hand. It took five full-grown men to pry him off.

I don't know what was going on in the mind of old Marc, maybe it was just a bad day. But I do know that if you chain your cousin to a tree his whole life, he may not be right in the head. Regardless, even sane chimps are powerful bullies ever on the lookout for a chance to gain the upper hand. Evolutionary psychologist Denise Cummins[2] puts it bluntly: "the struggle for survival in chimpanzee society is a struggle between dominance and the outwitting of dominance, between recognizing your opponent's intentions and hiding your own." Chimp politics are a Machiavellian arms race for the manipulation of minds. If you can relate to this, you need to get out.

Only the most dominant individuals—sociopaths and those with absolute power[3]—openly attempt to rule through force and fear. The rest of us work to subvert and outsmart each other and muster some allies at our back. Humans take the arts of deception to new heights.

"If you are big enough to take what you want by force," Cummins continues,[4] "you are sure to dominate available resources. Unless your subordinates are smart enough to deceive you. Then you must use other strategies—deception, guile, appeasement, bartering, coalition formation, friendship, and kinship to get what you need." Our relations are a subtle blend of politics, veiled pressure, and a great deal of stealthy gossip and reading between the lines—but for the most part, we do our best, trying to be the good people our parents taught us to be.

The bizarre thing is not that dominance relationships exist; it's that we so rarely act on them. Those who are dominant or influential are generally not even aware of them. But trust me, those struggling on the receiving end know. Physical altercations are rare in our daily dealings, and we rarely come to blows. Our politics are mainly bluster, or quietly sharing information with others about the transgressions of bullies, mooches, and thieves around us in order to marginalize them.[5] It is dangerous to reveal our machinations, and we work hard to hide it, even from ourselves.

Still, our lives do remain shaped by dominance, try as we might to suppress, subvert, and mask it. Your smile is a modified chimpanzee fear grimace, an appeasement gesture not unlike a hamadryas baboon presenting his rump. A smile relieves tension, and lets folks know they are safe with us.

What's the business takeaway? Just that beneath it all, you and your coworkers are a bunch of damn dirty apes. Smart ones, civilized, polite, and considerate. And a smile means more than you think it does.

Chapter Thirty-One
You Say You Want a Revolution?

Revolution is not something fixed in ideology, nor is it something fashioned to a particular decade. It is a perpetual process embedded in the human spirit.
—ABBIE HOFFMAN

Genetically, we are 98% chimpanzee, of course, and like them we live in social hierarchies—there are domineering individuals who will rule by force and fear if they can. That is the ape in us. But the remaining 2% is premised on helping and sharing.

Tomasello's research shows that even as toddlers, we have an instinctive urge to help and to share—surprising, I know. It is hard-wired into us. We may fall short administering it kindly and fairly, but we do know the math in our bones. Even preverbal babies look aghast when a plate of cookies isn't divided evenly between two older playmates or someone needs help and doesn't receive it. Young children and teenagers are quick to inform us if something's not fair—a concept that would seem irrelevant to a chimpanzee unless it faced a beating for it.

Very few social mammals have any notion of sharing or helping—who gets what is simply mediated by pecking order. Hens scurry out of the way of more dominant chickens, and when a group of chimps make a kill, the most dominant members eat first while the rest beg for scraps. The most desirable allies and booty calls get a calculated hand-out. Individuals are master politicians—their lives revolve around gaining the upper hand.

I imagine our ancestors' fortunes waxed and waned, but by sharing the work and taking care of one another, we persisted. Think about it: how else could we have survived the Pleistocene—a time of great climate fluctuations—while following herds of game with our grand-mothers in tow, on just two legs? Lose one and you're a monopod. A bipedal chimp would starve if he so much as sprained an ankle—nobody's bringing that guy breakfast in bed.

Superorganisms like us share the spoils as a matter of course. Shar-ing is fundamental to our strategy: termites and leafcutter ants share their underground nests; honeybees share defense; swarm-raiding ants flush out prey together. All superorganisms jointly construct and defend their nests, and all share the group's reproductive success. This is how we weather life's ups and downs. Members pool costs and ben-efits, sharing both work and wealth—a highly effective and flexible insurance policy.

They are also vigilant and protective of this commons. The queen scent-marks members—those who share the work of maintaining the colony and help her reproduce their collective success—with a signature chemical cocktail, gathered and distributed by her retinue of workers. Any ants lacking the chemical mark are aggressively excluded as competitors or parasites. The ants can be thus confident their nestmates are members of the colony, and rest assured that their futures are bound together. Their purpose and identity are nearly one and the same.

Principle #11. Choose good partners, share work and wealth, and protect collective value from parasites.

Millions of years in dominance hierarchies are not easy to shake off, however, and our own superorganisms rest on an uneasy bed of suppressed primate politics. Maintaining them requires a few work-arounds. Instead of sharing a chemical signature, we've repurposed our neural circuitry for perceiving patterns and signals towards belonging, manipulation towards shared intention, and mind-reading towards empathy and self-consciousness. One of the few things all people share, as Darwin noted,[1] is the hot blush of physiological shame that comes over us when we imagine being seen violating our group's norms and values. We care what other people think about us. That much is baked into our DNA.

Chapter Thirty-Two

Our Lips Are Sealed

Can you hear them? They talk about us. Telling lies,
well that's no surprise.
—THE GO-GO'S

Passion was a fairly ordinary chimpanzee mother, of average size and social rank. She'd never done anything too unusual. Jane had watched her raise her daughter, Pom, from birth. She knew she wasn't the most attentive mother, but lately Jane had grown disturbed about her activities. Passion had been stalking other mothers into the forest, getting them alone, then stealing and eating their babies. She killed them with a single bite to the skull, consuming the flesh and sharing it with her children. The following year it was worse. Pom learned it from her mother, and now it was she who seized and killed the infants. Passion took possession of these corpses, and the whole family fed for hours, tearing off pieces and chewing slowly.

"It came to me suddenly," writes Goodall,[1] "that in three years only a single infant in the Kasakela community had lived more than one month." Ten infants had disappeared over a four-year period. In each case, the mothers had tried desperately to elicit help from the alpha male, screaming in despair, looking from him to their deviant attackers in panic, but he never seemed to understand or care what they tried to say. Much like domestic assault among human men and women, the serial infanticide continued unabated.

Trivers' reciprocity paradigm[2]—*you scratch my back, I'll scratch yours*—grows value, but you can't just go around assuming everyone is kind and good. They aren't. You have to protect yourself from the inevitable bullies, thieves, and free-riders. How do we know which partners are safe?

Reputations lower the cost of trust. Each of us has a dossier on past actions maintained by the people we live and work among. Generous, stingy, mooch, helpful, lazy, or a jerk.

Acquiring a reputation requires repeated interactions, which only happens in small groups with fixed membership, long lives, and good memories. Pom was always careful around her mother when she herself gave birth. But most species can't leverage the power of extended reputation in any collective sense because they can't share information about the past or third parties. Our reputations are constructed through gossip. This requires us to have a name and language—chimps have neither.

Only a few species can do this. Bottlenose dolphins address each other with signature whistles and use that whistle when the individual isn't around—gossip! They remember their friends' whistle names for a long time, over 20 years in some cases. Parrots bestow names on their chicks soon after hatching, and other parrots will address them with it for the rest of their lives.

Crows are known for keeping score in this way.[3] When researchers at the University of Washington began a study requiring them to tag the crows, they donned heavy browed caveman masks. It seemed wise to conceal their identities from these clever birds they shared a campus with. The crows began dive-bombing those who wore the masks—but not just those crows they tagged. Birds that had never seen the masks and who weren't around previously began attacking as well. Nor were they just telling other crows to "get the guy in the mask" because other masks elicited no response. Not even Dick Cheney! How did the other crows know who to go after? They must have been told. Apparently, they can describe us in detail.

This suggests they keep a running tab on reciprocation. Why else would you need a name? Now, trust isn't limited to people you know, because their reputation precedes them. *I'll take my chances scratching your back because I've heard you're a good backscratcher.*

With names and language, reputations become exponentially more informative. Now one trusted friend can vouch for another or tell us who to keep an eye on. Folks tell tales not just about what we saw someone do, but about what a friend told us someone did. This is powerful stuff—a distributed, shared memory of the tendency of those we encounter to reciprocate and share, dominate, hoard, lie, or shirk obligations. Few of us have five-star ratings, and minor transgressions happen all the time. We tally each other's failings until a pattern emerges. Gossip is how our extended social networks keep score.

But still it still only scales so far. You have to trust the person you hear it from.

The largest circles of trust, and those most relevant to the teeming way of life we wish for, invoke *network reciprocity*. This occurs in groups that only accept people with a good reputation for back-scratching. Now, everyone can go around doing good deeds willy-nilly, because others can be relied on to do the same, despite not knowing their history of reciprocation. Now you can safely pay it forward with strangers. Cooperative groups dramatically outcompete selfish ones, and social capital—the sum of trust we have for others in our group—grows quickly, letting us get big things done together.

How do we achieve that?

The answer, says theoretical biologist Robert Axelrod,[4] is lengthening the "shadow of the future." We behave differently when our reputation precedes us. In some cultures, our honor is worth dying or killing for, because it determines whether trustworthy people will do business with us.

Values differ radically from one culture to another, but all work to grow and maintain a cultural commons in which helping and sharing pencils out. The fossil record suggests our ancestors acted on this quite ruthlessly, by executing moral transgressors. We tamed humanity with spears, stones, and the lure of a nice hot bowl of soup.

Chapter Thirty-Three

Fuhgeddaboutit

On the whole human beings want to be good, but not too good,
and not quite all the time.
—GEORGE ORWELL

Over the years, a variety of simple game-like scenarios have been devised for modeling social decisions. The Tragedy of the Commons and the Prisoners' Dilemma are the most famous. Developed by the RAND Corporation in 1950, the Prisoners' Dilemma has become the foundation of cooperation studies, used in fields as diverse as mathematics, sociology, biology, and economics. Here's how it goes: two partners in crime are arrested and independently given the opportunity to confess. If neither does, they each serve a shortened sentence. If one rats out the other, the informant goes free while the other serves a longer sentence. If both accuse the other, both serve hard time. Played once, the temptation is to rat and hope your partner does not. Most likely, both of you will suffer. In real life, however, we play our social games again and again with the same people. A rat earns retaliation, while cooperators earn trust and subsequent resilience. When players know they'll play again, tactics change. The shadow of the future looms large when our reputation affects our access to the soup.

Robert Axelrod held a contest to determine which social strategies would do best. He solicited small programs from other theorists, each like an individual with a different social tactic, and pitted them against one other in a repeating game of Prisoner's Dilemma in which the most successful strategies in each round generated more copies to compete in the next round. Which strategies would succeed? All the top performing strategies were nice—they were never first to rat on their partner. Being nice worked, and cheaters gradually dwindled and disappeared. The nice strategies, however, were also susceptible to being taken advantage of.

The winning tactic was surprisingly simple. Tit-for-Tat: always cooperate on the first move, then simply reciprocate what the other player does. Be nice when they are nice and avoid exploitation by immediately retaliating against a rat. Other strategies attempted to sneak in an extra point here and there with a random cheat, but these were no match for good old transparent Tit-for-Tat. The tactic wins not by beating other players, but by eliciting trust through consistency and transparency. Success in the game of life went to those who were predictably nice but evaded exploitation. They started by cooperating, and were never the first to defect, but they didn't get suckered either.

But it's easy to fall off the warm-fuzzy wagon, especially when the likelihood of miscommunication is high. When this happens, retaliatory spirals allow devious strategies to gain the upper hand. In this case, the winning strategy is a variant of Tit-for-Tat: Forgiving, Generous, Tit-for-Tat. Always extend a hand, assume your partner will return the favor, forgive them once if they don't, and then randomly forgive again every now and then. *Fuhgeddaboutit!* It's worth taking a few lumps to restore Tit-for-Tat, because cooperative clusters rapidly grow value for their members. Generous assumptions are in everyone's best interest.

Transparent information flows can also quickly rectify misplaced retaliation. Transparency reduces risk, and alliances thrive on it. In fact, it changes the very nature of the game: if everyone knows how cooperative and conscientious everyone else is, and that affects their access to the soup, folks start competing to acquire and maintain good reputations. Cooperators want to work with other cooperators; cheaters are cut out. Making transaction histories visible turns the Tragedy of the Commons—where we compete to get the most for what we put in—into an Assurance Game,[4] where we compete for an invitation to make and eat soup. We can smell that good soup bubbling away, and we want to join in for a taste.

Transparent, consistent action succeeds in the long run, where poor communication, tricks, lies, and inconsistency trigger spiraling erosion of value. Of course, such transparency isn't to everyone's liking, particularly not the deceptive parasites and freeloaders that thrive under cover of darkness. Coincidentally, these are also usually the ones with the power to prevent information from flowing. Maintaining transparency requires collective insistence.

Axelrod's competition showed it's pretty easy to tip the scales in favor of cooperation by lengthening the shadow of the future and increasing transparency. Cooperation wins when we know we'll be repeating our games and held accountable for our actions. The key to making stone soup is transparency and peer accountability. The villagers see what's going on in the square, smell the soup, and observe their neighbors contributing.

Networks and their value expand dramatically this way. If you stick to the strategy, your network will likely grow and prosper. Cheats and parasites get pushed to the periphery, and clusters of cooperation nucleate like nascent snowflakes. If good people can stick together while marginalizing free-riders, snowflakes snowball into an avalanche of good deeds and social capital. Big things happen quickly, and everyone makes more.

The Tragedy of The Commons is a finite game—zero sum. One winner, many losers. Eventually, everyone loses. But an assurance game is infinite. Everyone wins if we share the wealth and work fairly. The more winners, the more soup. It isn't pie. This is superorganism logic.

Of course, success primarily depends on the strategies you are playing against—who are you hanging around? Nice strategies succeed when they're played with other nice people, which is why folks teach their children the value of kindness—being thoughtful and considerate, sharing and helping others. Because that's what good people do, and we want our children to be welcome in those more exclusive circles.

Hopefully you've surrounded yourself with good people, because "bad neighborhoods" have a snowball effect too. Selfishness—like cooperation—is self-perpetuating. If the people around you are only out for themselves, you will have to eye them skeptically. We don't survive as easy marks. Parasites are real, and superorganisms are at risk.

But even if your organization is full of sharks, however, you can still grow the social capital you need to get things that matter done. Help nice people in your organization find each other and grow "network reciprocity" around them as a self-managed and protected commons. Let them choose their own teams based on reputation. Move towards good people and set good boundaries. Then you can safely do the right thing and assume those around you will too.

Chapter Thirty-Four
Maintaining Our Collaborative Commons

Many leaders are tempted to lead like a chess master,
striving to control every move, when they should be leading
like gardeners, creating and maintaining a viable ecosystem
in which the organization operates.
—FORMER GENERAL STANLEY MCCHRYSTAL

When groups are cohesive and distinct, cooperation within them tends to increase as more cooperative teams thrive and spread faster. Yet, modern hunter-gatherers are "universally and all but obsessively" insistent on living as free-willed equals. They "love their personal freedom and cherish independence of thought and action above all else."

Without diversity and independence, our collective intelligence fails and regenerative value erodes.

This requires actively cultivating a field in which diverse people feel inspired to show up as themselves, with all their unique gifts, because they know that our compelling shared purpose requires it. Maintaining this commons—because that's what it is—requires our distributed leadership. Everyone can mediate conflicts and point out transgressions of the group's value-based rules. Everyone can foster norms of creativity, inquiry, curiosity, and respectful listening. Everyone can be an ally, the more of us the better.

Leaders need to create safe physical and virtual spaces where everyone is assumed to have something of unique value to give. At Pixar, the animated film company known for its culture of creativity and innovation, CEO Ed Catmull elicits collective genius with a superorganism-like approach. Rather than try to force people to innovate, he sets the stage for it to flower by cultivating a no-penalty innovation culture where people contribute freely because they aren't afraid of being humiliated. The company's entire culture revolves around this premise.

Cultivate workplaces that acknowledge and celebrate differences— not because it's the politically correct or legally-mandated thing to do, but because they are important collective assets. Help like-minded people find each other and make their stone soup visible. Everyone wants to be seen and being seen helps us show up. Let everyone know they are uniquely appreciated and that they belong and are needed. Publicly acknowledge individual contributions and milestones, and dish out credit like candy at Halloween. Pay attention to who isn't speaking or being heard, and point out who is missing at the table. Let folks know the agenda in advance so introverts can think about it ahead of time and even email their thoughts. Ask open-ended questions and be inclusive of different styles and personalities—you don't know what you don't know.

Set the expectation that none of us have all the answers, but together, we just might.

Chapter Thirty-Five
Miss Manners

Politeness and consideration for others is like investing pennies
and getting dollars back.
—THOMAS SOWELL

Each group has their own ways of behaving, speaking—things like wearing dreadlocks, speaking in tongues, using cloth diapers, sporting a colored bandanna, asking if your food has touched gluten, or openly carrying semi-automatic weapons in the local Home Depot. These cement our shared identities, history, and beliefs, nudging us to cooperate with others who share them. If I see someone else on the freeway with an "iHeart ants" bumper sticker, I'll honk and wave and let them go ahead of me on the freeway exit.

Like us, each fungal cell seeks its tribe. The hyphae grow and spread as they search for a mycelium to join, but they will only fuse with others roughly like themselves. Like spies exchanging an elaborate set of escalating passwords, the fungi verify their potential partners by matching a dozen genes. Only the right partners can pass the test.

That's also why people hold onto beliefs that are so verifiably false. They are part of their identity, the way they define themselves in the world and find allies who share their values. It's a basic biological lock-and-key protection mechanism that protects collective value and confers immunity from outsiders. As signals become more distinctive, fewer partners can pass the test, and they can be trusted more.

Social norms, values, and rules are sometimes adaptive, but more often fairly accidental and arbitrary, like accumulating neutral mutations and junk DNA. It really doesn't matter what the markers are, just that we share them. They are membership badges that help us identify safe partners, allowing us to safely pool our scraps and protect our collective value from parasites, freeloaders, and competitors.

Collections of territorial markings, graffiti, brands, and slang evolve and adapt just as our immune systems and the mating dances of birds do, because that is essentially what they are. Cooperative partners have to protect themselves from parasites and freeloaders through lock-and-key tests. It doesn't necessarily matter what is being matched, just that they are an exclusive fit. Think of birds' increasingly elaborate mating dances, as they weave and bob and call. It's a test, designed to filter out subpar mates seeking a free ride on fitter genes.

This looks a lot like our own conformity bias—from high school onward, we tend to hang out with and copy others like us. Conformity makes evolutionary sense in a cooperative society. It's easier to trust partners that are like you. It feels safe. Usually, the most common behaviors are the right ones anyway, which is why they are so common. Follow along with those around you and you'll probably come out okay.

The desire for collective acceptance, and the consequence of its withholding is strong in us. Expulsion is a death sentence; being shunned a disability. This fear of exile plays out in our own organizations, where people only share their experiences and ideas, even anonymously, if they think they are "normal" for that group. If we think we are weird or don't belong, we generally hide our true nature and repress our urge to create.

Traditionally, such repression is just fine with organizations. Our personal lives don't belong at work—it isn't professional. Most corporate cultures don't care for oddballs. Eliminating them is a piece of our industrial hangover. It's hard to scale with deviants from standard in the mix. These are loose screws and defects needing to be weeded out. That's what quality control and standard operating procedures are all about. They are standard for a reason.

Norms can have serious consequences. Salish Sea orcas are dwindling because their rarified upbringing dictates they eat only the rare Chinook salmon. They turn their rostrums up in disgust at plentiful but plebeian Sockeye and Pinks. They also refuse to mate outside their group and are inbred and unhealthy as a result. The old rules hold for these blue bloods. They live by the old traditions.

Constrained norms are also a problem for companies that rely on swarm creativity and collective intelligence to regenerate value. If everyone hides their special sauce, how do we know what normal even is? We fear judgment and ostracism from our group, so we keep the weird stuff at home—which is why I work there. Why risk it?

The only problem with that—besides the damper it puts on creativity and collective intelligence—is that freeloaders and cons are even better at playing this game. If all partners start to look alike, it's easier for parasites to blend in with the crowd. Suddenly, strange variants look more attractive—they keep security sharp. Cooperative groups must escalate it continuously to prevent parasites from gaining entry.

It turns out the odd ducks who opt out of social action help cooperation spread. In a simulation game with three possible social strategies—contributing, cheating, or sitting out—cooperation is much greater than if there are only two possible strategies. Voluntary participation increases cooperation.

Sometimes it's physically impossible for one DNA blueprint to accommodate the whole range of likely environmental conditions. In this case, nature hedges its bets by maintaining a few different states in the population. Some individuals remain dormant, as seeds, spores, or eggs—sleeping until conditions improve. Maybe seeds can survive a bitter winter or wildfire while adult plants die. Opting out of social cooperation is like a dormant state; it increases the range of conditions a superorganism can tolerate. If lots of parasitic cheaters are sneaking around, avoiding collaboration protects you. People that don't engage can't be cheated. They don't get the benefits of cooperating, either, but they do provide a buffer zone where potential cooperators can sit out quietly until parasitic conditions improve.

Slime molds illustrate this nicely, according to my friend Dr. Darja Dubrovic[1] (what's cooler than being an expert on social amoeba?). Most of the time, individual amoeba slink through the soil seeking food, but when they get hungry, they sound a chemical alarm that draws most cells to come together. They fuse into the blob we know and love, sliming off into the proverbial sunset for someplace warm to spore out. Not all will get lucky in life's lottery, however. Some are relegated to the sterile stalk where they sacrifice their own reproductive success to raise someone else's lucky spores onto the wind. Joining the slug is a crapshoot. A few random individuals skip the slug, taking their chances by staying single. Maybe conditions will improve—they are willing to take that bet. In particularly volatile environments, more amoebae opt out. The slug-makers and slug-watchers are hedging their bets.

There's always more than one way to skin a cat. Diversity is nature's insurance plan.

Chapter Thirty-Six

Bonobo Revolution

If they are so successful, why haven't parasites taken over the world?
The answer is simple. They have. We just haven't noticed.
That's because successful parasites don't kill us, they become
part of us, making us perform all the work to keep them alive
and help them reproduce.
—DANIEL SUAREZ

A nother thing all foraging peoples seem to share is the way they work to subvert power-seekers. Groups work diligently to prevent the big-headed from gaining a foothold. One !Kung San man (! denotes a clicking sound unique to the !Kung San) explains. "When a young man kills much meat, he comes to think of himself as a chief or big man, and the rest of us as his servants or inferiors. We can't accept this. We refuse one who boasts, for someday his pride will make him kill somebody. So we always speak of his meat as worthless."[1]

Taking a would-be big man down a peg begins with a little poking fun, drawing attention and shame to his misplaced arrogance, and gradually escalates into cool greetings, silence, and general mocking and shaming until he apologizes and changes, or leaves. Things can get serious—the group may even prevail on the man's male kin to execute him (a way of avoiding cycles of clan-based revenge).

Some inkling of these dynamics can be seen in our closest primate relatives as well. If a low-ranking male chimpanzee has caught his own prey or is courting a favorite girlfriend, he will refuse to give up his righteous booty no matter who tries to take it from him—his conviction drives him to stand up for what's "right." Emboldened by conviction or a little backup, chimps will indeed push back.

The primate literature is full of stories about lowly individuals submitting to authority while quietly biding their time to turn the tables. Chimps even have a specific vocalization for the moment when their oppressor chases them up a tree but can't reach them anymore. Their outraged waa-barks translate unmistakably into the same thing we say with a finger from the safety of our cars. Chimps don't like being bossed around any more than we do. A young male chimp with big-man ambitions will cover his fear grin with his hands so the boss doesn't see, but he clearly resents submitting to him.

Low-ranking apes (mostly females, interestingly enough) occasionally team up to resist the authority of dominant chimps. At Gombe, a gang of feisty females prevented their old tyrant, Goblin, from making a comeback after his hiatus following an injury. Bonobo females are famous for keeping swaggering males in their place.

Even females in one captive gorilla harem collaborated to prevent a new silverback from taking over—they preferred their hot young male.

These anecdotes hint at the evolutionary origins of our own moral communities, and the wellspring and evolutionary dynamics of solidarity, righteous indignation, and the smoldering embers of resistance. Individuals of low rank in these species know when something is not right, and it does occasionally embolden them to fight together, but collective notions of right and wrong are mostly absent from the animal kingdom. Chris Boehm[2] sees moral codes and resistance to authority as coalitions—weaker individuals joining forces to prevent domination by the strong, like bonobo females pairing up to take on pushy males. Seen this way, the evolutionary roots of helping and sharing are suddenly very clear. Our moral communities are built on the collective power of subordinates who don't like being taken advantage of or pushed around.

At Yerkes National Primate Research Center in Atlanta, a group of chimp females rejected a whole series of would-be alpha males and beat some quite badly. Eventually, they did accept a harmless little fellow, but they controlled him completely, cooperatively preventing him from attacking any males they wanted to mate with. This weakling also worked hard to settle conflicts in the group: the women chose a peacekeeper!

Peacekeeping is a surprising function of African ape alphas. Silverback gorillas in particular tolerate little squabbling. Dominant male chimps and bonobos assert authority to keep the peace, to the whole group's benefit. When experimentally removed from zoo colonies, these societies come apart at the seams. Aggression skyrockets and tensions run high; these are not restful places.

But these few tales were unusual enough to warrant appearing in a scientific journal—other apes don't typically conspire to redirect society. When staff at the Arnhem Zoo called their chimpanzees in for dinner one fine summer evening, one pair of teenagers refused to come in. It was just too nice out. The practice at the zoo was not to feed the troop until everyone was inside for the night. The other chimps made their disapproval for the pair very clear, and when the lollygaggers finally did come in some hours later, they were housed separately to prevent reprisals. The next morning, everyone was released into the exhibit and the foot-draggers were soundly beaten—by each chimpanzee, one at a time. Theirs was not a moral offense but a personal affront. In chimp society, everyone exacts their own personal revenge.

The closest suggestion we have to anything resembling a moral code comes from a single bonobo incident witnessed in the wilds of Zaire some years ago. One young male—the son of the dominant female—jumped too close to a mother of low rank and may even have tried to snatch her new baby. The mother screamed bloody murder, and the whole troop turned on the youth in a violent assault. He was never seen again. His previously high-ranking mother was eventually found hiding high in a tree—a violation "so massively defended that even the highest echelons of society won't dare go against it."

We are constrained by our moral compass—a kind of collectively upheld big alpha that helps keep one another honest, like shoaling sardines repelling would-be predators by imitating bigger fish. Shame—that deep physiological response we get when we imagine being seen doing something people disapprove of—looks an awful lot like the response of a submissive animal to a more dominant one. Don't hurt me, I submit.

Chapter Thirty-Seven

A Rat in Our Midst

Even in the smeared boundary between chemistry and biochemistry,
between prelife and life, competition and cooperation coexisted
in an intricate dance, driving ever-widening
cycles of complexity and abundance.
—MARTIN NOWAK

Nothing is fair in love or war, and even cooperating parties seldom benefit equally. I can assure you competition, predation, and parasitism are real and to be anticipated. Many collaborations are more like Mexican standoffs than a gift exchange. Evidence suggests the algal partner in a lichen would do better if they wrested free from its fungal overlord. Even our helpful gut bacteria turn against us if our immune systems grow weak. Opportunists are always waiting in the wings.

When the mycorrhizal fungi initiate the process of connecting to a plant, the potential partners enter an escalating chemical dance of inquiries and replies, establishing trust before making a commitment. They need to be sure of their partner, because the relationship is prone to cheating. The fungi could shower the plant with nutrients, only to have the plant default on its sugar payment. Other times, the plant doesn't want the partnership, because humans already doused the fields with fertilizer. Then it's like trying to avoid an aggressive street beggar smearing your windshield with a dirty rag. The fungi don't have a choice—they cannot survive without sugar. They are forced to parasitize the plant. The fertilizer deters their partnership, turning normally helpful fungi into a begging, stealing blight. Humans really hate that! Chemically fertilized land can even lose its fungal networks altogether. As freshwater becomes scarcer, and the need to sink carbon more dire, we may wish to rethink this strategy, and encourage these underground networks to resume their work throughout the soil.

Superorganisms are plagued by parasites. If you're an ant, the most terrifying villain imaginable is the *Cordyceps* fungus. Its airborne spores settle onto you, commandeering your brain and turning you into a zombie. Bewitched, you trudge obligingly up a plant stalk, digging in your mandibles to dangle over the colony's trails like the Jolly Roger—the flag of treason. Meanwhile, the fungi consume you from the inside-out, until your lifeless shell explodes in a rain of deadly spores, onto your sister ants below.

Other ant species practice slavery—another kind of parasitism. These ants raid the colonies of closely related species, stealing their eggs and larvae, to put them to work for the benefit of their own colony's future. Some species can't even feed themselves without these slaves. Other species never even try to start a colony of their own. Their queen simply attaches to the queen of the other species, sterilizing her. The host workers care for the false queen's eggs by mistake, oblivious to their queen's wasting. Captive workers have a devious resistance strategy, though. They selectively kill their captors' female larva, reducing their oppressors' future success.

Leafcutter ants are locked in battle with the micro-fungus *Escovopsis,* which attacks their own fungal crops. The ants scour their gardens constantly, plucking out the invaders and reinoculating their crops on sterile compost, dusted with a fecal mixture of twenty different herbicides, fungicides, and growth hormones. The ants have a backup plan, too—an antibiotic bacteria they cultivate on their backs. Finally, deep in the nest, workers patrol constantly, collecting and killing foreign spores in a special cheek-pouch sterilization chamber. The toxic waste gets dumped in a pile outside the nest, where only the oldest garbage dump grannies work. With these defenses, the ants keep *Escovopsis* in check, but never fully eliminate it. Temporary 99.9% relief works best for long-term control, much as the triple cocktail works against HIV—keep the enemy on its toes with a variety of attacks. Otherwise, it's virtually guaranteed that remaining 0.1% will thrive once you've eliminated their competition. Now you've got superbugs.

These are examples of parasitism by one species on another, but being cheated on by members of your own social group has powerful consequences as well. Upon returning from my long sojourn in the Bering Sea, dreaming nightly of my hard-earned pile of cash, I discovered that my boyfriend—now my ex-husband—had quit his job as soon as I left and talked his way into collecting all my checks.

There is plenty of deception in nature. Hamadryas females and followers hide behind rocks for the occasional forbidden tryst, and chimp subordinates cover their mouths to suppress their passionate cries. The leader male is oblivious to this cuckoldry—he just assumes the infants born in his reign are his own. Humans play the field the same way if they can. Professor Jolly had to quit asking his Intro to Physical Anthropology students to map their family's blood types. The 20% "spontaneous mutation rate" wasn't demonstrating the laws of heredity the way he'd intended.

If cheating is inevitable, then how can we hope to share the work and wealth for a better future? Garrett Hardin[1] asked himself this question back in 1968 and devised a rhetorical scenario to explore it. He imagined an open pasture where any farmer could freely graze his livestock. He made the assumption that each farmer would maximize his own self-interest by maximizing his use of the pasture, despite knowing it could only support so many animals. Hardin showed that the resource would inevitably be overgrazed or cordoned off, ruining the commons to everyone's detriment. He could see no solution to the problem. Whenever users benefit from a common resource but pay no cost to maintain it, the resource is doomed.

The Tragedy of the Commons is inevitable in theory. There is no mathematical hope for our global climate or fisheries. Each of us will use as much as we can, because someone else will if we don't. It isn't fair for someone else to profit while we hold back, so we reject our conscience. Mr. Nice Guy will get his clock cleaned.

Seems cut and dried. We will all hang separately. It's as inevitable as math.

There's just one problem with Hardin's scenario. People share resources all the time: African tribal pastures, irrigation districts in Nepal and Spain, forests in Japan, lobster fisheries in Maine, and tens of hundreds of generations of indigenous forest stewardship. Economist Elinor Ostrom[2] saw this, and concluded that if practice doesn't work in theory, then clearly the theory is wrong.

Ostrom analyzed these successful commons, searching for features they shared. It turned out that all worked the same way: the resource's boundaries were clearly defined, and users had to commit to a defined set of rules, determined and enforced by the members themselves. Anyone who didn't agree to obey these rules was excluded, and users gradually and collectively levied escalating sanctions against any violators. Meanwhile, the resource's overall health was monitored and made visible to all, and each member's usage history was visible as well. That's it. This simple set of structures and processes allowed users to grow and maintain healthy commons. The keys were transparency and accountability, with accumulating reputations and escalating enforcement.

Ostrom won a Nobel prize for her important work. What's interesting is that these patterns are exactly what we see in superorganisms, and it is mirrored in the land use and social structures of foraging peoples. We already know how to maintain ecological and cultural commons to grow possibilities for future generations.

Chapter Thirty-Eight

Crime and Punishment

Associate with men of good quality if you esteem your own reputation;
for it is better to be alone than in bad company.
—GEORGE WASHINGTON

A mong traditional foraging peoples, leaders act as peacekeepers, but it's a difficult role. There's a reason no one stepped forward to announce themselves to those European explorers. Any hint of arrogance, bossiness, or boastfulness would automatically disqualify them from leading, and could get them ridiculed and ostracized. They are in the awkward position of needing to avoid the appearance of wanting power or even caring about it. Constantly at risk of overstepping their nonexistent authority, these leaders fill a vulnerable role. When you can't tell people what to do, then listening, logic, and oration are your only leverage. Moral authority is invested in you by the collective.

In settled tribes, where stockpiles and inequities grow, there is another kind of leader. This one excels in hunting, warfare, and economic success—he is admired, emulated, and feared. Such high-ranking individuals punish subordinates easily. Think of Stalin, Saddam Hussein, or the Roman emperors. Who cares what those below you think?

Dictatorships work, but they are pyramids requiring constant and expensive policing—even if you can get citizens to narc on each other. This isn't a recipe for infinite growth, however, because there is much distrust and social capital is low. You might get order, but nobody will volunteer more than the minimum. You won't get stone soup.

Most of us are conscientious, but given a choice between a group that punishes free-riders and one that does not, most people initially choose the punishment-free zone. But soon enough they change their minds. They aren't taken advantage of as much among the punishers, and overall cooperation is higher—the soup is tastier and there's more of it. But few folks want to pay the cost of punishing a cheater, especially if we are likely to see them again. Acting against a bully is risky, and punishers are generally avoided and have few friends. Most of us would rather pay taxes and let someone else to do it.

Reputations and gossip lower the cost of monitoring and sanctioning each other, but even these expanded circles of trust only scale so far. Quite often, we never even meet the members of our global organizations and fast-moving teams or the people we do transactions with on the Internet. How can we grow the trust we need on this scale?

The solution might be a mycelial one.

Harvard law professor and open-source proponent Yochai Benkler[1] observed that breaking information into digital packets would let us distribute the cost of maintaining this collective value at negligible cost to any one individual. This was one of 2011 *Time* magazine's "10 ideas that will change the world." You're probably thinking—so this guy wrote down the recipe for stone soup and made it into *Time* magazine? Basically. Commons-based peer production mitigates the Tragedy of the Commons at scale.

Welcome to the Mycelial Age, in which *"transaction costs are distributed among participants, along with mechanisms of tracking trust and ensuring reciprocity and transparency among large numbers of relatively anonymous online strangers."*

—Peter Gloor

Digital networks allow us to scale our accounting mechanisms and make them transparent. Companies like eBay and Amazon do this all the time by asking buyers and sellers to rate their transactions, aggregating these reciprocation histories into a score. A five-star rating indicates the individual is a consistently honest and reliable person—a transferable, tangible asset, because high-rated sellers can charge higher prices.

What if we created digital reputations and allow people to select those they would like to work with based on them? Cooperators could walk away from one team and join a better one, if everything was visible and transparent.

In the era of Facebook and LinkedIn, we see the same people and names all over the place. We belong to so many overlapping social networks. Seeing that we have friends and interests in common can increase the shadow of the future enough to trigger cooperation between strangers. The more groups there are, the easier it is for cooperators to escape cheaters—just move to a nicer group.

Marina Gorbis, Director of the Institute for the Future and author of *The Nature of the Future,* talks about layering and embedding digital reputations into our financial transactions to create a blended economy driven by commons. She calls it "socialstructing," a way to build better futures by deinstitutionalizing production, infusing social ties and human connectedness into our economic life, and redefining established paradigms of work, productivity, and value in the process. Alternately, as she warns, it might turn us all into "modern serfs on Zuckerberg's plantation," where "instead of turning market transactions into social flows, we could be turning social interactions into market commodities," generating wealth for Facebook shareholders with our donated time and content.

Theoretically, we can aggregate all kinds of behavioral data into our digital fingerprints, and that might even allow us to keep our personal information private. Maybe airport security and police don't really need to know anything about us beyond our actual performance history. Right now, communities are in despair over profiling and hair-trigger stereotype-based decisions. Is there a superorganism inspired solution here?

Recently, I ran this notion by a fiend (this is not a typo). He suggested I call this digital reputation app "the Superorganism User Experience," or SUE—as in Sue Me, because that is what would happen. But it turns out an app like this is actually out there already. Peeple[2] was initially described as "Yelp for people: the only social networking app where your character is your currency." It allowed you to rate folks based on your professional, personal, and romantic interactions with them. Released in October 2015, Peeple enjoyed a brief stint as the Internet's most hated app before it was yanked. Cofounder Julia Cordray received death threats, and critics called it invasive and objectifying. In short, it would "usher in a hellish age of pervasive mutual surveillance." The app reappeared in 2016, with anything contentious or vaguely useful carefully removed. Problem solved.

I still think the idea has merit. It could be voluntary. We know opting out works from an evolutionary standpoint, and we could rate our interactions instead of the character of others. Did they do what they said they would? Were they polite? Fair and honest? You could ask someone, "Hey, are you on SUE? Do you wanna rate our interaction?" And point your phones at each other and rate away.

Implementing cooperation fingerprints would probably be easier within organizations. Could we use this accounting system to rate and review interactions with our team members? Who needs an annual review when we could just build them for each other throughout the year? How much did you contribute? How reliable were you? How pleasant, how creative? And what if your pay depended on that rating? Such reputation fingerprints would keep us accountable to each other, instead of the shareholders, while growing transferable social capital for the team. You might choose to work with highly rated people on a specific problem without knowing them personally. Maybe whole industries or supply chains could link their reputation databases, allowing global cross-platform teams to emerge. Imagine if we had the power to self-organize our work lives this way, distributing the cost of protecting our collective soup from parasites, forming trustworthy teams around any project or challenge we deem worthy? Extra-cooperative groups might emerge within our distributed economy, and the boundaries of these cooperative clusters expand as we strive to join them. They would be exclusive, but neither zero sum nor finite. Now our commons begin to grow.

Chapter Thirty-Nine

Expanding Our Superorganisms

. . . all things are one thing and that one thing is all things—plankton,
a shimmering phosphorescence on the sea and the spinning
planets and an expanding universe, all bound together by
the elastic string of time . . . look from the tidepool to the stars
and then back to the tidepool again.
—JOHN STEINBECK

A single sloth may host a thousand different species, not including the bacteria in its gut. The leafcutters outsource their digestion to another kingdom of life, while hosting fungicide-secreting bacteria on their backs. The soil itself is built from lichen's intimate fungus and alga partnerships, while the fungal networks underground trade nutrients and water with Earth's green sugar factories that feed us all. We are all knit together in a living, breathing fabric.

Species intertwine, and cooperation spreads. Symbiosis is everywhere. But everywhere you look, folks are inflicting depravity on each other and the life around them. How can we possibly get 7 billion people to suppress their rapacious appetites? Are effective superorganisms a futile concept? Should we build walls, or tear them down?

How does nature do it?

Those little black Argentine ants from the prologue are now a massive super-colony with little interest in warfare—there is no more "us and them" in their adopted lands. How did this happen, and is it something we might mimic?

Well, it's true you can drop an Argentine ant from San Diego in a colony in Spain and it'll get along fine. That's because anyone who was different got dismembered long ago. They are genetically homogeneous where it counts. Not only do I suspect this is morally incompatible with the future we'd like to see, it's evolutionarily unstable as well. These super-colonies have only been around since the '40s, and mathematical simulations suggest their conformity makes them sitting ducks for parasitic invasion. Sooner or later, one species or another will discover how to mimic their scent to gain entry to their nests, then run amok in the endless larval chambers devouring the young. Maybe this is what's going on at Fox News.

Our immune system offers another model. This flexible, open-ended system patrols our bodies in a highly distributed way, protecting us from hostile invasion. But it's much more than a way to keep outsiders out. This isn't an in-or-out passport scan at a border checkpoint. These microbes build our immunity, and our systems don't work without them.

Our systems tolerate diverse foreigners very well. Nine of every ten cells in your body aren't even you, if you ignore all those red blood cells, which lack DNA. 90% of you is actually bacteria and other microbes. They aren't you, genetically speaking, but you need them all the same. Some perform your digestion while others help protect you from invading pathogens. Newborns drink mother's milk but can't actually digest it. *Bifidobacteria* do it for them. Microbes turn our genes on and off, shake hands with our immune system, help digest our food, and even fiddle with our neurochemicals. Our very personalities are formed by interactions between our genes and theirs. These creatures aren't living on us, they are us[1]—*drop the hand sanitizer!* We are lichens, in a literal way.

Part Six

Make More Life with Your Life: Regenerative Value

Try to leave this world a little better than you found it.
—ROBERT BADEN-POWELL

Chapter Forty

Reincarbonation

Big fleas have little fleas,
Upon their backs to bite 'em,
And little fleas have lesser fleas,
And so, ad infinitum.
And the great fleas, themselves, in turn
Have greater fleas to go on;
While these again have greater still,
And greater still, and so on.
—THE SIPHONAPTERA, NURSERY RHYME

Once a month, my dad took me to the Scripps Aquarium[1] for a member night slide show and visit behind the scenes. Zebra-striped lionfish arched venomous spines out of the tanks at us, while the secretive Pacific octopus glared, flipping a disgusted tentacle, or darting angrily into his cave. According to Ancient Hawaiian legend, the octopus is the only living survivor from a past universe. Staring into his goat-slit eyes, it wasn't hard for me to believe. He did seem a lone, hyper-conscious alien from a bygone time and place.

My dad was an architect. His specialty seemed to be housing those on the receiving end of dominance hierarchies: aquaria, zoos, college dorms, and military barracks. I loved going to the construction sites, especially the ones at Sea World. Scampering along the planks above the Shark Exhibit—the world's first aquarium with a glass tunnel running through it—while my dad paced out lines and chatted with the foreman I could have touched the grey figures that circled lazily below. These prehistoric forms had cruised mostly unchanged like this, for 400 million years.

When I think of "sustainability," my mind goes to creatures like these—sharks and octopi. They've been around a very long time in essentially this form, because their ways of life work.

Once, when the revolutionary new ice-cleaning conveyor belt stopped working at the Penguin Exhibit, my dad brought me to help him spray ice for them (he also used this as a teachable moment as to why I should not pursue architecture as a career). The penguins seemed to think our feet were eggs (or they just didn't like cold rears). They squatted on our feet while we disgorged slush from a wide canvas hose. Watching them trip and waddle so comically, I thought how much of their birdness they had given up in order to survive out there on the Antarctic ice. But underwater, they sped like silvery missiles after the darting shoals of fish. They were perfectly honed to this situation. What I remember most about that day, though, is the little green pan of goo we had to step into before we could enter the exhibit: our humanity had to be sterilized to make the birds safe from us. They had survived millions of years in the merciless Antarctic wind, but we could kill them in a careless instant.

Humanity weighs heavily on many of us. If we just ate less, drove less, traveled less, used less, were less—but we bit the apple, and were cast from the garden in penance. I don't believe this kind of thinking is going to work. How can we do good things in our time on Earth if we fundamentally see ourselves as sinners apart from the rest of living things? This is self-loathing of biblical proportions—this way lies the Unabomber.[2] Even worse, this ambivalence is embedded in our language, which means it's embedded in our hearts. When we say, "How would nature do it?" we are not including humanity. We say our children have a "nature deficit,"[3] or speak of Biophilia—the innate human affiliation for things alive. While useful on some level, these ideas contain the implicit belief that we are apart and other. Nature is out there, and we are inside.

I don't believe we can regenerate abundance until we cast this shame away. We aren't children apart from nature, lost in a bad divorce. We're just getting on with the business of living the way people do—which isn't all that different from the way ants and termites and naked mole rats do it. You may say—*of course we are part of nature! We've just forgotten, because nature is outside and we live in air-conditioned houses—we just need to go outside!* I certainly relate. But nature isn't outside. It *is* us, inside and out. The termites live in air-conditioned houses too, after all.

The great biologist E. O. Wilson estimates that all the ants on earth are about equal to us in biomass, yet they aren't drowning in plastic waste or choking on the air they exhale. If they can do it, why can't we? I don't see why not. Smart phones are our antennae, cities our coral reefs, skyscrapers our termite mounds. The Pacific Garbage Patch teems with new kinds of plastic-eating microbes just as earlier bacteria and fungi once cracked the code on fallen trees. It's the universal math of life—every individual of every species struggles to survive and reproduce, and so do we. The difference is simply that the other superorganisms build their compounding wealth on infinite things—sunlight and carbon, diffuse specks of water and nutrients, complexity, diversity, connection, and trust. Their teams grow from the edges out, in modular, self-managed units that seek and respond to opportunity and risk on the front lines, while they leverage symbiotic partnerships to convert their collective value. By focusing on shared purpose, building with infinite stuff, and spilling the value they create out into the larger ecosystems they are part of, they feed the life that feeds them, compounding their future potential. This is no pyramid scheme—these are infinite things. The fungi have done it for over a half-billion years and are as close to immortal as living things get. This is regeneration.

Pattern 5: Superorganisms regenerate the systems they depend on

Principle #12. Build with abundant things, feed the life that feeds you, and grow future potential.

For many, nature seems like a bottomless fountain. The fish in Senegal glitter like jewels in our nets. The trees we cut to build or burn in Indonesia dangle their fingery leaves before us, each a tantalizing arm's-length from the last. The bush meat we snare in Cameroon hoots and taunts, while the Amazon and Pacific seem to stretch on forever. We know less about the ocean's depths than the surface of Mars. People I've met in African bush villages or South American jungle enclaves are often afraid of "the bush"—a place where snakes slither, leopards and jaguars prowl. Little boys throw stones at things that rustle in the shadows, and the Congo writhes on in the heart of darkness. The forests of Sierra Leone and Europe are alive with big bad wolves and witches. In many places, nature is an irrelevant distraction, contrary to the essential work of scratching out a living to save oneself and one's family. In India's Sundarban mangrove islands, you're more concerned with saving yourself from nature—in the form of a tiger. In North America, world's greatest gobbler of energy and layer of waste, nature is an abstract "out there" best reserved for Shark Week.

Meanwhile, executives keep the shareholders happy by dipping into a treasure trove of minerals and oil—producing an endlessly-expanding Santa's sack of cast-off debris and emissions. Perverse wealth incentives keep us in intractable gridlock, circling a drain of our own device. We can see it coming clear as day, but seem virtually powerless to make it stop. As long as trees grow slower than interest compounds, we'll have no rational choice but to turn living things into money until nothing is left.[4]

Other than sunlight and the occasional meteorite, what we have is what we've got. Planet Earth is our collective Easter Island unless we start mining asteroids in outer space, shipping space barges of garbage, siphoning carbon emissions off into the cosmos, and lassoing ice comets...or change our way of life. Summers get hotter, the polar vortex fiercer, hurricanes, floods, and droughts more destructive. We can't keep doing it this way.

So how would nature do it? Look around. She's doing it now. Indigestible nutrients have always gotten themselves concentrated in one place or another—often thanks to the gathering power of superorganisms, which have specialized in unlocking diffuse untapped value for a very long time. The more nutrients accumulate, the greater their potential for making hungry creatures go. It's not worth chasing a single plankton, but a bloom of krill feeds a lot of whales.

Earlier humans were nomads, like the driver ants today. We hunted the plains, picked the low-hanging fruit, burned the wood on the ground, spun the stick and moved on. After a while, the land rebounded and we cycled back around, like the aardvark.

With agriculture came settlements, however, and with it, inequity, hierarchy, and explosive population growth. Today, our cities are many millions strong, and like leafcutter colonies, we process huge quantities of wild resources. This is what we call "economic value."

Like us, the ants and termites and underground mycelia change the environment to suit themselves instead of letting it change them. Their footprints on the land are not small either. The difference between their way of life and ours is simply that they build with infinite things, regenerated from scattered scraps of waste. We, on the other hand, are still building with finite things, dug and sucked from the ground as our waste collects untapped.

Just 7% of our plastic gets recycled; billions of barrels of yesterday's sunlight pumped from the ground and thrown carelessly out in forms no other species can yet digest, like handfuls of gold dust tossed out of reach. All this carbon traps heat like a greenhouse, altering the climate for the entire planet. The frequency and strength of extreme droughts and floods increases, and weather patterns shift. Ice shelves melt and sea levels rise, coastlines are erased and countless lives displaced. Large-scale migrations and bloody conflicts erupt as whole ecosystems shift, contract, and blink out—forgotten. Biodiversity, complexity, interconnection, and resilience dwindle. As resources become scarcer, prices rise, and the gap between the haves and the have-nots increases. Economic volatility, social unrest, and vulnerable supply chains plague us.

Our imaginations, collaborativeness, and flexibility exploded our ancestral populations, ranges, and niches—out of Africa and onto every landmass on earth. But today, billions of people have little of anything. They've lost the resource base their ancestors cultivated and relied on. Instead, they gather densely in cities, hoping to become cogs in the manufacture-consumption-waste machine. And as you know, when anything worthwhile accumulates, you can bet something or someone—probably a superorganism—is trying to unlock it. Crime stalks the urban poor and bloody revolution threatens the rich. Business as usual puts everyone at risk.

The first step to getting out of a hole is to stop digging. But meanwhile, we're literally choking on yesterday's sunlight. What an incredible energy and nutrient bonanza, the likes of which hasn't been seen since fungi discovered how to digest wood.

If you've ever stood beneath a rainforest elder—an old mossy, epiphyte-encrusted fig tree, for instance—you know about the nature of abundance and waste. Monkeys and parrots chatter and leap noisily overhead, taking a bite or two of each fruit and then dropping it. Clearly none of them got the memo about the starving children in

Africa, because there's an obscene amount of waste. But below the tree, the circular economy rolls on. The litter is quickly consumed by an army of arthropods and fungi, tiny deer and tapirs. Falling debris collects in the elbows of branches, offering nutrients to bromeliads that become breeding pools for frogs and insects. This is a richly diverse and wholly interconnected web, pulsing with irrepressible life—and you don't even want to know what goes on after dark.

Once upon a time, there was no such thing as garbage—there was only food.[5] This is still true today. Every creature's waste becomes food for another. Nutrients flow from the dead to the living in a raw soup of energy and matter, passing through our temporary bodies in sprawling webs of digestion. Waste is precious and always reclaimed.

Dung beetles make their entire living on this principle. They are honed to transform others' dross into gold—a warm wet place to cradle their eggs or a delightful breakfast treat. To the ancient Egyptians, dung beetles were sacred. Each represented Khepri, God of the rising sun himself, who deposits semen in his holy dung ball each day, re-creating himself from nothing, to roll the sun across the sky into darkness and be reborn anew. The scarab, tumbling his dung home in little balls, represents renewal, transformation, and resurrection of the dead into new forms among the living. He is the tumbling, flying, living symbol of reincarbonation.[6]

Dung is a concentrated patch of precious moisture and nutrients, so the scarabs move fast, rolling their fragrant treasures off as quickly as they can. A fresh elephant cake will attract some 4,000 dung beetles just minutes after slapping the ground, with another 12,000 on the way.

With that kind of competition, you roll fast and hard.

As a biologist, I have no doubt our waste will be collected and rolled away at some point. That's what nature does. The dead become the living and the sun rolls across the sky. If history is our guide, we can expect our waste to be used by something, sometime. But why let the bacteria and fungi enjoy all the profit?

For 3,000 years, Chinese peasants have raised carp in artificial ponds, using the rich mud to fertilize their mulberry bushes, whose leaves feed their domesticated silkworms. After the silk is spun, the dung and pupae are fed to the fish. The Cardboard-to-Caviar project similarly turns restaurant waste into horse bedding, which is then fed to worms, which are fed to fish, whose caviar is served at the restaurant.

Ford Motor Company's historic River Rouge factory is more ambitious. Smokestack scrubbers remove particulates, while a 5,000 square-foot rooftop garden absorbs water and provides insulation, solar panels and fuel cells. Native plants absorb industrial toxins from the soil.

Other locales are trying to redesign the whole manufacturing ecosystem to eliminate waste completely. Denmark's Kalundborg industrial park hosts an oil refinery, whose flare gas heats a power plant. The drywall factory consumes waste gypsum, while the excess steam sterilizes the machinery in a pharmaceutical plant. In Chicago, architect Gordon Gill's ambitious decarbonization plan links all 450 big buildings into an ecosystem that leverages the network for savings. Such interconnection could reduce energy consumption by 20%.

A report from the Ellen MacArthur Foundation[7] and consulting firm McKinsey points out just how much value our trash has. Europe alone could save some $630 billion Euros a year if they put their nutrients back into the system. Boosting the recycling rate to 20% would yield an additional 3 or 4% GDP. Refurbishing smartphones alone would reduce manufacturing energy costs by $4M, saving 100,000 metric tons of carbon emissions and $475M in materials a year.

But too often it seems the circular economy chases its tail rather than compounding wealth. Value is lost in each conversion, and the reuse-reduce-recycle plan is really just a temporary solution, a patch delaying the inevitable until the über-rich can board their space shuttles like rats fleeing a sinking ship. *[Oh wait, we're here!]* Yes, efficiency saves money, which can be reinvested for growth, and companies like

HP, Epson and Xerox have realized huge cost savings from it. But it doesn't address the fundamental issue. Doing less harm is tediously incremental and relies on voluntary abstinence and bitter judgment from those who do their best while the rest of humanity parties on in blissful oblivion with their plastic water bottles and space cocks. It's only half the picture. I don't think saying no to dessert while resenting those who take two is going to get us where we need to go. It's the Tragedy of the Commons all over again. We're going to need some mighty boundless optimism and love for one another if we're to adapt to our finite reality. Philosopher Bertrand Russell[8] said it best:

Love is wise, hatred is foolish…If we are to live together and not die together, we must learn a kind of charity and a kind of tolerance, which is absolutely vital to the continuation of human life on this planet.

He also said this—which is a kind of personal mantra for me: *"When you are studying any matter, or considering any philosophy, ask yourself only what are the facts, and what is the truth that the facts bear out? Never let yourself be diverted either by what you wish to believe, or by what you think would have beneficent social effects if it were believed. Look only and solely at what are the facts."*

So, what *are* the facts? How does nature do it?

Green things are Earth's primary producers, converting raw sunlight into energy, which fixes atmospheric carbon into sugar. Plants are the base of life's pyramid. The more they make and grow, the richer this planet becomes. We can do it too.

Michael Pollan's Sahara Forest Project uses sunlight and saltwater to produce freshwater, clean energy, and food—while regenerating life in the desert. That's interesting. But let's scale it up and make things as the plants do. We have the Internet and photovoltaics—we are converging on the plant's recipe for infinite growth using our own mycorrhizal networks to feed them. Imagine—if we could make everything from CO_2 like the plants do. Might our skies have some to spare?

If bacteria won't eat our mess fast enough, we must do it ourselves through carbon negative manufacture. New Light Technologies captures methane-based carbon to make "Air Carbon," a thermoplastic material that performs just as petroleum-based plastic does. Dell uses Air Carbon along with Ecovative's mushroom packaging, and Sprint makes phone cases with it. Petrochemical distributor Vinmar International has committed to buying a billion pounds of Air Carbon a year for the next 20 years.

But what we really need is a mycelial solution: distributed manufacture, with local feedstock and energy. How about 3D printers in every neighborhood, powered by local sun and wind, eating our waste, making what we need in place? 3D printers easily eat recycled plastic, but why not start out with something fully digestible from the get-go, something the rest of nature can eat too? Bring that carbon we've tossed away back to the biosphere. Think of vast colonies of tiny coral reef polyps, secreting calcium carbonate cement with dissolved carbon, or the distributed network of termite-tummy bioreactors digesting scraps of discarded waste, or the forests carpeting the Amazon and Congo, converting CO_2 into wood through a vast blanket of greenery.

Now, imagine the bonanza for all of Earth's creatures if we reclaimed all our carbon. Imagine if human consumption was good for the planet. Given enough time, it's inevitable. Whether we'll be around to see it is less certain.

Chapter Forty-One

The Tail Grows Back

*How paramount the future is to the present
when one is surrounded by children.*
—CHARLES DARWIN

As an intrepid beanbag biologist, I spent my time foraging for books in the hidden thicket at the back of my kindergarten class—the library nook, where I hoped the teacher wouldn't notice me. I consulted the most advanced references I could find—*In the Shadow of Man, Watership Down, The Voyages of Dr. Dolittle, Flight to the Mushroom Planet*, and anything—anything—about Middle Earth. But one day, hiding from Dick and Jane in the stacks, I found a book titled the *Code of Life*,[1] an illustrated account of Watson and Crick's discovery of DNA (Rosalind Franklin even made an appearance, bringing the boys tea and transcribing their notes). It was like a message in a bottle had just washed up on the shores of my desert island! I pulled the crumbling cork to discover Earth-shattering old news—there was a code of life??? I suspected I wasn't supposed to know about this. Guilty as a tomb raider, I pulled the beanbag over me and huddled out of sight. When I finally lifted my head, everyone had gone home, and the classroom was locked! No matter. I'd discovered the code of life.

The following year they put me in a different school.

This was a public one too, but we were expected to read college textbooks and do a science project each year. Finally, we would learn something!

I would need to go Downtown—to the Central Branch of the San Diego Public Library system. My mom clutched my hand, looking London-fierce in her crocheted poncho and wooden sandals and perfectly spherical Angela Davis hair, as we politely stepped past street people in various states of horizontal. *Dear me. Oh, no thank you.* She was always properly British.

Inside, the old men managed to stay upright in their chairs and not talk to the voices in their heads. This was a library after all. It was sacred.

My projects led me there every fall, scouring the shelves for ideas and leads. One year, I stumbled across an ancient black tome, with the enticing word *REGENERATION* stamped in weathered gold on the faded linen spine. It was written by one Dr. TH Morgan, in 1901. Inside were hand-illustrated pictures of the most adorable cross-eyed flatworms! I checked out the book and mail-ordered a jar of *Planaria* worms from the North Carolina Equipment Supply, whose advertisement I'd seen in the back of the *Journal of Irreproducible Results*[2] (which I thought was the coolest thing since punk).

The worms cruised in endless circles around my mom's cupcake tub, eating the hard-boiled egg yolks I fed them. They never uncrossed their eyes, by the way—proof-positive that if you keep making that face you will stick that way.

Morgan's writing was a little heady; the topic of regeneration was swimming in the deep end even for him. But he had some neat experiments in there: he cut the worms in half and documented their heads and tails growing back a little each day. I tried Dr. Morgan's experiment, and it worked!

What was it about them? Was it a special cell that could regenerate this way? Or something they produced? Maybe I could isolate this regenerative substance. Did some parts grow back faster than others? Inquiring minds wanted to know. I tried slicing them up different ways, but the wriggly little beasts were wild and hard to handle—scrunching up in balls and refusing to play. I don't know if it was Dr. Morgan or me, but I hit on the idea of laying each one on an ice cube to make it lie straight, and then sliced each one into eight tiny pieces with a scalpel and put each one in a numbered compartment in an ice tray. How many days until the cross-eyes were whole again?

Eventually, Dr. Thomas Hunt Morgan gave up trying to figure out the mystery of regeneration and moved on to lower-hanging fruit: he won a Nobel Prize for discovering that chromosomes were the basis of heredity. Twenty-five years later, Watson, Crick, and Rosalind Franklin discovered DNA. Twenty-five years after them, I stumbled on the long-lost code of life! It seemed like kismet.

This was my introduction to regeneration, unless you count the alligator lizards in the canyon below my house. They were big and not a little intimidating. If you grabbed one wrong it would muscle out of your hands, leaving a wriggling tail behind before turning to hiss and look daggers at you. I once found one with a half-regrown stump, and I left them alone after that. What if a cat got it and I'd used up its extra life?

Regeneration is mysterious and complex, but nature continually self-organizes to repair and regrow itself, even as its beings evolve and change. The massive glacier in Alaska's Glacier Bay has been in retreat for 200 years, relinquishing bare rock to tenacious lichens and liverworts. These pioneers cling to the exposed surface, digesting the rock to make soil. Weeds blow in and find purchase there, stabilizing the ground for fungal networks to settle. Once these underground webs are established, they move water, nitrogen, and nutrients to bigger plants. Creeping shrubs appear, nursing tiny seedlings into forests of alder. These give way to magnificent spruce and cedar forests, the most massively productive ecosystems on earth. Eventually, bacteria and fungus will digest all this carbon, regenerating an expanding spiral of life.

Superorganisms harness this process in miniature. In the Kalahari, termites concentrate locked-up energy and nutrients, and partner with their fungi to release it. The grass surrounding the mounds becomes tender, drawing grazers that fertilize the soil with their dung—to be carried away by busy beetles. Herbivores attract predators, who leave carcass remains for a lively host of decomposers who further enrich the soil, thus supporting more vegetation—which feeds the fungi which feed the termites and so on. The termites are doing more than just recycling nutrients. They are improving—transforming—the entire landscape, regenerating opportunity for a wide range of residents. The mounds rise above the yearly flood water, for instance, acting as snorkels and sheltering many plants and animals. Rainwater soaks deep into their tunnels, aerating and protecting topsoil, stored for the long dry season.

"Life creates conditions conducive to life," as they say. But that is not the termites' purpose; it is merely a byproduct of it. Their purpose is to launch the next generation of termites into a world of abundance and potential. For that to happen, their wealth must compound. Regenerating systems around them allows them to do that.

Chapter Forty-Two
Ecosystem Engineers

Life creates conditions conducive to life.
—JANINE BENYUS

An army of bizarre elephantines worked to shape the land throughout the Pleistocene. Big ones and small ones, woolly ones and bald ones, even one with a spork on his face (yes, Mother Nature invented that timeless cafeteria combo of fork and spoon long ago).

Elephants have a dramatic impact on their environment and everyone in it. Their muddy wallows draw many animals (and their predators), and they are important seed dispersers, plucking inaccessible fruit, carrying the seeds in their massive stomachs to disperse over great distances. Some seeds will only germinate if deposited within a moist elephant sprouting kit. Dung beetles love them of course, as do the lucky honey badgers that find their fragrant larvae-rich truffles. Most profoundly, their habit of bulldozing trees gradually transformed many of the world's woodlands into the mosaic of savanna grasslands we see today, creating opportunities for other species. Large, hoofed grazers thrived as the wet fruit-filled forests our ape ancestors relied upon dwindled.

Ecologists often speak of keystone species that support many others, like the center-stone of a Renaissance arch. Pull it away, and many others will fall. Fig trees are like this—many other species would fail without them. But ecosystem engineers like the elephants reshape the whole environment, provoking a cascade of new opportunities and dilemmas. They are destructive, but ultimately their disturbance opens space for new diversity, potential, and abundance.

Life on earth is a litany of spiraling successions, disruption and shifting opportunity. In the earliest days, bacteria dined on sulfur and fumes, exhaling carbon dioxide waste. They were so successful that their CO_2 accumulated in the primordial atmosphere, until other cells stumbled onto photosynthesis. Those green things claimed that carbon, exhaling a new waste product in the process: oxygen, which tragically poisoned the earth for earlier bacteria. Their gasping survivors were forced to crawl off and hide in the toxic cracks of the world, while new life came out to breathe it. Some plants grew and shaded others—the race for sun was on. Wood allowed trees to grow strong and tall—nothing could eat that wood. Its carbon accumulated over vast millennia—becoming the subterranean fossil fuels we use today—until fungi and bacteria cracked the code. Unlocking the value in accumulated waste can indeed transform everything for those that came before.

Humans are one of the most dramatic ecosystem engineers this planet has ever known, of course. Our footprint is not small. Like ants and termites, we change our environment to suit ourselves. Termites don't like hot, dry conditions any more than you'd like to be stuck in the Mojave Desert naked without a water bottle, but they thrive in the Kalahari nonetheless, even though it rains just a couple of inches a year. They simply modify their mounds, the same way we open and close our shutters, curtains, and windows.

Our modern way of life—dredging up vast stores of buried carbon—is a radical innovation that has changed the world forever. But are we creating opportunities for more life with it? The cockroaches, pigeons, and rats would probably endorse us, but mostly we've wreaked havoc. This is our great extinction event, just as the photosynthetic bacteria brought about before us. What will rise from the ashes?

Being a poetic soul, I like to imagine ancient fungi and ants going down the same kinds of rabbit holes we do today, changing every ecosystem they touched to the displeasure of other species. But today, these disruptive innovators have settled in to provide critical life support for every Earthling to come. Can we do this? I believe we can—because we must. The option is not one we can survive. And besides, all our ancestors have succeeded. It's in our blood.

Like photosynthetic bacteria oxygenating an anaerobic world, our waste brings mass extinction. Can we regenerate new life with it? Maybe. It's a slow process though: plastic-eating bacteria, genetically engineered what-if-ers. But how is this any different from wood-eating fungi, the ants breeding tame, wingless aphids, or mosquitoes inserting various viruses into their hosts? I don't know the answer to that, but I do know that as superorganism apes, we have the unique ability to imagine the futures we want, dream our collective dreams, and reverse-engineer them together. We can do it consciously, purposefully, regenerating richer futures, filled with more life and potential.

What kind of footprint will we leave behind?

Chapter Forty-Three
The Snuggle for Survival

Contemplate an entangled bank, clothed with many plants of many kinds, with birds singing on the bushes, with various insects flitting about, and with worms crawling through the damp earth those elaborately constructed forms, so different from each other, dependent on each other in so complex a manner, have all been produced by laws acting around us.
—CHARLES DARWIN

So now we return to our initial question: how would nature build infinite wealth on a finite planet? I think you know—she is doing it now. Nature is driven by a compelling purpose: to regenerate the future. She makes more life with her life. Superorganisms like the ants and honeybees do this by building with infinite things—sunlight and carbon, the complexity, diversity, density and strength of our connections, trust and transparency. We can always find and make more. We are designed to thrive in landscapes of scarcity by pooling scraps of value that aren't worth the effort for other creatures, converting them into something with more potential.

Superorganism societies grow from the edges out, in modular, self-managed units that seek and respond to opportunity and threat on the front lines. This isn't a circular economy, it is a spiraling one, like the Nautilus shell or a head of sunflower seeds: the value they create spills out into the larger ecosystem, feeding the life that feeds them.

Principle #12. Build with abundant things, feed the life that feeds you, and grow future potential.

What I refer to as "teeming" is a new way to do business and structure our whole society. It may seem daunting, but I don't think it is actually that hard. We are superorganisms too, after all—this way of life feels natural to us. It's the way we like to work and the way we work best.

Superorganisms don't evolve often—maybe half a dozen times in the history of the world. We are indeed quite special. But once the transition occurs, superorganisms cannot go back to the every-one-for-themselves program. Populations that try will blink out and fail. Superorganisms are one of life's most disruptive innovators, and they thrive all around because of it—on our countertops, our gardens, and even our organizations. We have all the ingredients we need to make stone soup.

Life's simple rules can seem inscrutable, but they are absolute nonetheless. A clock winding down; seeds in the rainmaker sifting from one level to the next; sunlight streaming through leaves, through proteins and genes, inexorably into dust. Eons of time and sifting will continue sculpting energy and matter into these wondrous but temporary vessels until each of us returns to stardust. It's evolution, and we are part of it. Species come and go. Some children live and some die. We gobble resources as fast as the algae blooming and crashing on our polluted shores, and our way of life cannot survive. Perhaps whole branches of humanity will be pruned away from this tree of life, leaving something quite different behind. There may be much tragedy and heartbreak, but the march of the penguins goes on until it stops. The same laws of diversity, symbiosis, or discarded life govern our days. Evolution will be what it is.

Meanwhile, beauty and goodness, morality and meaning are what each of us chooses to make it. Art, poetry, song and dance, love and family, kindness and humor—these things have no real value beyond the pleasure, richness, and comfort they give one another in our short time here. And what more could we want, anyway? Simply more of it, for our children and all the children of Earth, no matter how distant our ancestors.

I think Charles Darwin had it right. He lost a daughter the same as me, and I think we've trodden some of the same ground getting here. In the last pages of the *Origin of Species*, he asks himself—as I have many times—what meaning there could possibly be in her death. He walks, and finds himself lost in a forest rich with trees and singing birds, and feels his heart swell with nature's unspeakable beauty. Here is his answer. Each of us are amazing apes—bursting with art, music, and invention—and just one among millions of end twigs generated by billions of years of growth and pruning. Each of us is an improbable miracle. Each of us dies, and it's unbearable for the loved ones we leave behind, but this process of living and dying is what sculpts, in Darwin's words, "the endless forms most beautiful and most wonderful" that thrive all around us. The simple magic of evolution continues in us all.

This is the magic that excites me to work for better things. We all have this capacity to imagine better futures, and the human spirit is nothing if not persistent. The star-nosed mole sees seismic vibrations with his 22 pink snout tentacles, while the mimic octopus changes color and shape to match 15 different animals on cue. Similarly, we ant-like apes can do things other species would never dream of. The magic of what could be drives us on.

What folks think "should be" isn't really all that interesting to me, but I delight in trying to understand what actually is, and I get really excited about what could be. Every vision brings a dream of the future our children might inherit.

The future is uncertain, but whatever we must do, know that millions of ancient and implacable mentors have done it before you. Reach out and introduce yourself, because "life did not take over the globe by combat, but by networking." When diverse individuals come together around a few simple rules and a compelling shared purpose, there is a moment—a turning point—when a new pattern suddenly appears. You never know when.

Notes

Prologue

1. Steinbeck, 1945.
2. Trivers, 1985.
3. I wrote him a letter telling him about my various passions and asked if he'd write me a recommendation for the Bio-Anthropology PhD program at Harvard. He called me (it was like getting a phone call from the POTUS, I was that excited), and said, "Where are you getting this crazy stuff? I'll recommend you just to inflict you on them."
4. Hölldobler and Wilson, 2009.
5. Invasive Species Specialist Group, 2016.
6. White, 1958.

Introduction

1. Goodall, 1986.
2. "Take four hundred chimpanzees and put them in economy class on a seven-hour flight. They would, in all likelihood,...stumble off the plane at their destination with bitten ears, missing fur, and bleeding limbs. Yet millions of us tolerate being crammed together this way." (Nowak and Highfield, 2011: xvi.)
3. Crespi 2014; Hölldobler and Wilson 2009. I'm not the first to think this. The brilliant evolutionary biologist Bernard Crespi and Ed Wilson have both written about it. Crespi 2014; Hölldobler and Wilson 2009.
4. Kingsley, 2002; Henson, 1912.
5. Dobzhansky, 1973. The great population geneticist Theodosius Dobzhansky said it best! *"Nothing in biology makes sense except in the light of evolution."*
6. "Life did not take over the globe by combat, but by networking" (Margulis and Sagan, 2001:11).

The Mycelial Way: A Quick Guide to "Teeming"

1. Thompson, 2008b.

Chapter One: Supersaurus Wrecks
1. Hesselbein and Goldsmith, 2009.

Chapter Two: Ask a Local
1. Darwin Correspondence Project, 1846.
2. Ask Nature, 2015.
3. Harman, 2013. The following examples and many, many more can be found in Jay Harman's captivating book, *The Shark's Paintbrush*. Highly recommended!
4. N. R. Bogatyrev, O. Bogatyreva, 2014: 297-314.
5. Hölldobler and Wilson, 2011.
6. Johansen and Ronn, 2014.

Chapter Three: The Meek Shall Inherit the Earth
1. Tomasello, 2009.
2. Wheeler, 1911.
3. Wilson and Hölldobler, 2005.
4. Hölldobler and Wilson, 2011.
5. Crespi, 2014.
6. Stamets, 2005.
7. Bingham and Simard, 2012.
8. Rayner, 1991.

Chapter Four: The Sacred Desert Monkey
1. C. J. Jolly, 1970: 5-26; C. J. Jolly, 2009: 187-199.
2. Macho, 2014.
3. Kummer, 1995.
4. In an interview, CBS's Bob McKeown once accused Marlon Perkins of perpetrating the same kinds of tricksies the Disney-lemming directors had. Perkins asked McKeown to turn off the camera, then punched him in the face. He was nearly eighty.
5. The Afar women wear necklaces strung with varying numbers of large round beads. These are quite beautiful, and have a waxy, almost transparent, quality. Through a translator I asked a woman if she would be interested in a trade. The woman was horrified, and so was the translator. Not only were these beads her dowry, gifted from her husband to indicate her worth to him, but each had been painstakingly sliced, rolled, and mummified from the scrotum of a neighboring tribesman, killed in his tent by her suitor to prove his love.

6. C. N. Simonti, et al., 2016. This ancient genetic legacy still affects us, according to John Capra, who discovered associations between Neanderthal DNA and a wide range of traits, including resistance to UV radiation and pathogens, and increased risk of nicotine addiction, and faster blood coagulation, and wound sealing. Today, these genes increase our risk of stroke, pulmonary embolism and complications in pregnancy.

7. Marks, 2002. Many—perhaps most—genomicists seem unaware that no biological basis for race exists. They regularly lump their populations into blacks, whites, and Asians for genetic disease correlations, but it is totally unhelpful to try to correlate diseases with an imaginary family tree. Most of the genes in these "populations" have been moving around like water through the human protoplasm for a very long time. There is simply no biological basis for race beyond a few location-specific genes for skin and eye color, hair type, malarial immunity, and altitude tolerance. These genes are adaptations to the environment they evolved in, and they are pinned-in-place by selection.

8. Rhizomes are root-like cords of fungal webs, and Jon Marks' blog, Anthropomics http://anthropomics.blogspot.com is a great read!

Chapter Five: All for One and One for All

1. Some linguist, I can't remember who, recently declared that the plural for octopus is *octopodes*, because octopus is Ancient Greek—octopi would only apply if the word was Latin. But guess what? If you're talking about the genus *Octopus*, it is Latin, because it's a scientific name. So even though it comes from the Greek, if it's *Octopus vulgares*, the common octopus, then I can say octopi to my heart's content. And I will.

2. An animal is judged self-aware if they can pass the Mirror Self-Recognition Test, which goes like this: the animal gets to know itself in the mirror. Then, they are anaesthetized and a dot of paint is applied to their forehead (or genitals if you're a dolphin, because apparently they're into that). When the animal wakes up, it usually gets aggressive with the guy in the mirror, just like before—it thinks another animal is looking at them. A very small number do something quite different, however—they touch the mark. Chimps pick their noses and make faces in the mirror, bottlenose dolphins check their privates and stick out their tongues, elephants and orcas, Eurasian magpies, and bizarrely, some ants try to clean off the dot. Half of human children can pass it by eighteen months.

3. According to the Cambridge Declaration on Consciousness, written by Philip Low and publicly proclaimed on July 7, 2012, at the Francis

Crick Memorial Conference on Consciousness in Human and non-Human Animals. It was signed by participants that very evening, in the presence of Stephen Hawking, and memorialized by CBS *60 Minutes*. The octopus was specifically welcomed into the sentient club.

4. Drucker, 1988: 35-53.
5. Darwin's issue was a different one. He saw how cooperation could evolve in a superorganism society as a whole, but he couldn't see how the different castes could evolve along different paths.
6. Genes were purely selfish (Dawkins, 1976) until theoretical biologists David Sloan Wilson and Eric Sober and mathematician Martin Nowak (Nowak, et al. 2010.) did the math. Genes and individuals may indeed be selfish, but sometimes groups are sufficiently cohesive to compete against each other. Then, more cooperative groups outcompete selfish ones. E. O. Wilson agreed. It's still contentious stuff, and I wouldn't be surprised if blows have been thrown over it.

Chapter Six: Our Magic Friendship Number

1. Dunbar, 2016
2. Peter, 1969. The Peter Principle is a concept in management theory formulated by Laurence J. Peter, who said that promotions are made based on performance in current roles, not the abilities the new role requires. Thus, employees only stop getting promoted once they stop performing effectively. Managers rise to the level of their incompetence.
3. Boehm, 1999.
4. Literally! We just whacked 'em, according to Christopher Boehm.
5. O'Donnell et al., 2015; Sasaki and Pratt, 2012.

Chapter Seven: The Tao of Superchimp

1. T. D. Wilson et al., 2014: 6192. Subjects were asked to spend ten minutes or so alone with their thoughts—no phones or other activities were permitted. They were wired up and given the chance to shock themselves during the thinking period if they desired. Even when people said they would pay money *not* to feel that shock again, a quarter of the women and two-thirds of the men zapped themselves when left with alone with their thoughts. One guy pressed the button 190 times.
2. When I shared this with my perennially obscure father, he just raised an eyebrow and said "The crows are calling my name, said Caw." But an Italian gentleman told me all the mamas in Italy complain about this.

3. His name is an acronym for Avian Language Experiment, which I think says more about scientists than parrots.

4. Alex looked at himself in the mirror and asked, "What color?" then learned the word "grey." Existential, no?

5. Humanity loves to get down. Music is extremely ancient—one of the few human universals we can clearly identify. It uses the exact same neural circuitry as speech, and quite probably preceded it. Wouldn't you love to attend a *Homo erectus* rave? I bet they were fantastic. Did they have glow-sticks? You never know.

6. Anthropologist Paul Mellars of Stony Brook University says the focus on exaggerated sexual features fits with other artifacts found from the period, including phalluses.

7. In fact, Baran later said the Net's biggest threat wasn't the Soviet Union at all—it was the phone company.

Chapter Eight: The Maker Instinct

1. Johansen, 2012: 29-47. Bob Johansen speaks eloquently on this.

Chapter Ten: The Power of Self-Organization

1. When the Human Genome Project presented the first rough draft of a complete human DNA sequence in 2000, the vast majority—97 percent of its 3.2 billion bases—appeared to have no function. Back in the 70s, Francis Crick himself (the co-discoverer of DNA's double-helical structure) suspected most of our genes were little better than junk.

2. In 2003, the University of Plymouth used a £2,000 grant to study the literary output of real monkeys. They left a computer keyboard in an enclosure with six Celebes crested macaques for a month. The monkeys produced five pages, mostly consisting of the letter S—until the alpha male smashed the keyboard with a stone. The other monkeys finished the job by urinating and defecating on it. The researchers concluded that "monkeys are not random generators, they are much more complex than that."

3. Population geneticist Sir Ronald Fisher said it well—"Natural selection is a mechanism for generating an exceedingly high degree of improbability" (Fisher, 1930).

4. Laloux, 2014. Much of this chapter is inspired by Frederic Laloux's excellent book, *Reinventing Organizations.*

5. Semler, 2004.

6. Reingold, 2016.

Chapter Eleven: Scattered, Squandered Scraps

1. Shirky, 2010.
2. Diamandis and Kotler, 2012.
3. Internet Live Stats.
4. United Nations, 2013.
5. Anderson, 2015.
6. Leber, 2012.
7. G.A.N. Wright and L. Mutesasira, 2001.
8. Yunus and Weber, 2007.
9. Drive My Car, 2017; Tx Zhuo, 2015.
10. Johansen and Ronn, 2014, 74.

Chapter Twelve: Think for Your Own Damn Self

1. Seeley, 2010: 183-184.
2. Fisher, 1930. Richard Dawkins called Sir Ronald "the greatest biologist since Darwin." He invented modern statistics and population genetics, and revived the idea of sexual selection, which nobody had thought about since Darwin. He also saved millions of people from starvation with his modern crop-breeding programs. On top of that, Fisher was a Professor of Eugenics at University College London, and the Eugenic Review's book reviewer. A committed eugenicist, he attributed the fall of civilization to the diminished fertility of the British upper class, and did his single-handed best to save it by having eight children of his own.
3. Biological philosopher Stuart Kauffman conceived the Adjacent Possible while trying to mathematically represent a random walk to the present. I'm not sure that was a useful exercise, but it's a great concept. Steven Johnson also explored this idea of an "ever-present set of opportunities at the boundaries of our reach," saying "the adjacent possible is a kind of shadow future, hovering on the edges of the present state of things, a map of all the ways in which the present can reinvent itself." These boundaries grow as you explore them, says Johnson—each decision opens new possibilities. "Think of it as a house that magically expands with each door you open. You begin in a room with four doors, each leading to a new room that you haven't visited yet. Once you open one of those doors and stroll into that room, three new doors appear, each leading to a brand-new room that you couldn't have reached from your original starting point." Johnson, 2010: 31.
4. Shirky, 2010.

Chapter Thirteen: I Feel Like Making Stigmergy

1. All examples from Surowiecki, 2004.
2. As related by Shirky, 2010.
3. Gorbis, 2013; Johansen, 2012.

Chapter Fourteen: Simple Rules and Tipping Points

1. As reviewed in Miller, 2010.
2. Milgram, 1977. The six degrees of separation concept originates from Stanley Milgram's 1967 "small world experiment." Milgram sent packages to 160 random people in Omaha, Nebraska, and asked them to forward it to a friend or acquaintance they thought could bring the package closer to a certain Bostonian. There were rules—they could only mail it to someone they knew on a personal, first-name basis. On average, it took six mailings to get it there. In 2008, Microsoft showed the average chain of contacts between users of its NET Messenger Service was 6.6 people.

Chapter Fifteen: Fairy Rings

1. Gloor, 2006.

Chapter Sixteen: Shared Purpose

1. We know of only two exceptions: ravens try to get others to look at things, and chimps nudge other chimps and point to the spot they want scratched. Frans de Waal relates that sometimes, at Yerkes Primate Center, two chimps will suddenly stand up and hurry out of the building together, heading for an experimental setup that requires them to cooperate to extract food. It seems to him they somehow discussed it and made a decision to try it. Jane Goodall also reports that sometimes, when male chimps see colobus monkeys on the other side of their valley, their hair bristles, and they reach out and touch one another, then set off on a hunt.
2. Marzluff and Angell, 2012.
3. Hill, 2014: 92.
4. C.K. Prahalad and S.L. Hart, 2006, 54-67. This article discusses new business models aimed at providing goods and services to the world's poorest people.
5. In Hesselbein and Goldsmith, 2009: 141.

Chapter Seventeen: Toss It Up and See What Sticks

1. G. W. Rouse, S. K. Goffredi, and R. C. Vrijenhoek, 2004: 668–671.

These animals were only just discovered in 2002—at 2900 meters (that's 10,000 feet) below the surface, in a deepwater canyon in the Monterey Bay.

2. Kim and Mauborgne, 2005. The authors argue that companies can succeed not by battling competitors, but rather by creating "blue oceans" of uncontested market space. These strategic moves create leaps in value, while unlocking new demand and making the competition irrelevant.

3. https://hbr.org/2009/12/the-innovators-dna. The Innovator's DNA. JH. Dyer, H Gregersen, CM. Christensen. Dec. 2009. Harvard Business Review.

Chapter Eighteen: It's Sexy Time
1. Johnson, 2010: 45.
2. Dyer, Gregersen, Christiansen, 2011.

Chapter Twenty: Going Viral
1. Hill, 2014: 158.
2. Gloor, 2006.
3. Krause et al. 2015.
4. Gladwell, 2002.
5. Satell, 2013.

Chapter Twenty-One: Brewtopia
1. Nowak and Highfield, 2011.
2. Johansen and Ronn, 2014: 32.
3. Maintaining the collective value these networks create requires protection, however. The General Public License prohibits the appropriation of public software code, along with the Open-source Initiative. The Creative Commons license does this in a broader sense, enabling networks to protect their openly shared, common resources while still allowing collective intelligence to play with them.
4. Gorbis, 2013.
5. Hippel, 2005.

Chapter Twenty-Two: We Meet in the Middle
1. Laloux, 2014.

Chapter Twenty-Three: Surfing the Edge
2. Bogatyreva, 2015.

Chapter Twenty-Four: Are You a Grizzly or an Aardvark?

1. NBC via Associated Press, 2006. I know this because I was stuck on a fishing boat watching tapes of *When Grizzlies Attack* on repeat for four months—after I wisely tossed my copy of *Blue Velvet* overboard. My one act of willful littering. Fishermen love grizzly attacks, and they love *Blue Velvet* too, but it just isn't a great idea to watch it with them. "Wild find: Half grizzly, half polar bear: Hunter bags what expert 'never thought would happen' in wild." MSNBC.MSN.com. May 11, 2006.

Chapter Twenty-Five: Lead Like a Superorganism

1. L. Swedell, et al., 2011: 360-370.
2. Kummer, 1995.
3. Boehm, 1999: 61-62.
4. Gloor, 2006.

Chapter Twenty-Six: Freaks, Geeks, and Folks Like Me

1. Bogatyreva and Shillerov, 2015.
2. Gordon, 2010. We know they do: Camponotus mirabilus nests in bamboo, constructing wicks to drain the water inside them. Aphaenogaster workers soak up crushed dead insect juices with leaves, then bring them back to the nest. Other ants cover food with leaves, hiding it while they recruit more nestmates.

Chapter Twenty-Seven: Please Don't Eat Me

1. American writer best known for his novels *All About Lulu, West of Here, and The Revised Fundamentals of Caregiving*, which was made into a film with a similar name.
2. C. Geertz, 1973: 49.
3. Eugenics wasn't confined to the horrors of Nazi Germany either, by the way. This was a serious academic discipline for fifty years—supported by American presidents and many well-respected thinkers and charitable organizations. Fine universities advocated forced sterilization of the deaf and blind, criminals, the mentally ill, and members of minority races. Between 1907 and 1963, more than 64,000 forced sterilizations were secretly performed in the US—unknown to the poor folks who visited the hospital for other reasons. North Carolina's aggressive eugenics program persisted until 1977.
4. Yvon Chouinard, CEO of Patagonia. My children hate it when I say this. For some reason it makes them nervous.

Chapter Thirty: Might Versus Right

1. *Chlorocebus sabaeus*, a lovely little monkey with golden-green fur, a yellow-tipped tail, distinguished whiskers, and, in the males, a delightful blue scrotum.
2. Cited in Cummins and Allen, 1998
3. For instance, the atrocities at Abu Ghraib or the Stanford Prison Experiment.
4. Cited in Cummins and Allen, 1998: 37.
5. De Waal, 2013: 69, 81.

Chapter Thirty-One: You Say You Want A Revolution?

1. Always ahead of his time, Charles Darwin homed in on shame and blushing as the only shared human social trait. Darwin, 1872: 309-346.

Chapter Thirty Two:

1. Goodall, 1986.
2. Trivers, 1985.
3. Marzluff and Angell, 2012. Ch 32 -2 ^^
4. Axelrod, 1984. Ch 32-3 ^^
   The Assurance Game uses trust to escape the uncertain outcome of the Prisoner's Dilemma. In an Assurance Game, transparency builds trust, increasing the likelihood of mutual cooperation. The hard part is finding the threshold of trust that triggers it. Move to ch 33 4

Chapter Thirty-Three: Fuhgeddaboutit

1. Trivers, 1985.
2. Marzluff and Angell, 2012. Ch 32 -2 ^^
3. Axelrod, 1984. Ch 32-3 ^^
   The Assurance Game uses trust to escape the uncertain outcome of the Prisoner's Dilemma. In an Assurance Game, transparency builds trust, increasing the likelihood of mutual cooperation. The hard part is finding the threshold of trust that triggers it. Move to ch 33 4

Chapter Thirty-Five:

1. Dubravcic, Baalen, and Nizak, 2014. VVV move to Ch 35

Chapter Thirty-Six:

1. Lee, 1984: 49.
2. Boehm, 1999: 124.

Chapter Thirty-Seven: A Rat in Our Midst

1. Hardin, 1968: 1243-1248.
2. Ostrom, 2015.

Chapter Thirty-eight

1. Benkler, 2006.
2. Takcam, "Peeple App."

Chapter Thirty-Nine: Expanding Our Superorganisms

1. S. F. Gilbert, J. Sapp and A. I. Tauber. 2012.

Chapter Forty: Reincarbonation

1. Now called the Birch Aquarium.
2. Ted Kaczynski, also known as the "Unabomber," is a domestic terrorist, nature-centered anarchist, and mathematical prodigy. A one-time Berkeley professor, Kaczynski engaged in a nationwide bombing campaign against people involved with modern technology, mailing homemade bombs to his targets, over a twenty-year period. He killed three and injured twenty-three more. The moral of the story? Don't think so hard.
3. Louv, 2005; Kellert and Wilson, 1993.
4. J. Brown-Hansen, 2015. Thanks to the brilliant Jamie Brown-Hansen for explaining this to me. See https://www.greenbiz.com/article/community-credit-next-generation-financial-architecture for more of her work on bio-inspired financial architecture.
5. For a nice vision of a biologically-inspired circular economy, I recommend Hutchins, 2012, and McDonough and Braungart, 2002: 2013.
6. Janine Benyus talks a lot about reincarnating our materials, and I made up this term to describe that process.
7. All examples are cited in the Ellen MacArthur Foundation's reports. See https://www.ellenmacarthurfoundation.org/publications for their latest publications.
8. BBC's 1959 Face to Face interview with Bertrand Russell, video, https://www.youtube.com/watch?v=1bZv3pSaLtY. My middle school hero!

Chapter Forty-One: The Tail Grows Back

1. Try as I may, I sadly cannot find this book or anything about it.
2. This awesome satirical geek-newsletter got some attention from the American military in 2001, when a copy of a 1979 article, entitled

"How To Build An Atomic Bomb In 10 Easy Steps" was found in Al-Qaeda's abandoned Kabul headquarters. Apparently they'd actually been reading it and trying to figure it out.

References

Adams, Richard. 1972. *Watership Down.* London: Rex Collings Ltd.

Adamson, Joy. 1960. *Born Free, A Lioness of Two Worlds.* New York: Pantheon Books.

Ask Nature. 2015. "Mist Platform Technology." *Biomimicry Institute.* Accessed March 2, 2017. https://asknature.org/idea/mist-platform-technology/#.WKztZRIrKV4.

Anderson, Mark. 2015. "How Aerial Tech is Bringing the Internet to Everyone, Everywhere." *Air & Space Magazine.* http://www.airspacemag.com/flight-today/06_on2015-internet-from-above-180956600/?no-ist. Accessed March 2, 2017.

Antrosio, Jason. 2012. "Denisovans, Neandertals, Archaics as Human Races." *Living Anthropologically,* http://www.livinganthropologically.com/anthropology/denisovans-neandertals-human-races/. Last updated August 7, 2012. Accessed March 2, 2017.

Axelrod, Robert M. 1984. *The Evolution of Cooperation.* New York: Basic Books.

Beale, Bob. 2003. "Humungous Fungus: World's Largest Organism?" *ABC News in Science.* http://www.abc.net.au/science/news/enviro/EnviroRepublish_828525.htm. Accessed March 2, 2017.

Benkler, Yochai. 2006. *The Wealth of Networks: How Social Production Transforms Markets and Freedom.* New Haven, CT: Yale University Press.

Benyus, Janine M. 1997. *Biomimicry: Innovation Inspired by Nature.* New York: Morrow.

Bingham, M. A., and S. W. Simard. 2012. "Mycorrhizal Networks Affect Ectomycorrhizal Fungal Community Similarity Between Conspecific Trees and Seedlings." *Mycorrhiza* 22: 317-26.

Block, Susan. 2014. *The Bonobo Way: The Evolution of Peace through Pleasure*. Beverly Hills, CA: Gardner & Daughters.

Boehm, Christopher. 1999. *Hierarchy in the Forest: The Evolution of Egalitarian Behavior*. Cambridge, MA: Harvard University Press.

Bogatyreva, Olga, and Alexandr Shillerov. 2015. *Biomimetic Management: Building a Bridge Between People and Nature*. North Charleston, SC.: CreateSpace Independent Publishing Platform.

Cameron, Eleanor, and Robert Henneberger. 1954. *The Wonderful Flight to the Mushroom Planet*. Boston: Little, Brown, & CO.

Chimpanzee Sequencing, and Consortium Analysis. 2005. "Initial Sequence of the Chimpanzee Genome and Comparison with the Human Genome." *Nature* 437: 69-87.

Cooperrider, David, Diana D. Whitney, Jacqueline M. Stavros. 2008. *The Appreciative Inquiry Handbook: For Leaders of Change*. San Francisco: Berrett-Koehler.

Crespi, B. 2014. "The Insectan Apes." *Human Nature Nat* 25: 6-27.

Cummins, Denise D., and Colin Allen. 1998. *The Evolution of Mind*. New York: Oxford University Press.

Darwin, Charles. 1872. *The Expression of the Emotions in Man and Animals*. New York: D. Appleton & Company.

Darwin Correspondence Project. 1846. "Letter to Leonard Jenyns, 17 October 1846." *University of Cambridge*. http://www.darwinproject. ac.uk/letter/DCP-LETT-1009.xml. Accessed March 3, 2017.

Dawkins, Richard. 1976. *The Selfish Gene*. New York: Oxford University Press.

Dewey, Caitlin. 2015. "Everyone you know will be able to rate you on the terrifying 'Yelp for people' — whether you want them to or not." https:// www. washingtonpost.com/news/theintersect/wp/2015/09/30/everyone-you-know-will-be-able-to-rate-you-on-the-terrifying-yelp-for-people-whether-you-want-them-to-or-not/?utm_term=.dd55c3a67069. Accessed March 4, 2017.

Diamandis, Peter H., and Steven Kotler. 2012. *Abundance: The Future is Better than You Think.* New York: Free Press.

Dobzhansky, Theodosius. 1973. "Nothing in Biology Makes Sense Except in the Light of Evolution." *The American Biology Teacher* 35: 125-29.

Drive My Car. 2017. "The Car Sharing Economy." http://www.drivemycar.com.au/Long-term-rental-in-the-car-sharing-economy. Accessed March 4, 2017.

Dubravcic, D., M. van Baalen, and C. Nizak. 2014. "An Evolutionarily Significant Unicellular Strategy in Response to Starvation in Dictyostelium Social Amoebae." *F1000Res* 3: 133.

Dunbar, R. I. M. 2010. *How Many Friends Does One Person Need?: Dunbar's Number and Other Evolutionary Quirks.* Cambridge, MA: Harvard University Press.
2016. *Human Evolution: Our Brains and Behavior.* New York: Oxford University Press.

Dunbar, R. I. M., Clive Gamble, and John Gowlett. 2010. *Social Brain, Distributed Mind.* New York: Oxford University Press.

Dunbar, R. I. M., Chris Knight, and Camilla Power. 1999. *The Evolution of Culture: An Interdisciplinary View.* Edinburgh: Edinburgh University Press.

Dyer, Jeff, Hal B. Gregersen, and Clayton M. Christensen. 2011. *The Innovator's DNA: Mastering the Five Skills of Disruptive Innovators.* Boston, MA: Harvard Business Press.

Dyer, Jeff, Hal B. Gregersen, Clayton M. Christensen, and Mel Foster. 2012. *The Innovator's DNA Mastering the Five Skills of Disruptive Innovators.* Grand Haven, MI: Brilliance Audio.

Fisher, Ronald Aylmer. 1930. *The Genetical Theory of Natural Selection.* Oxford: The Clarendon Press.

Fortey, Richard A. 1998. *Life: A Natural History of the First Four Billion Years of Life on Earth.* New York: Alfred A. Knopf.

Gilbert, S. F., J. Sapp, and Al Tauber. 2012. "A symbiotic view of life: we have never been individuals. *Quarterly Review of Biology*, vol. 87, no. 4. December 2012: 325-341.

Gladwell, Malcolm. 2002. *The Tipping Point: How Little Things Can Make a Big Difference*. Boston: Back Bay Books.
    2005. *Blink: The Power of Thinking Without Thinking*. New York: Little, Brown and Co.

Gloor, Peter A. 2006. *Swarm Creativity: Competitive Advantage Through Collaborative Innovation Networks*. New York: Oxford University Press.

Goodall, Jane. 1971. *In the Shadow of Man*. Boston: Houghton Mifflin.
    1986. *The Chimpanzees of Gombe: Patterns of Behavior*. Cambridge, MA: Belknap Press of Harvard University Press.

Gorbis, Marina. 2013. *The Nature of the Future: Dispatches from the Socialstructed World*. New York: Free Press.

Gordon, Deborah. 1999. *Ants at Work: How an Insect Society is Organized*. New York: Free Press.
    2010. *Ant Encounters: Interaction Networks and Colony Behavior*. Princeton: Princeton University Press.

Grootaert, Christiaan, and Thierry van Bastelaer. 2001. "Understanding and Measuring Social Capital: A Synthesis of Findings and Recommendations from the Social Capital Initiative." World Bank. Social Capital Initiative Working Paper No. 24.

Hardin, Garrett. 1968. "The Tragedy of the Commons." *Science*, vol. 162, no. 3859, 1243-1248.

Harman, Jay. 2013. *The Shark's Paintbrush: Biomimicry and How Nature is Inspiring Innovation*. Ashland, OR: White Cloud Press.

Hesselbein, Frances, Marshall Goldsmith, and Leader to Leader Institute. 2009. *The Organization of the Future 2: Visions, Strategies, and Insights on Managing in a New Era*. San Francisco: Jossey-Bass.

Hill, Linda A. 2014. *Collective Genius: The Art and Practice of Leading Innovation*. Boston: Harvard Business Review Press.

Hippel, Eric von. 2005. *Democratizing Innovation*. Cambridge: MIT Press.

Hölldobler, Bert, and Edward O. Wilson. 2009. *The Superorganism: The Beauty, Elegance, and Strangeness of Insect Societies*. New York: W.W. Norton.

2011. *The Leafcutter Ants: Civilization by Instinct*. New York: Norton.

Hutchins, Giles. 2012a. *The Nature of Business*.

2013. *The Nature of Business: Redesigning for Resilience*. Gabriola Island, BC: New Society Publishers.

Institute for the Future. 2007. *The Future of Work: Perspectives*. White Paper. *Technology Horizons Program*. Palo Alto: IFTF.

International Energy Agency. 2014. "Modern Energy for All." *World Energy Outlook*. http://www.worldenergyoutlook.org/resources/ energydevelopment. Accessed March 4, 2017.

Internet Live Stats. "Internet Users." http://www.internetlivestats.com/ internet-users. Accessed March 4, 2017.

Invasive Species Specialist Group. 2016. "View 100 of the World's Worst Invasive Alien Species." http://www.issg.org/worst100_species.html. Accessed March 4, 2017.

Johansen, Robert. 2012. *Leaders Make the Future: Ten New Leadership Skills for an Uncertain World*. San Francisco: Berrett-Koehler Publishers.

Johansen, Robert, and Karl Ronn. 2014. *The Reciprocity Advantage: A New Way to Partner for Innovation and Growth*. San Francisco: Berrett-Koehler Publishers.

Johnson, Steven. 2010. *Where Good Ideas Come From: The Natural History of Innovation*. New York: Riverhead Books.

Kellert, Stephen R., and Edward O. Wilson. 1993. *The Biophilia Hypothesis*. Washington, D.C.: Island Press.

Kim, W. Chan, and Renée Mauborgne. 2005. *Blue Ocean Strategy: How to Create Uncontested Market Space and Make the Competition Irrelevant*. Boston: Harvard Business School Press.

Kingsley, Mary Henrietta. 2002. *Travels in West Africa*. Washington, D.C.: National Geographic; Reprint Edition.

Klein, Jeff. 2012. En*theos Radio interview of Brian Robertson. "It's Just Good Business," March 9, 2012, 2012. http://www.entheos.com/radio/shows/Its- Just-Good-Business.

Krause, Jens, Richard James, Daniel W. Franks, and Darren P. Croft. 2015. *Animal Social Networks*. New York: Oxford University Press.

Kummer, Hans. 1995. *In Quest of the Sacred Baboon: A Scientist's Journey*. Princeton: Princeton University Press.

Laloux, Frederic. 2014. *Reinventing Organizations*. Brussels, Belgium: Nelson Parker.

Lee, Richard B. 1984. *The Dobe Ju/'hoansi*. Belmont, CA: Wadsworth.

Lieberman, Robin Sol. 2016. *The Charisma Code: Communicating in a Language Beyond Words*. Ashland, OR: White Cloud Press.

Lofting, Hugh. 1922. *The Voyages of Doctor Dolittle*. Lippincott, Williams & Wilkins.

Louv, Richard. 2005. *Last Child in the Woods: Saving Our Children from Nature-Deficit Disorder*. Chapel Hill, NC: Algonquin Books of Chapel Hill.

Macho, Gabrielle A. 2014. "Baboon Feeding Ecology Informs the Dietary Niche of *Paranthropus boisei*." PLoS ONE, vol. 9, no 1. http://journals.plos.org/plosone/article?id=10.1371/journal.pone.0084942. Accessed March 4, 2017.

Margulis, Lynn, and Dorian Sagan. 2001. "Marvellous Microbes." *Resurgence* 206, 10-12.

Marks, Jonathan. 2002. *What it Means to be 98% Chimpanzee: Apes, People, and their Genes*. Berkeley: University of California Press.
2015. *Tales of the Ex-Apes: How We Think About Human Evolution*. Oakland: University of California Press.

Martin, Roger. 2007. "How Successful Leaders Think." *Harvard Business Review*.
2009. *The Opposable Mind*. Cambridge: Harvard Business Review Press.

Marzluff, John M., and Tony Angell. 2012. *Gifts of the Crow: How Perception, Emotion, and Thought Allow Smart Birds to Behave Like Humans.* New York: Free Press.

McDonough, William, and Michael Braungart. 2002. *Cradle to Cradle: Remaking the Way We Make Things.* New York: North Point Press. 2013. *The Upcycle.* New York: North Point Press.

Miller, Peter. 2010. *The Smart Swarm: How Understanding Flocks, Schools, and Colonies Can Make us Better at Communicating, Decision Making, and Getting things Done.* New York: Avery.

Morgan, Thomas Hunt. 1901. *Regeneration.* New York: The Macmillan Company.

Nakagaki, T., H. Yamada, and A. Toth. 2000. "Maze-Solving by an Amoeboid Organism." *Nature* 407, 470.

Nowak, M. A., and Roger Highfield. 2011. *SuperCooperators: Altruism, Evolution, and Why We Need Each Other to Succeed.* New York: Free Press.

Nowak, Martin A., Corina E. Tarnita, and E. O. Wilson. 2010. "The Evolution of Eusociality." *Nature* vol. 466, no. 7310, 1057-062.

O'Donnell, S., S. J. Bulova, S. DeLeon, P. Khodak, S. Miller, and E. Sulger. 2015. "Distributed Cognition and Social Brains: Reductions in Mushroom Body Investment Accompanied the Origins of Sociality in Wasps (Hymenoptera: Vespidae)." *Proceedings B of The Royal Society* 282, no. 1810. Doi: 10.1098/rspb.2015.0791.

Ostrom, Elinor. 2015. *Governing the Commons: The Evolution of Institutions for Collective Action.* Cambridge: Cambridge University Press.

Pascale, Richard T. 1999. "Surfing the Edge of Chaos." *Sloan Review MIT.* http://sloanreview.mit.edu/article/surfing-the-edge-of-chaos. Accessed March 4, 2017.

Pascale, Richard T., Mark Millemann, and Linda Gioja. 2000. *Surfing the Edge of Chaos: The Laws of Nature and the New Laws of Business.* New York: Crown Business.

Peter, Lawrence. 1969. *The Peter Principle: Why Things Always Go Wrong.* New York: William Morrow and Co.

Reingold, Jennifer. 2016. "A Radical Shift Left Zappos Reeling." *Fortune.* http://fortune.com/zappos-tony-hsieh-holacracy. Accessed March 4, 2017.

Robertson, Brian J. 2015. *Holacracy: The New Management System for a Rapidly Changing World.* New York: Macmillan Audio.

Sagarin, Rafe. 2012. *Learning from the Octopus: How Secrets from Nature can Help us Fight Terrorist Attacks, Natural Disasters, and Disease.* New York: Basic Books.

Salk, Jonas. 1973. *The Survival of the Wisest.* New York: Harper & Row.

Sandberg, Sheryl. 2013. *Lean In: Women, Work, and the Will to Lead.* New York: Alfred A. Knopf.

Sasaki, T., and S. C. Pratt. 2012. "Groups Have a Larger Cognitive Capacity than Individuals." *Current Biology* 22, no. 19, R827-9.

Satell, Greg. 2013. "How Disruption Happens." *Digital Tonto.* http://www.digitaltonto.com/2013/how-disruption-happens. Accessed March 4, 2017.

Seeley, Thomas D. 2010. *Honeybee Democracy.* Princeton: Princeton University Press.

Semler, Ricardo. 2004. *The Seven-Day Weekend: Changing the Way Work Works.* New York: Portfolio.

Senge, Peter M. 2010. *The Necessary Revolution: Working Together to Create a Sustainable World.* New York: Broadway Books.

Shirky, Clay. 2010. *Cognitive Surplus: Creativity and Generosity in a Connected Age.* New York: Penguin Press.

Sober, Elliott, and David Sloan Wilson. 1998. *Unto Others: The Evolution and Psychology of Unselfish Behavior.* Cambridge: Harvard University Press.

Stamets, Paul. 2005. *Mycelium Running: How Mushrooms Can Help Save the World.* Berkeley: Ten Speed Press.

Steinbeck, John. 1945. *Cannery Row.* New York: The Viking Press.

Surowiecki, James. 2004. *The Wisdom of Crowds: Why the Many are Smarter than the Few and How Collective Wisdom Shapes Business, Economies, Societies, and Nations.* New York: Doubleday.

Sutherland, Rory. 2013. "Rory Sutherland Knows how to Save marketing." *Wired.* http://www.wired.co.uk/article/rory-sutherland-knows-how-to-save-marketing. Accessed March 5, 2017.

Takcam. "Peeple App." http://www.takcam.com/peeple-app-review-julia-cordray. Accessed March 5, 2017.

Thompson, Clive. 2008a. "Is the Tipping Point Toast?" *Fast Company.* https://www.fastcompany.com/641124/tipping-point-toast. Accessed March 5, 2017.

Thompson, Ken. 2008b. *Bioteams: How to Create High Performance Teams and Virtual Groups Based on Nature's Most Successful Designs.* Tampa, FL: Meghan-Kiffer Press.

Tomasello, Michael. 2009. *Why We Cooperate.* Cambridge: MIT Press.

Trivers, Robert. 1985. *Social Evolution.* Menlo Park, CA: Benjamin/ Cummings Pub. Co.

Tse, Sarah. 2015. "2,200 Year Old Termite Mound Discovered in Central Africa." *The Science Explorer.* http://thescienceexplorer.com/nature/2200-year-old-termite-mound-discovered-central-africa. Accessed March 5, 2017.

Turner, J. Scott. 2000. *The Extended Organism: The Physiology of Animal-Built Structures.* Cambridge: Harvard University Press.

United Nations. 2013. "Deputy UN Chief Calls for Urgent Action to Tackle Global Sanitation Crisis." *UN News Centre.* http://www.un.org/apps/news/story.asp?NewsID=44452&Cr=sanitation&Cr1=#.WKzwIBIrKV7. Accessed March 5, 2017.

Vodafone Global Enterprise. 2013. "Invisible Infrastructure: The Rise of Africa's Mobile Middle Class." Vodafone. http://www.vodafone.com/business/global-enterprise/invisible-infrastructure-the-rise-of-africas-mobile-middle-class-2013-08-22. Accessed March 5, 2017.

Waal, Frans de. 2007. *Chimpanzee Politics: Power and Sex Among Apes.* Baltimore, MD: Johns Hopkins University Press.

2013. *The Bonobo and the Atheist: In Search of Humanism Among the Primates.* New York: W.W. Norton & Co.

White, T. H. 1958. *The Once and Future King.* Glasgow, UK: William Collins, Son.

Wilson, D. S., and E. O. Wilson. 2007. "Rethinking the Theoretical Foundation of Sociobiology." *Q Rev Biol* 82, 327-48.

Wilson, E. O., and B. Holldobler. 2005. "Eusociality: Origin and Consequences." *National Academy of Sciences* 102, no. 38, 13367-71. DOI: 10.1073/pnas.0505858102.

Yunus, Muhammad, and Karl Weber. 2007. *Creating a World Without Poverty: Social Business and the Future of Capitalism.* New York: PublicAffairs.

Zappos Insights. "Holacracy and Self Organization." https://www.zapposinsights.com/about/holacracy. Accessed March 5, 2017.

Zhuo, Tx. 2015. "Airbnb and Uber Are Just the Beginning. What's Next for the Sharing Economy." *Entrepreneur.* https://www.entrepreneur.com/article/244192. Accessed March 5, 2017.

Acknowledgements

This book required a lifetime of study and support—all of it dependent on a variety of welcoming superorganisms.

I'd like to thank the biomimicry community, ultimately set in motion by Janine Benyus' 1997 book and the tireless work and vision of Dayna Baumeister to make it come to life. These women are my ultimate heroines and guiding lights. Thanks to Janine for seeing my potential and encouraging me, and to Dayna, who mentored me through my many idiosyncrasies. Hopefully your lessons—a rigorous and methodical approach to bioinspired innovation, opportunities to practice biomimicry in the real world, and critique to tether my intellectual wanderings to Earth—have been put to good use here. Thank you, Dayna and Janine!

Thanks to my cohort of Biomimicry Professionals—the first to achieve the Masters of Science at Arizona State's Biomimicry Center, and companions on my journey. Special thanks to those who read early drafts of this manuscript: Michael Dupee, Estelle Martinson, Rachel Hahs, Jane Toner, Joe Zazzera, Lisa Dokken, Brennen Jensen, and Diana Hammer. Extra special thanks to Ana Carol Freitas at Cultura Creativa and Daniela Esponda for their brilliant design skills.

Thanks also to members of the biomimicry community who offered helpful comments, guidance, and exciting conversations along the way—Jamie Brown, Jacques Chirazi, Chris Garvin, Michelle Fehler, Colin Mangham, Tim McGee, Bowine Wijffels, Ilaria Mazzoleni,

Prashant Dhawan, Josh Stack, Leon Wang, Thomas Baumeister, Anuj Jain, Megan Schuknecht, Jennifer Schill, Denise DeLuca, Curt McNamara, Claire Janisch, Toby Herzlich, Karen Allen, Taryn Mead, Erin Leitch, Zeynep Arhon, Delfin Montanana, Mark Kerbel, Marc Weissburg, Al Kennedy, Richard James MacCowan, Katherine Collins, Darja Dubravcic, and Nan Woodman.

Thanks also to Holly Harlan, Beth Rattner, and members of the Biomimicry Leaders Network who provided huge support and encouragement—particularly to Colleen Mahoney and Amy Larkin, who offered friendship, a nexus of connection, advice, and a place to stay!

Deepest gratitude to my early reviewers, in particular to Jay Harman and Francesca Bertone, Michael Dupee, Frans de Waal, David Sloan Wilson, Peter Gloor, Ken Thompson, Giles Hutchins, Eric Corey Freed, Denis Hayes, Gil Friend, Katherine Collins, Nikolay Bogatyrev and Olga Bogatyreva, Tatyana Kanzaveli, Zem Joaquin, John and Barbara McDonald, Jill Fehrenbacher, Patric Palm, and David Moya.

Many thanks to those who provided me with opportunities to get my thoughts out to the broader public. There have been many, but special thanks to Norbert Hoeller, Marjan Eggermont, and Tom McKeag at Zygote Quarterly; Jill Fehrenbacher at Inhabitat.com; David Pescowitz, Marina Gorbis, and Mark Frauenfelder at the Institute for the Future; Jerry Michalski at REX; Joanna Gangi at the International Living Future Institute; Nick Aster at Triple Pundit; Joel Makower and Elsa Wenzel at Greenbiz; Janet Salazar and Constance J Peak at Impact Leadership 21; and Erin Connelly and Adiel Gavish at AskingNature, the Biomimicry Institute's blog.

Special thanks to those who took a chance on providing me with opportunities to grow and develop the knowledge and experience I've been so blessed to acquire, including Cliff Jolly, Todd Disotell, and Eric Delson at the New York Consortium for Evolutionary Biology; Celeste DeWald at the California Association of Museums; Gaylene

Xanthopoulos at the Leadership Edge; Camille Primm, the ultimate career coach; Dayna Baumeister at Biomimicry 3.8, as well as Charlie Rodi and Nancy Mancilla. Mostly, I know I've failed to meet your expectations, but this book would never have happened without your helping hands. Thank you.

Thanks, too, to those who provided me with critical mentoring, conversations, support, and inspiration: Camille Primm, Bob Trivers, Cliff Jolly, Jane Phillips Conroy, Bill Lester, Joe Nyiri, Gaylene Xanthopoulos, Lynn Friedmann, Dayna Baumeister, the San Diego Writers Ink, Bill McDonough, Roger Bingham, Amanda Caniglia, Naila Chowdhury, and Janet Salazar. Special thanks to John McDonald and his wife Barbara, for sharing so many brilliant conversations and ideas and believing it is possible to apply biological concepts to create a better future for everyone. Your patience and support has been astonishing and I will never forget it.

I am deeply grateful to all those who contributed to my Kickstarter campaign to fund the writing of this book. Please know that I am deeply touched by each of you. Thank you so much for believing in me. You're the best! Jim and Maggie Barker, Gil and Gail Woolley, Sheen Fischer, Brennen Jensen, Colleen Mahoney, Paul Telfer, Krista Nordstrom, Jonathan Katz, Katherine Collins, Todd Disotell, Chris Garvin, Mindy Jodoin, Greg Simmons, Toby Herzlich, Lynn Zucchet, Sarah Simmons, Michael Dupee, Deanna Hesford, Chuck Templeton, Dayna Baumeister, Elisha Long, John McDonald, Peter Lawrence, Jill Sandman Newell, Martin and Judy Sandman, Jacques Chirazi, Kathy Zarsky, Erin Ellis, Marie Bourgeois, Anjan Prakash, Daniela Marshall, Nancy Mancilla, Jack Mevorah, Theresa Millard, Danyelle Comer, Jill Fehrenbacher, Shawn McDonald, Cheryl Spector, Adib Dada, Harry Uvegi, Randall Anway, Norbert Hoeller, Reza Sadeghi, Fernanda Litt, Chris Bryan Ligerman, Josh Marks, Emily Kennedy, Gretchen Hooker, Leon Wang, James Turner, Susan Swartz, Sean Daly, Linda Nicholes, Sara Stinson, Audrey Seymour, Ryan Tanakit, MiMi DeMirjian, Dorna Schroeter,

Jane Phillips-Conroy, Valerie Kosheleff, Sarah Spicci, Yuka Yoneda, Carol Thaer, Daniela Esponda, Nan Woodman, Niki Singlaub, Christine Bagwell, Kathy Brann, Prashant Dhawan, Estelle Martinson, Lisa Dokken, Melissa Jawaharlal, Mary Hansel, Al Kennedy, Rachel Hahs, Beth Cordasco, Jamie Brown, Daniela Ivanova, Victoria Keziah, Karen Johnson Rossin, Karen Allen, Jane Toner, Steve Lieberman, Jackie Lowe Stevenson, Scout Wilkins, Joe Zazzera, Patrick Baumann, Hatton Littman, Lisa Schlotterhausen, Gamelihle Sibanda, Jonathan Pinzon Kuhn, Jo Fleming, Daphne Fecheyr-Lippens, Jorge Kanahuati, Michael Callaway, Codrin Kruijne, Peggy Chu, Anders Sahl Hansen, Trine Hundevadt, Susan Okerstrom, Ana Carolina De Freitas Alves, Jennifer Hendricks, Saskia van den Muijsenberg, Erin Rovalo, Curt McNamara, Sherry Ritter, Torrey McMillan, Venugopal Kanneboina, Tim McGee, Jason Antic, Sam Rye, Tim Pilbrow, Brian McDonald, AJ Wacaser, Amy Coffman Phillips, swissnex San Francisco, Elouard Claire, Doug Paige, Kris Callori, Ilaria Mazzoleni, Tessa MacKay, Alena Iougina, Kelly Siman, Faye Yoshihara, Praveen Gupta, Diana Hammer, Jennifer Siegwart, Richard James MacCowan, Angeleno Nic, Carlos Fiorentino, Allison Alberts, Naima Solomon, Darel Engen, Dixie Hudson, Nan Renner, Myra Benoist, Mauricio Ramirez, Beth Rattner, Francesca Bertone, Bob Parks, Olga Bogatyreva, Robin Sol, Steve McCoy, Victoria Avi, Maria Luisa Gutierrez, Eugene Eccli, John Krigbaum, Eric Dargent, Carol Sanford, Ryan Raaum, Eugene Harris, and Jose Guilabert Bravo. Thank you for being part of my superorganism!

Deepest thanks to my team—those who put the nuts and bolts of this book together. To my dear publisher, Steve Scholl, for providing editing and patience and excitement and everything else, Stephen Sendar for believing in me and helping me see the bigger vision, and Christy Collins for design in the trenches. To Rebecca and Mike at Ocean Beach Business Center. Special thanks to amazing editor Anastasia Hipkins, and to Beverly Trainer for developmental edits. To Beau Casey, for rockin' it daily; Ana Carol Freitas for fantastic design; to videographers

Bryan Tanori and Marshall Thompson; and to Carmen Serrano who pretty much kept my world afloat and gave our family so much (much-needed) love while I slogged through all this as a single mother!

Infinite thanks to my dearest friends, who have stuck with me through thick and thin, even when they secretly wondered what the hell I was doing. To Paul Telfer, Trish Reed, and Jane Toner—thank you for taking part in life's adventures with me. You've made them so much more fun. Here's to many more! To Reza Sadeghi—how lucky I am to have met you, you've taught me so much. To Lynn Zucchet, Deanna Hesford, Mindy Jodoin, Jennifer Siegwart, Jill Sandman Newell, and Krista Nordstrom for unconditional love and tireless support through the best of times and the worst. Each of you has helped make me a better person, and knowing you always have my back makes all the difference. And to Robin Sol Lieberman, how blessed I am to have met you in the jungles of Veracruz, and to discover life's many twists and turns overlapping so delightfully. Here's to many more wildings and greater adventures.

Last and most important, deepest and most grateful thanks to my family. To Liz Shepherd Callanan and Sarah and Alan Simmons; to the baffling and inscrutable brilliance of the amazing Desmond, Ingo, and Roan; and most of all, thank you to my mother Margaret and to my father James Barker. Without your love, guidance, teaching, and help in so, so many uncountable ways, we all know I'd be lucky to be bagging groceries. Love you!!!

About the Author

Dr. TAMSIN WOOLLEY-BARKER is an evolutionary biologist, bioanthropologist, and biomimicry pioneer with an extensive background in corporate strategic and organizational design, bio-inspired innovation, and sustainability. She is the Dean of Geoversity School for Biocultural Leadership in Panama, Founding Director of the Borrego Institute for Living Design adjoining the Anza Borrego Desert Wilderness, and CEO of TEEM Innovation Group, LLC, working to rehumanize organizations, revitalize communities, and regenerate cultures and ecologies using evolutionary principles. Visit TEEMLab.com for more.